To Joyce —

With appreciation !

Guy Louis Rocha

Sally Zanjani

The Ignoble Conspiracy

Nevada Studies in History and Political Science

The following titles are available

No. 8
Eleanore Bushnell and Don W. Driggs,
The Nevada Constitution:
Origin and Growth
(Sixth Edition) 1984

No. 11
*W. Shepperson, N. Ferguson,
and F. Hartigan,*
Questions from the Past
1973

No. 14
Ralph J. Roske,
His Own Counsel:
The Life and Times of Lyman Trumbull
1979

No. 15
Mary Ellen Glass,
Nevada's Turbulent '50s:
Decade of Political and Economic Change
1981

No. 16
Joseph A. Fry,
Henry S. Sanford: Diplomacy and Business in Nineteenth-Century America
1982

No. 17
Jerome E. Edwards,
Pat McCarran: Political Boss of Nevada
1982

No. 18
Russell R. Elliott,
Servant of Power: A Political Biography
of Senator William M. Stewart
1983

No. 19
Donald R. Abbe,
Austin and the Reese River Mining
District: Nevada's Forgotten Frontier
1985

No. 20
Anne B. Howard,
The Long Campaign:
A Biography of Anne Martin
1985

No. 21
Sally Zanjani and Guy Louis Rocha,
The Ignoble Conspiracy: Radicalism on Trial
in Nevada
Fall 1986

No. 22
James W. Hulse,
Forty Years in the Wilderness: Impressions of
Nevada, 1940–1980
Summer 1986

No. 23
Jacqueline Baker Barnhart,
The Fair But Frail: Prostitution in San Francisco, 1849–1900
Summer 1986

No. 24
Marion Merriman and Warren Lerude,
American Commander in Spain: Robert Hale
Merriman and the Abraham Lincoln Brigade
1986

NEVADA STUDIES IN HISTORY AND POLITICAL SCIENCE

THE IGNOBLE CONSPIRACY

RADICALISM ON TRIAL IN NEVADA

SALLY ZANJANI AND GUY LOUIS ROCHA

UNIVERSITY OF NEVADA PRESS

RENO, NEVADA

1986

NEVADA STUDIES IN HISTORY AND POLITICAL SCIENCE NO. 21

STUDIES EDITOR
Wilbur S. Shepperson

EDITORIAL COMMITTEE

Don W. Driggs   Joseph A. Fry
Jerome E. Edwards   A. Costandina Titus

Library of Congress Cataloging-in-Publication Data

Zanjani, Sally Springmeyer, 1937–
   The ignoble conspiracy.

   (Nevada studies in history and political science;
no. 21)
   Bibliography: p.
   Includes index.
   1. Preston, Morrie Rockwood, 1882–1924—Trials,
litigation, etc.   2. Smith, Joseph William,
b. 1870–   —Trials, litigation, etc.   3. Trials
(Murder)—Nevada.   4. Picketing—Nevada.   I. Rocha,
Guy Louis, 1951–   .   II. Title.   III. Series.
KF224.P74Z36   1986   345.73'02523   85-31830
                             347.3052523
   ISBN 0-87417-103-2 (pbk. : alk. paper)

The paper used in this book meets the requirements of American National Standard for Information Sciences—Permanence of Paper for Printed Library Materials, ANSI Z39.48-1984. The binding is sewn for strength and durability.

University of Nevada Press, Reno, Nevada 89557 USA
© Sally Zanjani and Guy Louis Rocha 1986. All rights reserved
Cover design by Dave Comstock
Printed in the United States of America

CONTENTS

ACKNOWLEDGMENTS

Uncovering the story behind a trial that occurred nearly eighty years ago would have been impossible without a good deal of assistance. Our greatest debt is to the late Louis Rockwood Lebel, who graciously shared with us his recollections of his family and of Morrie Preston. We are saddened that he did not live to see the book to which he contributed so much. Esther Lebel and other family members also assisted us greatly. Among the colleagues in several states who helped us trace the movements of principal figures, R. P. Baker, Arkansas History Commission, and John Gonzales, California State Library, were especially helpful.

Our endeavor to solve the mysteries linked to the Preston-Smith trial received valuable aid from several sources. Richard Johnston generously permitted us to examine his extensive research on the careers of Thomas Bliss and William Claiborne. William Rowley, professor of history at the University of Nevada, Reno, offered welcome advice on the location of significant information on George Wingfield. Staff members at the Nevada Historical Society and at Special Collections, University Library, University of Nevada, Reno, provided many courtesies.

No small measure of our gratitude is due to Nicholas Cady, acquisitions editor at the University of Nevada Press. His editorial guidance played a vital part in making the book we had envisaged a reality.

INTRODUCTION

Even today the great labor trials that made headlines during the first two decades of the twentieth century occupy a distinctive place in Western history: Big Bill Haywood in 1907, Morrie Preston and Joseph Smith in the same year, James B. McNamara in 1911, Joe Hill in 1913, Tom Mooney and Warren Billings in 1917. The earlier trials, Haywood and Preston-Smith, shared common roots in the increasing radicalization of Western hard-rock miners that developed from the struggles in Idaho and Colorado during the 1890s and early 1900s, yet each trial involved a crime of violence tangled in a unique set of circumstances. Haywood and his associates were accused of conspiring to assassinate former Idaho governor Frank Steunenberg; Preston and Smith of killing a restaurant owner in a Nevada picketing dispute; McNamara and his brother of setting a bomb that gutted the *Los Angeles Times* building and killed twenty-one people; Hill of a Utah homicide committed in the course of an armed robbery; Mooney and Billings of a San Francisco bombing that took the lives of several bystanders at a patriotic parade.

The outcomes ranged from Haywood's acquittal to Hill's execution before a firing squad, and the judgments historians have subsequently reached upon these trials have also varied widely. Although most now concur with the jury that acquitted Haywood, some have been puzzled by the extraordinarily convincing performance of chief prosecution witness Harry Orchard, and even more serious questions have been raised concerning the innocence of Hill; the McNamaras changed their pleas to guilty, setting off a wave of disillusionment among their partisans; Mooney and Billings, by contrast, eventually stood forth exon-erated. While Haywood's future role as an IWW leader has secured him a permanent niche in American history, our collective memory of the others has been as uneven as the outcomes and has shown a greater relation to the harshness of the punishment than to the probable guilt of the central figure. Hill, whose conviction aroused international protest in his own time, was the inspiration long after his death for both an enduring song and a novel and remains probably the best known today. As for Mooney, Billings, Preston, and Smith, though labor faithfully agitated on their behalf for years and their names were once familiar to many, they are now forgotten except by a few specialists in the field.

Despite these wide differences in crimes, outcomes, probable guilt, and historical judgment, it is possible to detect common patterns in the origins and conduct of several of these cases which suggest that it may be useful to consider them as something more than discrete events. The Haywood, Mooney, and Preston-Smith trials all hinged on a mysterious witness of doubtful character. Both the Haywood and Preston-Smith trials chiefly devolved upon alleged union conspiracies behind a seemingly simple crime. Still more fundamentally, these trials were real-life dramas that played an important role in shaping public attitudes. In much the same way that large segments of the public in the 1970s became acquainted with the Symbionese Liberation Army and Amer-ica's revolutionary fringe primarily through the kidnapping and trial of Patty Hearst, the public of an earlier day saw the widespread conflict between labor and management personified by a few individuals in these labor trials. Although the struggles of Western workers from the 1890s through the First World War occurred on many levels, such events as the mass arrests at Seattle and the deportations from Bisbee failed to crystallize around an identifiable hero—or villain, depending on the source. The labor trials, by contrast, were ready-made melodramas, in which the defendant came to embody the union as surely as John D. Rockefeller symbolized capitalism or Boss Tweed exemplified corrup-tion among urban officials. Some who read the press reports on Haywood's trial envisaged him as a sinister thug halted from his career of surreptitious violence by a few fearless lawmen, others as a fine, strapping young union leader kidnapped by scheming capitalists de-termined to enslave the working class. But for readers with prejudices of all persuasions these trials became the stage on which the fundamental conflict between the radical Western unions and the business world was played out. For this reason, the consequences of the labor cases reverberated beyond the individual fate of the man on trial, a circumstance that was often clearly recognized by the participants: had Haywood been found guilty of plotting Steunenberg's death, the radical unions would have stood condemned of conducting a campaign of terror throughout the West. Thus conviction in the broader forum of public opinion could have immediate effects far beyond the courthouse. Rarely was the effect of a trial in shaping the public image of a union so evident as in Nevada following the Preston-Smith case.

In retrospect, it is clear that much of the historical importance of the Preston-Smith trial stemmed from its symbolic uses in influencing public attitudes during the year that preceded the suppression of Nevada's radical labor movement. In Goldfield, as in Colorado and Idaho's Coeur d'Alene, the sequence of events involved the formation of a mine owners' association, which soon cemented alliances with state politicians, and the use of troops to destroy the unions. Turning to the military to accomplish what economic methods had failed to effect was a *political* move and one which, as historian Melvyn Dubofsky has observed, depended on isolating labor from its allies psychologically. During this isolation phase, the Preston-Smith trial was an important publicity device the mine owners used to convince the public that the union was a dangerous and violent movement that should be extirpated. Distortions of the Preston-Smith case by newspaper editors helped incite hysteria and develop popular support for the mine owners' next move, military force.

When federal troops moved in to suppress Goldfield's radical unions a little more than six months after the Preston-Smith trial, it was a serious defeat for radical labor in the Intermountain West. The struggle that labor historian Vernon Jensen has termed "one of the most unique and most bitter labor wars in our industrial relations history" was over, and the unit that some in the Western Federation of Miners (WFM) considered the "strongest, most progressive and advanced" local was lost to the federation. Nevada's mines, a center of labor activity since the Comstock days, ceased to sustain the unions, and labor's fighting front shifted to other states. The loss was a particularly heavy blow to the anarcho-syndicalist Industrial Workers of the World (IWW), who long looked back on Goldfield as the Camelot where their dream of organizing all wage earners in One Big Union had briefly come to life. According to Paul Brissenden's classic history of the IWW, it was here that the union made "the first notable application of the principles of revolutionary industrial unionism." Goldfield had helped the IWW cling to life in the early days, and its memory continued to inspire union members during the years of suppression that lay ahead. How much more the living reality might have nourished them can only be surmised; nonetheless, the men who stifled Nevada's radical unions in the cradle had no difficulty imagining the strength the radicals might have attained in time. Spies inside the union had reported to the mine owners that the radicals saw Nevada as a wealthy but thinly populated state that could easily be taken over for the establishment of Socialism.

Not only did the Goldfield debacle have a discernible impact on the union movement in the West, but its effects extended into the political sphere. In 1907, when Joseph Smith, one of Nevada's leading Socialist politicians, and Morrie Preston, a dedicated Socialist and a promising public speaker, stood trial, American Socialism was a rapidly growing movement with high hopes for Nevada, a small state where a favorable shift in the already substantial Socialist proportion of the vote might well be achieved. In Milwaukee, as David Shannon has noted in his history of American Socialism, the secret of success for the Socialists was their close alliance with the unions; no such nexus was to be permitted to develop in Nevada. With the destruction of the WFM and the IWW in Goldfield, the leadership of the state Socialist party shifted away from the union radicals to more conservative, middle-class politicians in the northern part of the state, and the character of the party altered correspondingly. Although Nevada Socialist candidates did increasingly well at the polls through 1916, the part had lost a dedicated cadre of organizers when the radical unions were driven from Goldfield. The increment their efforts might have provided to edge Nevada Socialist candidates for high office into the winning column was also lost, together with the momentum these additional victories might have lent to the national movement.

It was against this background of Socialist challenge and union strife that the Preston-Smith case became a cause celebre, albeit before a much more limited audience than the Haywood or Mooney trials. We should bear in mind that there was a time when two sessions of the Nevada legislature passed resolutions advocating clemency for Preston and Smith, reflecting a degree of public outrage over a criminal trial that to the best of our knowledge has never been duplicated in Nevada. Big Bill Haywood came to plead with state officials on their behalf, and Socialist Labor party leader Daniel DeLeon sought to focus national attention on Preston by nominating him for the presidency of the United States. The Preston-Smith case loomed large in the resolutions passed at the national conventions of two radical labor organizations, the WFM and the IWW. While local newspapers warned against freeing the "assassins," workingmen throughout America deluged the Nevada supreme court with petitions urging clemency for Preston and Smith. The intense feeling that centered on these two men three-quarters of a century ago clearly signaled that many of their contemporaries believed they had suffered a terrible injustice, yet the unresolved clamor and the ensuing years of silence have left the Preston-Smith case insufficiently understood. The time has arrived for a careful assessment to determine how their conviction occurred, whether an injustice in fact took place, and why it mattered so much to so many people.

I

THE TENTH OF MARCH

Darkness had fallen, and Goldfield's lamps were already burning at a few minutes after seven as the short, heavy-set "walking delegate" from the IWW stood on the board sidewalk in front of John Silva's Nevada Restaurant, ready to persuade customers to take their business elsewhere. The IWW was boycotting the restaurant because Silva had docked the wages of a waitress who left without notice. The union maintained that a worker was entitled to a day's pay for a day's work. The union man wore brown boots, with his corduroy trousers tucked into the tops in miner's style, and he had turned the collar of his corduroy coat up around his neck against the cold wind that whipped through the streets ahead of the approaching storm. His snub-nosed face beneath straight, blond hair was clean shaven and boyish, with wide, pale gray eyes. His name was Morrie Rockwood Preston. In his pocket was an Iver Johnson .38 caliber gun.

Through the large, wooden-framed windows that lined the front of the building, Preston could see Silva, wearing an old vest over his shirt, seated at a table with several customers who boarded at the restaurant. Members of the rival AFL carpenters' union, they had refused to honor the IWW boycott. Preston had just dissuaded carpenter W. R. Dixon and shingler Fred Luxinger from entering when he saw Silva jump up and rush into the kitchen to take down the pistol that hung from a nail on the wall. Dixon warned Preston, "Look out, he's coming with a gun!" As the Portuguese restaurant owner approached, Preston backed away against the sidewalk railing and took out his .38. "Go on. I kill you," said Silva, standing in the doorway and pointing his gun at Preston. "You mind your own business." Dixon and Luxinger raced out of danger, heading toward the firebell at the end of the street. The ringing of the bell was Goldfield's alarm for trouble of any kind. Preston moved forward in an effort to reach the spot where the sidewalk railing ended and a step led down to the street. He thought Silva tried to shoot him as he advanced, but nothing happened. During the instant's reprieve gained when Silva's gun failed to go off, the young picket fired in panic at the restaurant owner. Silva, shot once in the stomach, turned, staggered back inside, and fell to the floor. By midnight he was dead.

Preston walked away toward Union Hall. Jackson Lee ("Diamondfield Jack") Davis and Thomas Bliss said they saw a group of union leaders who had awaited Preston in front of the Hoffman Saloon move forward to surround him protectively like a corral and walk him to Union Hall, but other witnesses denied this, and also denied that Davis and Bliss were on the scene. A miner who passed Preston walking alone in the street spoke to him but he did not seem to hear. The man remembered that Preston had a "sickly smile" on his face.

The incident on March 10, 1907, at the Nevada Restaurant had all the earmarks of a commonplace frontier shooting, not to be condoned but easily to be understood. In the tense atmosphere accompanying the labor troubles that month, Goldfield was an armed camp, and the young union delegate had shot too hastily, believing that Silva was about to shoot him. Until the day he died, Morrie Preston would claim that it was nothing more than this, a simple case of shooting in self-defense. But it would end with not only Preston but also Joseph Smith, Vincent St. John, Dan Roudebush, Jerry Sexton, Elmer Vice, Ben Donnelly, Harry Rogers, A. J. Johnson, and Harry Jardine—a roster of Goldfield's most militant labor radicals—under indictment for conspiracy to murder John Silva, the first on an alleged assassination list that was said to include several leading mine owners and businessmen.

II

THE GOLDEN AGE

From the East and the West we are marching;
Can't you hear the swift, hurrying feet?
They are coming to deal retribution
And the right shall not suffer defeat.
We shall strike like a flash of forked lightning
As it shoots from a dark, cloudy sky
Dealing death to a system of robbery;
BUT OUR COMRADES WE'LL NEVER LET DIE.

We will number our soldiers in millions,
And your blood like a river shall flow,
While the death dew shall cling to your valleys,
And the red stain shall shine on the snow;
Our masters shall make full restitution,
We swear it by GOD upon high;
We will fill all your graveyards with tombstones;
BUT OUR COMRADES WE'LL NEVER LET DIE.

—from a poem by "Reuben True" in *Miners' Magazine,* March 1907, on the approaching trial of William Haywood, Charles Moyer, and George Pettibone.

"I was born in Memphis, Tennessee about 26 years ago [September 28, 1882]," wrote Morrie Preston in 1908, summarizing in a single sentence nearly all we are likely to learn of his early life, "at an early age removed to Arkansas, and was compelled to support myself which I did by selling newspapers, and trying to get some schooling; later I removed to Los Angeles, California and made good headway in school when I was again compelled to quit to aid in the support of the family."[1] Preston wrote that he came of Scotch-Irish ancestry, and the blunt, handsome features of his boyish face, with its generous mouth and wide, gray eyes, clearly affirmed his origins. He tells us nothing, not even the occupation, of the father he never knew. Frank James Preston had died when his son was a year old, leaving Morrie and his Georgia-born mother, Kate, the last remnant of a family shadowed by bereavement. Already in her forties, Kate Preston was poor, widowed, no longer young, and she had buried two of her three children.

In 1898 Morrie and his mother moved to southern California, then returned briefly to Little Rock in 1900 before settling permanently in Los Angeles later that year. Kate was now nearing sixty and more heavily dependent than ever on her young son. Soon after the initial move to California, and in the midst of his struggles to finish high school while he worked as a paper boy to support the two of them, Morrie met a strong-minded widow named Lillian Mary Burton, who was soon to supplant his mother in his affections. Their arrangement was partly economic, to be sure: Morrie and Kate probably needed a home, and Lillian needed Morrie's earnings to aid in her long struggle to make ends meet by giving elocution classes and by whatever other means came to hand. Yet the deep emotional bond that developed between them outweighed practical considerations. Morrie found something that had been lacking in his own mother in this strict and capable schoolmistress, whom not everyone found easy to get along with. In the presence of Lillian, nearly twenty years her junior, Kate seems to have dwindled away to a ghost, even before her death sometime after 1903. One of Lillian's nieces who visited the home in this period was not even aware of Kate's existence and thought that Morrie was a bright orphan her aunt had taken in from the street.[2] Soon Morrie was calling Lillian "Mother," and so she appeared in the eyes of the unions, the press, and the public at the time of his trial, though her black hair and her dark brown eyes showed no familial resemblance to the blond, gray-eyed Morrie.

In this devoted and studious boy, Morrie's new mother must have found an equally satisfactory son. From the night when she thought she sensed a holdup man lurking in the bushes and Morrie went forth to combat the menace, Lillian had gratefully turned to the boy as the male protector missing in her life since her second husband had died and her grown son left home.[3] Already sixteen at the time of his initial move to

Los Angeles, Morrie had long outgrown the mischievous pranks of boyhood. And he brought none of the worries associated with Lillian's rebellious and dangerously attractive daughter, Zora Etta. Possibly Morrie's only adolescent flaw from the maternal point of view was his Socialism, but even that may have seemed like a safe abstraction, less upsetting to Lillian than having a daughter who was growing to fancy herself an artist and a Bohemian.

Not much is known of Lillian's background. Her elocution classes suggest some education and aspiration to gentility. Born in Wisconsin, the eldest daughter of sawmill worker Levi Nunnaley and Mary Frost Nunnaley, both early midwestern pioneers, Lillian had also lived in Nebraska and Iowa. She was married to a man named Davis, to whom she bore a daughter and a son. The Nunnaleys apparently moved to southern California in 1885, and it is probable that Lillian soon followed with her children. Her second marriage to Burton and his death remain obscure. All that is absolutely clear about Lillian is her deep devotion to Morrie Preston and her unwavering belief in his innocence.

When Morrie gained a new mother, he also acquired a sister two years younger than he—the beautiful, black-haired Zora, with deep-set, dark eyes, wide mouth, and a dimple in her cheek. Years later he loved her as something more than a sister, and it is likely that he loved her that way from the very beginning. As a teenager, Zora was packed off to a convent school, which Lillian evidently hoped would curb her head-strong, mercurial temperament, instill pious and domestic virtues, and postpone the temptations implicit in her beauty. This formidable task proved beyond the powers of the good nuns, and Zora emerged from the convent as intractable as ever. The one lasting artifact of her convent training was her artistry at sewing, which was to stand her in good stead when she worked as a dresser to the Hollywood stars in the 1920s.

At seventeen, in 1901, she was married to Gottlieb Fischer, with the blessing of her mother, who no doubt hoped that a stolid, German-immigrant farmer could succeed where the nuns had failed. Initially, the domestication of Zora proceeded apace. The following summer a mid-wife was called to Lillian's Hope Street house to aid in an agonizing birth that produced a boy weighing more than twelve pounds. Morrie had already assumed the role of nurse whenever need arose in the household, and no doubt it was he who cared for Zora while she recuperated. She named the baby Louis Rockwood, giving him Morrie's middle name.[4] Proof of her love for Morrie was revealed in that name, but the greater proof lay more than six years ahead in a future neither of them could possibly have envisioned.

Friends and neighbors who knew Morrie in Los Angeles in this period later remembered him as "exceptionally bright" and "honest to a fault," a quiet, industrious boy who worked at night after school. Though he may have dreamed of becoming an engineer, his impoverished circumstances did not allow the luxury of higher education. When he later found a job as a nonunion telephone lineman, his short, burly figure in overalls and cap became a familiar sight on the neighborhood repair wagon. He had shown no radical leanings then. In the words of a neighbor, "To our knowledge he had no anarchistic views, but, on the contrary, manifested a great proneness for scientific subjects," constantly attending lectures at the Academy of Sciences of Southern California.

Just one hint emerges from this period that Preston was already something more than an industrious student and devoted son. Dr. George Pitzer, who had often seen him as a schoolboy in 1900, wrote, "He was a very sociable young man, quiet, free from anything like a vindictive spirit, but of very strong convictions, and conscientious to the last degree."[5] Strong convictions, perhaps springing from the anger of youth at the injustices of the world, marked a familiar rite of passage in late adolescence. It was a phase most often safely crossed, but there were still places at the turn of the century where the man with strong convictions carried more dangerous baggage than the man with a gun.

By 1906 Zora's marriage to Gottlieb had turned troubled. She bore him another child, who died in infancy, but she seems to have returned to her mother's house for long periods. The inevitable hostility between Morrie and Gottlieb had now reached a "yelling stage" that made it unmistakable, even to little Louis. Around this time Zora began to pursue a variety of careers learned neither at the convent nor at Gottlieb's hearth. She became fairly successful as a masseuse, convincing her clients that the magical touch of her perfectly manicured hands could restore youth and beauty. Her greatest talent may have been her ability to convince. Perhaps she was already setting herself up as a seeress of numerology, burning incense in the cottage behind Lillian's dwelling where she held her seances, using her hypnotic, deep-set eyes and her natural acting ability to create a sense of occult powers and accepting monetary "love offerings" for her services. She could tell a client's age, she could read the future, and—what was of even more immediate utility—she could predict the movements of the stock market. Her wealthy clientele included many stockbrokers seeking mystical guidance for their chancier speculations, and it is not improbable that those interested in mining stocks were full of excited talk about Goldfield.[6]

From them or another source, Morrie contracted the boomtown fever that sent him away from home for the first time in his life, breaking his routine of steady work, an evening walk home with Zora from her massage salon, and avid attendance at scientific lectures. No young man was likely to embark for Goldfield without dreams of vast wealth, and it is possible that Morrie also harbored the secret hope that things might greatly change if he could return to Zora a prince instead of a pauper. What, after all, could a telephone lineman possibly offer but a drab life of drudgery with little appeal to a glamorous woman? In the autumn of 1906, just after his twenty-fourth birthday, bearing strong convictions and large hopes, Morrie embarked on his great adventure.

The mining camp in the southern Nevada desert toward which he headed was the new El Dorado—Goldfield. The very word seemed synonymous with fortune and high adventure, and it drew young men as the glimmering vision of California had drawn an earlier generation in 1849. Shoshone prospector Tom Fisherman had made a strike in the Joshua tree-studded desert east of the Malapai mesa in 1902. Four years later it had burgeoned into a camp of perhaps twenty thousand people, clustered in hastily erected frame buildings, bottle houses, cabins, tents, cave dwellings, and blankets spread on the gravelly sand, amid a forest of mining headframes.

To a young man like Preston, new to the mining booms and away from his family for the first time, it must have seemed boundlessly exciting. He found some rough carpentry work putting up screens at the Miners' Union Hospital. The doctor in charge apparently thought him likeable and willing, for shortly afterward he was asked to remain at the hospital as a nurse. But at about this time, Preston found something more than work or excitement, something that was to derail his life from the respectable track on which a hardworking and personable young man, with a little more education than most and some aptitude for public speaking, was so clearly pointed—if he had stayed at home with Lillian in Los Angeles. In Goldfield, Morrie Preston found the combined WFM (Western Federation of Miners) and IWW (Industrial Workers of the World),[7] and the former nonunion telephone lineman suddenly emerged in the shock troops of America's most radical union at the very moment when a critical showdown was beginning.

The showdown in which chance would compel this young man to play a prominent role was the climax of years of struggle following the formation of the WFM at Butte in 1893. The ensuing industrial wars at the Coeur d'Alene (1899), Telluride (1901), and Cripple Creek (1903) mines had served to radicalize the WFM, a trend culminating in the formation of the IWW in 1905 at a Chicago convention. The new union's primary organizer, the WFM, then transformed itself into the mining department of the IWW.

It soon became clear that the "fighting faith" of the anarcho-syndicalist IWW was of an even redder hue than that of its Socialistic parent organization. The IWW, as Wallace Stegner has perceptively noted, was a "militant church," which commanded "all the enthusiasm, idealism, rebelliousness, devotion, and selfless zeal of thousands of mainly young, mainly migrant workers." The ultimate goal of the Wobblies, or Wobs, the common terms for IWW members, was to destroy capitalism and establish a stateless workers' commonwealth of self-governing unions assisted by technical experts. This revolutionary change was to be accomplished by combining the entire working class, including Asians, women, Negroes, and unskilled, marginal workers, whom the American Federation of Labor (AFL), with its craft union orientation, was not yet ready to embrace, into the One Big Union and advancing through "direct action." The IWW defined direct action broadly to include efforts by workers to improve their lot by virtually any means, from conventional strikes through passive resistance and sabotage to the ultimate general strike, which would at last place workers in control of the means of production. The Wobs gloried in these strikes, both as a means to debilitate the capitalist enemy and as a method of fostering a sense of power among workers. In Stegner's words, "It was conflict of the bloodiest kind that kept the IWW together. . . . Its greatest single contribution was the production of martyrs."[8]

This taste for combat was soon manifested in a series of strikes launched by the IWW in an effort to capture AFL affiliates. The WFM, the only viable, if increasingly uneasy, department of the IWW, had affiliated with the AFL in 1896, but friction over the AFL's conservatism and unwillingness to aid the WFM during the Leadville strike had prompted the WFM to withdraw the following year, and the two had remained rivals. AFL leader Samuel Gompers, fearful of the WFM's even more radical offshoot, had already directed AFL affiliates not to cooperate with the new union. The giant AFL, claiming more than 80 percent of America's two million union members, was the clear victor in these preliminary rounds over the tiny IWW, with a dues-paying membership that probably did not exceed forty thousand in 1905–6; indeed the early demise of the IWW appeared increasingly likely. IWW officials were compelled to report at the next convention that the new union had lost nearly every strike it undertook.[9] In this precarious situation, it is easy to see why events in Goldfield, where the IWW was in the process of winning its first important success, began to assume so large a significance to both friends and enemies of the beleaguered union.

Labor unions had begun their organizational campaigns in Goldfield on March 15, 1904, when the WFM organized Local No. 220. The AFL established a carpenters' local on September 22, eventually to be followed by a typographical union, their only additional success, despite tenacious efforts by their organizers and the support of mine owners endeavoring to use the AFL to destroy the radical unions. A third union, Local No. 510, was formed during the latter months of 1904 and functioned as a WFM auxiliary for about a year before being absorbed by the IWW after the appearance of IWW Local No. 77 in late 1905, probably in November. An IWW member later acknowledged that deporting AFL members who hired on as scabs during strikes helped to maintain the ascendancy of the WFM-IWW in this period: "It is true that the I.W.W. and W.F.M. did force some A.F. of L. members out of town and they were probably not provided with all the luxuries of modern civilization."[10] But the AFL hung on, and AFL carpenters even began carrying guns to their jobs when a fresh round of wrangling with the WFM heightened the tension during the days just before the shooting at Silva's restaurant.

Against this background of sharp union rivalry, two peculiar sets of circumstances intensified the friction in Goldfield labor relations. The first was the bad blood between mine operators and WFM miners who had dealt violently with each other in the industrial wars in Idaho and Colorado. Blacklisting by the mine operators and deportations of former scabs by the WFM kept these old animosities smoldering in Goldfield. The second source of labor friction was high grading, the theft of rich high-grade ore from the mines by miners who tucked chunks into their lunch buckets, their pockets, their specially constructed double-crowned hats, their mouths, and other places of ingenious devising. Some union radicals openly condoned high grading because it accorded with their belief that workers should enjoy all the fruits of their labor, while a good many others pursued it without the impetus of ideology. Saloonkeepers, gamblers, prostitutes, local merchants, and illegal assayers serving as fences found the added income from high grading lucrative, and many of Goldfield's citizens sympathized with the miners. In the long run, however, high grading was a practice certain to bring serious conflict with the mine owners.[11]

Despite these tensions beneath the surface, labor relations between WFM members and their Goldfield employers remained essentially amicable through the spring of 1906, but IWW militance soon began to ruffle the waters. During the last week of May 1906, seven months after the inception of the first IWW locals, the Wobblies sought higher pay for messenger boys at the Western Union telegraph office, and their first organized strike commenced. The outcome was a limited success for the messenger boys, who gained a small increase in wages, but a very important step for the IWW, which achieved recognition as union representative for the messenger boys during negotiations presided over by Governor John Sparks and Attorney General James G. Sweeney.[12]

Before the summer was over, the burgeoning IWW found its locals at odds with Lindley C. Branson's *Tonopah Daily Sun* and *Goldfield Daily Sun*. An ardent opponent of the IWW, Branson attacked the radical labor organization in the pages of the newspapers which he both owned and edited. In August 1906 the Goldfield IWW Newsboys' Union declared a sympathy boycott of the *Goldfield Sun* after Tonopah's IWW local declared the *Tonopah Sun* unfair. The newsboys refused to deliver the paper, and merchants were threatened with boycotts if they patronized it. WFM Local No. 220 promptly complied with a request from the Goldfield IWW to endorse its action, but neither the AFL typographical union nor the carpenters' locals honored it. The IWW accused the carpenters of scabbing on the newsboys and monopolizing Goldfield construction; their opponents countercharged that the militant union harassed and injured newspaper employees and aroused the anxieties of newspaper patrons by photographing them. As the gap between the AFL and the radical unions widened, the mine owners intervened to cast their weight on the side of Branson and the AFL by closing the mines for one shift to allow a vote on the boycott by the full membership. Despite this strong hint, the new vote sustained the IWW boycott. The Goldfield mine owners then locked out the WFM miners "until such time as the trouble was settled," which was intended to mean until the endorsement was withdrawn.[13] The drive to rescind appeared dashed on September 10, 1906, when IWW Local No. 77 merged with Goldfield Miners' Union No. 220 during a mass meeting in the big arena erected for the Gans-Nelson world lightweight championship prize fight. However, some leading mine owners apparently favored the combination because they hoped the conservative members of the larger miners' union would dominate the IWW.

A settlement followed hard on the heels of the merger. On September 14, after the Goldfield IWW agreed to withdraw the boycott at the request of their Tonopah counterparts, Branson capitulated and sold the *Goldfield Sun*, which was renamed the *Goldfield Daily Tribune* and removed from the unfair list some three weeks later when former *Sun* employees were finally terminated. His animus against the IWW sharpened by this encounter, Branson retreated thirty miles north to Tonopah, where he concentrated his resources on the *Tonopah Sun*. With its expensive $37,000 plant, large staff, and wide audience, Branson's surviving *Sun* for a time became one of the most successful and influential newspapers in the state and the source many Nevada editors used for information on events in Tonopah and Goldfield. The unified WFM-IWW had achieved a successful boycott against the *Goldfield Sun,* the Wobblies' second victory since coming to Goldfield. But they had also humiliated a powerful enemy who fed his spite to his newspaper and saw it thrive like a hound on red meat.[14]

During the winter following Branson's retreat, the Goldfield WFM-IWW elected two business agents to enforce its will. One was Morrie Preston, whose rapid rise to prominence in the union is the more startling because it occurred in just two months among men who were strangers, with whom he shared none of the fraternal memories of other mining camps that bound so many WFM miners together. The other business agent was a dark-haired man of thirty-six, with a receding hairline, brown eyes, an upturned nose, and a large handlebar mustache: Joseph William Smith. Born in London in 1870, Smith had emigrated to the United States by way of Canada in his late teens. Following a stint as a waiter in Chicago, he headed west to Denver, eventually arriving in California, where he married, and operated a restaurant in San Francisco. In early 1905 he opened another restaurant in the small town of Wadsworth on the Southern Pacific line in Nevada. The venture evidently met with scant success and was soon abandoned. The autumn of 1905 found Smith working as a waiter in Goldfield, where he quickly became a militant IWW activist, despite his background as a small businessman. When IWW Local No. 77 received its charter in November, Smith became the union's first secretary. It was Smith who organized the IWW local in Tonopah, and who walked into the office of the *Goldfield Sun* and warned the printers to join the IWW within twenty-four hours or be run out of town, thus attracting the enduring animosity of Lindley Branson. While Branson's editorial page snidely urged Smith's return "to his waiter's napkin or dish clout" and pounced on his reputed failure to obtain American citizenship before becoming a Goldfield town trustee, the Socialists chose Smith as a candidate for state office. The "rantings" of the man the *Sun* likened to a "foul buzzard" apparently made sense to many a wavering worker.[15]

The high-handed tactics of these two business agents aroused growing antagonism among Goldfield employers as the union expanded and consolidated that winter. Preston and Smith not only directed unaffiliated workers to join the union, they also issued orders to the employers in equally peremptory fashion, without consultation or negotiation. Smith, in particular, was resented as a "bully" for the "domineering, even insulting manner in which he laid down his mandates." The underlying principle behind those mandates was the IWW dictum "An injury to one is an injury to all," even when the injury was a trivial complaint to Morrie Preston from a waitress who had been docked a day's pay at Silva's restaurant. During those heady months when the union was tasting its power, such a complaint was enough to set a boycott in motion. IWW leader Vincent St. John was later to remember that winter as a golden age when employers sought an audience with union committees, instead of the other way around, and the wage scales the secretary posted on the bulletin board outside Union Hall became "the LAW." The employers, for their part, called it "tyranny."[16]

Beneath the surface of the golden age, however, two developments were under way in late 1906 and early 1907 that would prove more ominous to the union than the bristling hackles Smith was raising in the unpopular role of union enforcer. The first occurred in November 1906, with the arrival of St. John himself, a short, slight young man of thirty with a calm face and round, gray, slightly anxious eyes, once a revered figure in the WFM pantheon of heroes. He was a veteran of Cripple Creek, where he had led a strike in 1901 and gained a lasting reputation for violence. After the union was driven from Cripple Creek in 1903, St. John surfaced once more, working under the assumed name "John Vincent" but still familiarly known as "the Saint," in Burke, Idaho, where he became president of the WFM local. His work as an organizer in the Coeur d'Alene came to an abrupt halt nearly three years later when he was swept up in the unfolding drama of the Haywood case.

During the Christmas holidays in 1905, former Idaho governor Frank Steunenberg was killed by a bomb set at his garden gate in Caldwell, Idaho, by Harry Orchard. Steunenberg was not likely to be much mourned by union men, because he had presided over the union troubles in the Coeur d'Alene and had allowed the miners to be imprisoned in bull pens. Union involvement was immediately suspected in the bombing. Under the coaching of Pinkerton detective James McParland, an employee of the Mine Owners' Association, Orchard confessed that every unexplained mine explosion, death, accident, or fire in the Northwest, including his own murder of Steunenberg, had been plotted by the WFM leadership. Charles Moyer, president of the WFM, William D. Haywood, secretary-treasurer, and George Pettibone, a former union activist, were arrested and charged with plotting Steunenberg's death. St. John was also taken into custody, but efforts to connect him with Steunenberg's murder proved unavailing.[17]

By the time Idaho authorities could hold him no longer, St. John was extradited to Colorado on a flimsily contrived murder charge based on the battle between strikers and nonunion labor at Telluride five years earlier. "His persecutors are now contemplating charging him with the crucifixion of Christ," *Miners' Magazine* observed, "if they can only secure a 'confession' from some degenerate of a detective agency."[18] The charge was by now all too familiar to the WFM—conspiracy to commit murder. It was a charge the prosecutors would find themselves unable to sustain in the face of a defense ably conducted by St. John's attorney, Orrin N. Hilton, though the case dragged on for months. Judge Theron Stevens, soon to continue his career on the bench in Goldfield, eventually quashed the indictment, tartly noting that "a count for conspiracy can not be joined with a count for murder," and the prosecutors were compelled to move for dismissal.[19] St. John next appeared as one of the five WFM delegates at the IWW convention in Chicago, and the schism that was to separate him forever from the conservative members of the WFM rent the union.

Much of that 1906 IWW convention remains obscured by the dust raised in the fury of charge and countercharge, but the effects of the schism that occurred between radicals and conservatives are in no way obscure. The WFM executive board decided to deny support to either faction and declared its intention to reorganize the IWW, though the WFM formally remained the mining department of the IWW until the two unions separated in July 1908. Another effect of the WFM's disenchantment with the IWW was the instant transformation of St. John from a revered union hero, praised continually in the pages of *Miners' Magazine,* to a "viper" the WFM had hugged to its bosom to "warm it into life." He became a focus of hatred as harshly vilified by his erstwhile union friends as he had ever been by the mine owners.[20] And when St. John arrived in Goldfield with the unerring instinct of a homing pigeon, much of the fire he drew fell indiscriminately around him. He was cast beyond the pale, and with him went not only the other Goldfield firebrands, such as Harry Jardine, Ben Donnelly, and Sam Tregonning, but the entire union, the entire city. St. John's efforts to play a recessive role, by avoiding trouble, refusing to serve on committees, and trying to restrain his followers from coercive acts that might exacerbate the union troubles, were all to no avail. His very presence attracted danger, as he himself so clearly recognized. "Our enemies are moving with all the power at their command," he had already warned his followers. "We must be up and doing with a heart for any fate."[21]

The parent WFM usually sprang to the defense of its locals with ferocity, and the Goldfield union was one of particular importance, having leapt forward as the fastest growing local in the WFM during the closing months of 1906. But when Goldfield's ordeal began with a lockout the following spring, *Miners' Magazine* responded with nothing more than a single line, a Shakespearean aside, noting that "considerable trouble" was brewing but exaggerated press reports left the editor "unable to give the facts."[22] The reason for this resounding silence was not far to seek. In Goldfield, the place AFL organizer Grant Hamilton termed "the last stronghold of the IWW," those battle-scarred young soldiers in labor's army had rallied around the Saint. The dream had become reality; they lived the golden age; they filled the pages of *Miners' Magazine* with impassioned poetry; they signed their letters "John Brown," "Yours for the OBU," "Yours for Industrial Freedom," "Yours for the Revolution in our Time."

Thus St. John's arrival in Goldfield was, in retrospect, the first development with ominous repercussions for the union. The second, also in November 1906, was the incorporation of the Goldfield Consolidated Mines Company, organized by George Wingfield and U.S. Senator George Nixon and later augmented by a $1,000,000 loan from eastern financier Bernard Baruch. While the union appeared to retain the upper hand, winning a substantial wage increase after a strike the following month, the organization of Goldfield Con signaled the beginning of monopoly control in Goldfield.[23]

Prior to this date, high-grade ore and the prevalence of the leasing system had been conducive to both labor peace and union growth. A leaser, with only a few weeks or months in which to mine the high grade and make his killing, was perfectly willing to accede to any union demand. Enduring a strike while the clock ran out on his lease was the last thing he could tolerate, and the long run was no concern of his. No piece of machinery was too extravagant, no demand by labor too exorbitant. It was every man for himself, a system of rampant individualism in which common action against the budding union was a matter of vast indifference. Paradoxically, this very individualism

among the employers fostered the pure communalism of the One Big
Union. The IWW's success in Goldfield has sometimes been ascribed to
a brilliant and imaginative organizing effort. In fact, the IWW effort in
Goldfield was probably no more brilliant than in numerous other camps
where the union failed. The difference was that here propitious circumstances allowed them to succeed—at least for a time. Now, however, this early era of individualism was at an end, and management was
consolidating at the very time the union was rent by schism. The leasers
did not immediately disappear—according to one report, nearly three
hundred were still operating the following spring—but henceforth the
bulk of the bullion production was in the hands of the Florence Mining
Company, where Wingfield sat on the board of directors, and the giant
Goldfield Con.[24] The One Big Union faced the one big mining company, and it may well be no coincidence that the first major labor
difficulty in the mines of the district occurred shortly after the organization of Goldfield Con.

In George Wingfield, who *was* Goldfield Con in the same sense that
Louis XIV was the French state, the Wobblies faced one of the toughest,
coolest, and smartest customers they would ever encounter. An Arkan-
sas-born cowboy turned gambler, just thirty years old, Wingfield had
made some money in Tonopah before he gravitated to Goldfield and the
Mohawk Mine that was to become the nucleus of Goldfield Con.
Senator Nixon had provided part of the capital and the requisite prestige
to raise more with Baruch and other eastern financiers, and he paid an
occasional courtesy call on Goldfield, sometimes at junctures when his
talent for conciliation would prove particularly useful. But he was much
away in Washington. Wingfield—bristling with firearms, his bold,
handsome, somewhat irregular features characteristically expression-
less—was the man on the spot and the guiding spirit of Goldfield Con.[25]

The incorporation of Goldfield Con was soon followed by the establishment of a security apparatus, in which the lines of demarcation
between the mining company and the state were to become blurred
indeed. Governor Sparks's ready compliance with a request from Goldfield Con to send four state detectives to Goldfield during the December
1906 strike revealed two points of subsequent significance: Wingfield
clearly preferred to bypass local law enforcement officials and take his
business directly to the governor; and when he did so, his reception at the
capitol was a warm one. As a supplement to the state detectives,
Wingfield also engaged the Thiel Detective Agency. The following
September the state's police powers and Goldfield Con virtually
amalgamated when Clarence Sage, a Thiel detective, became the direc-

tor of both the Goldfield Con security forces and the state detectives. Sage's name would remain anathema to Goldfield miners for years to come.[26]

Detective Sage, later to be convicted of rape and manslaughter, was typical of the men with whom Wingfield surrounded himself. Another boon companion was Wingfield's bodyguard, Diamondfield Jack Davis, a gunman and convicted murderer. Also on hand was Sage's chum, George Gibson, shortly to be tried for a murder committed during a brawl in the tenderloin. Wingfield had only lately risen from the ranks of these frontier toughs, and when he was not cutting a fine figure as a mining millionaire at the tables of the rich and influential, he still clearly enjoyed their company. Their alignment with him was something more than old affinity buttressed by immediate necessity; indeed, for men who apparently refused to identify with the working class in an industrial economy and could not expect to continue their way of life in the Socialist utopia of the WFM-IWW, their choice showed a certain ideological consistency. "Workers of the world unite" was a theme with little appeal to the predatory riffraff who flourished in frontier boom-towns that had not yet completed the economic and cultural transition into urban industrial communities. Nor did working-class unity hold much attraction for the hired gun; although he worked for wages, he saw himself as an ally of his employer. Such men were the dark underside of the free enterprise system Wingfield championed. So, as the opposing armies began to assume a shadowy shape, it is not entirely surprising that the gunmen and petty criminals gravitated quickly and naturally to his side.

George Wingfield, unlike St. John and his cohorts, was not prone to composing manifestos. He was a secretive man, with the hooded expression of a good poker player, and he kept his own counsel. Yet he too must have been laying his plans, for he knew as surely as St. John that a critical struggle was at hand. The spies he had placed inside the union were bringing in reports that St. John saw Nevada as an isolated state of great wealth where the union could take control and gain possession of all property.[27] As the New Year of 1907 was toasted in Goldfield's famous Northern and the other brawling saloons, it was already apparent that this last of the great western boomtowns contained two groups of young men with very different ideas on the shape of the future.

If 1906 closed with economic boom and political polarization in Goldfield, it ended on a note of quiet prosperity and moderate reform in the nation as a whole. The Progressive movement was stirring. Theodore Roosevelt presided over the White House, the selective busting of trusts, and occasional displays of American power that swelled the patriotic breast. In Nevada, shortly after Morrie Preston's arrival, the equation was a little different. The urge to raise the banner of reform was not yet germinating in the mind of a young Goldfield lawyer named George Springmeyer, who would lead the Nevada Progressive party, and the new prosperity had nothing solid or conservative about it. It was a grand Saturday night revel, a splurge, the binge of a cowboy galloping into town with guns blazing at the end of a long trail drive. Left behind were the long years of deprivation between 1880 and 1900 after the decline of the Comstock, when Nevada's population sank by nearly a third and the production from her one important industry, mining, dwindled away. In the past were all the harsh expedients with which those who stayed on sought to survive those lean years: the long list of governmental reforms by which politicians strove to reduce a state government conceived in flush times to one within the means of starvelings; the temporary domination of state politics in the 1890s by the Silver party, through which the old guard deflected political protests into the safe channel of a single-issue pressure group; the dream of reclamation, to make agriculture succeed in the inhospitable desert where mining seemed to have failed.[28]

By New Year's Day 1907, economy and reclamation no longer mattered so much. The mining boom led by the Tonopah and Goldfield discoveries, and soon to be joined by the great copper mine near Ely, had brought so much prosperity that the state's population would nearly double in a single decade. Affluence spread out in ever-widening circles to the old ranching communities and commercial towns. Forgotten mining camps that had slumbered for years were alive once more with eager prospectors. Even Goldfield's radical union leaders were not immune to the frenzy. Several of them speculated in stocks and dealt in mining claims no less feverishly than other Goldfielders, trying to seize a piece of the capitalist world while awaiting the coming of the revolutionary utopia. Rumored discoveries of new mineral bonanzas crowded the pages of local newspapers, and if many proved less fabulous than their promoters claimed, this failed to dampen the bonanza spirit.

In the political arena, the Republican majority that had dominated the state from the Civil War until the 1890s was a thing of the past, the brief and ardent affair with the Silver party had grown cold, and Nevada had emerged as one of the Democratic islands in a nation where the Republicans were the traditional majority party. Critical in this political realignment was the vote of the miners streaming into the new boom camps. In

Goldfield alone, Democratic registration increased so massively that the national party awarded Major Minnemascot, the William Jennings Bryan mule, to the city after the 1908 election.[29] The Democratic margin in these camps might have been still larger had it not been for the introduction of a new political factor more potentially dangerous to the major parties than the Silver party had ever been—the Socialists.

Founded by Eugene V. Debs and others in 1901, the Socialist party sought the gradual transformation of the capitalist system through the democratic process. The new party immediately attracted a strong following within the WFM, which adopted Socialism as part of its constitution the following year. In his 1904 bid for the presidency, Debs became the first statewide Socialist candidate to appear on the Nevada ballot and drew 7.6 percent of the vote, a more notable showing than he achieved in the nation as a whole. "These are stirring times for living men," Debs told his followers during that campaign. "The day of crisis is drawing near . . . the old order can survive but little longer."[30]

In the next Nevada state election in 1906, the Socialist assault on the old order made a small but perceptible advance to nearly 10 percent of the vote; the party fielded both a full local ticket in Goldfield and a full state ticket. One of the most popular candidates was Joseph Smith, running for state treasurer, with the second largest vote accorded to any Nevada Socialist candidate in that election. The times were becoming too stirring for the comfort of many mainstream politicians, among whom one of the most preeminent was Theodore Roosevelt. In retrospect it is evident that the extreme concern of Roosevelt and others over the rising power of the Socialists was groundless, in view of the small Socialist percentage of the vote. But the political future was still clouded then, and the Socialists were arcing upward toward the zenith of 1912, when Debs would poll 6 percent of the national presidential vote and 1,200 Socialists would be elected to office on the state and local level. So high were the hopes that the Socialists themselves pinned on their future in Nevada that in 1912 the party's national organization launched a major electoral drive to win the state and succeeded in electing a Socialist state senator, an assemblyman, and twenty-nine county and township officials. In 1916 a Socialist colony was launched at Nevada City, the party polled nearly 30 percent of the vote for United States senator, and the Nevada Socialists wielded considerable political influence.[31]

The apprehensions of Nevadans of other political persuasions no doubt rose in tandem with Socialist hopes, for to them, in 1906, it seemed that the Socialists had a large potential constituency in the state, that in the avowedly Socialist WFM they possessed an active and dedicated cadre of organizers, already hard at work in building the party, and that the Socialist vote was creeping steadily upward, perhaps one day to attain majority status. Only half a century had passed since the rise of a new majority party in the Republicans, and the strength of the American consensus on democratic capitalism had not yet been tested against the Socialist challenge. So small was the Nevada electorate in 1906 that no state candidate polled as many as 9,000 votes, no winning margin was greater than 4,000 votes, and a relatively small number of voters could easily alter the balance. Not many who eyed this fragile electoral equation would be inclined to ignore the warning Debs sounded that year, "A mighty social revolution is impending—it is shaking the earth from center to circumference, and only the dead may be deaf to its rumblings."[32]

In Nevada those rumblings were especially audible on January 20, 1907, at the famous Bloody Sunday parade, held in commemoration of the failed Russian revolution of 1905 and the St. Petersburg massacre on Bloody Sunday. By order of the union, all mines, restaurants, and saloons were closed during the largest demonstration Goldfield had ever witnessed. While thousands watched from the sidewalks, the WFM-IWW paraded through the city to Miners' Union Hall, where St. John spoke from the balcony to an excited, cheering crowd. That night a mass meeting jammed Union Hall. Men, women, and children filled all the chairs, two hundred people stood in the center aisle, and many more crowded the stairs. Near the speakers hung a red banner inscribed to Haywood, Moyer, and Pettibone: "If they pack the jury to hang our men, we will pack hell full with them." This dreaded red flag of the Socialist revolution was to assume a large symbolic significance in the Preston-Smith trial.

Several battle-scarred young veterans of the years of bloody conflict that Sidney Lens has rightly termed *The Labor Wars* spoke from the podium that night—the fiery Sam Tregonning, St. John himself, and Robert Randell, a young man from Wyoming lately expelled from the United Mine Workers for defending the WFM. But noticed among them was a new apostle, whose swift and sudden rise to prominence in union affairs suggests considerable capacity for leadership, as well as an ability to ring the changes on union themes as well as any seasoned rabble-rouser on a street corner soapbox (Lillian's elocution lessons were bearing strange fruit). A short, burly figure rose, a pair of wide, gray eyes swept the hall, and Morrie Preston began what was to be his first and last major speech in Goldfield. He found conditions in America similar to those in Russia because both nations contained "the toilers

who produce and the capitalist class which robs workers and consumes."
He went on to exhort his listeners:

> Let us not be stopped in our purposes by the cry of "Anarchy." Those who
> try to intimidate us by throwing that word at us simply do so because they
> are utterly ignorant of the true meaning and purpose of anarchy and
> anarchists.
>
> The kidnaping of Moyer, Haywood, and Pettibone was endorsed and
> approved by the supreme court of the United States. This proves con-
> clusively that the same conditions exist here as in Russia, and the action of
> the supreme court in denying the writ of habeas corpus shows that in the
> future any man may be kidnapped, railroaded to prison and the gallows,
> and be murdered by legal prostitutes in the employ of capital, and all this
> with the sanction, encouragement, and aid of the highest court in this
> country.[33]

Within three months Preston's warning that "any man" might be rail-
roaded to prison by the capitalists was to gain a terrible prophetic
significance when he himself unwittingly provided the proof.

After Preston finished his speech, St. John rose to a standing ovation
and assured his listeners that if Haywood, Moyer, and Pettibone should
hang it "will explode the percussion cap of the coming revolution in this
country." He promised, "We will sweep the capitalist class out of the life
of this nation and then out of the whole world." The meeting concluded
with the passage of resolutions supporting the three imprisoned union
leaders and the Russian revolutionaries. "Your cause is our cause," the
Goldfielders declared to the Russians. "Your victory is our victory. We
have no enemy but the capitalist class! Our country is the world! Our flag
is the banner that is dyed red with the martyrs' blood of our class! Down
with capitalism! Long live the International working class republic!"[34]

Burning words, these from Union Hall. Perhaps they were only the
IWW variant of political rhetoric, no more to be taken seriously than the
conventional pieties of the mainstream politicians, and no more intended to be lived by. But it is easy to understand why contemporaries
took them very seriously indeed. It seemed that in Goldfield the IWW
was in the process of achieving the first stage of its program, the
organization of all workers in one big union. This was the working-class
rebellion in action, the planned process of creating the new syndicalist
society within the shell of the old. The next stage was the promised
revolution in which St. John would sweep the capitalists from the earth.
The union leaders had said it themselves. In the Nevada of 1906 a good
many people believed they meant exactly what they said.

III

THE TRIAL BEGINS

"Preston and Smith Indicted by the Grand Jury," read the March 29, 1907, headline in the *Tonopah Sun*. Above the headline was a large drawing of a thug wearing an IWW button. He had the close-cropped hair of a convict, a cauliflower ear, a frown, a malevolent squint, a grim, cruel mouth, and his heavy paw grasped a piece of paper with a skull and crossbones drawn upon it. "Motto. All men are equal. The Gospel According to St. John. De mines belongs to de miners and de gang—de millionaires is getting too thick around here—down wid de stars and stripes—dere is too many of our marters wearin de stripes—our cause is boosted by shootin men in the back—assassination is one of our specialties—we have got de whole state of Nevada on our list." Beneath the drawing was typed a quote from George Wingfield, "Compromise be damned." The *Sun*'s editorial urged Nevadans to "Exterminate the I.W.W."

The day after the shooting, Preston had walked with his attorney into the office of Justice of the Peace Isaac Solomon to give himself up. The *Sun* printed a false report on Preston's confession: an IWW committee had agreed to kill four men, including Silva, Wingfield, and Davis, and the prisoner was bitter because the others had not completed their assignments. Preston had made no such confession, but his attorneys would have done well to take note of this early hint that the shooting might metamorphose into a conspiracy case.

Union men faced an even more pressing danger when their opponents formed a Committee of Public Safety in the Montezuma Club. Security at the jail was so strict that even the constable on guard was not entrusted with a key; still, miners with guns formed a protective guard of their own around the jail. By the time the expected lynch party, dispatched by the Committee and led by Diamondfield Jack Davis, arrived at the jail shortly after midnight, they learned, "much to their disappointment and chagrin," that district attorney Henry Swallow had taken the wise precaution of moving the prisoners to the jail at Hawthorne, the Esmeralda County seat. The lynch party prowled on, their coil of greased rope in readiness, searching the streets of the city for the IWW leaders they hoped to hang. Ben Donnelly, St. John's right-hand man, was said to be hiding in the tenderloin. St. John himself, who had been expecting them for some time, was holed up in a cabin waiting with his rifle. "But they never came," he later wrote, "as they only cared to tackle unarmed and unsuspecting victims." The lynch party disbanded without finding any of their intended prey—at least none they cared to take on.[1]

At the end of March, Preston was indicted for the murder of Silva and for assault with intent to kill upon one of Silva's employees. Also indicted as an accessory to Silva's murder, as well as for the assault, was Joseph Smith. While Preston never denied shooting Silva, the evidence presented to the grand jury that indicted Smith remains obscure. The main witness against him during the trial would tell a story that completely surprised the defense. Smith had directed the boycott against the Nevada Restaurant and Silva had mentioned him—erroneously—in his dying declaration as the picket Preston replaced, but this hardly sufficed for his indictment as an accessory to murder. Perhaps the main reason for Smith's indictment was his prominent position. After the 1899 conviction of Paul Corcoran, financial secretary of the Burke, Idaho, WFM local, on a murder charge despite his absence from the scene of the dynamiting at the Bunker Hill concentrator plant, prosecutor James H. Hawley recalled that the object was not to punish small fry whose convictions were unimportant to the future of the region but to demonstrate that "the law would reach anyone," even a man of high standing in the community against whom the prosecutors lacked proof.[2] The indictment of Smith, a radical union activist, a town trustee, and a Socialist candidate for state office, may have been intended to beam a similar signal in Nevada.

If hard information on the case the state was building against Preston and Smith was scanty, rumors abounded. Four secret indictments on the Preston-Smith case had reportedly been returned by the grand jury but no arrests ensued. The IWW was said to be planning "an attempt at jail delivery" for the pair. On Easter Sunday, soon after the indictments, six heavily armed law officers appeared in the "rickety county bastile" at Hawthorne. According to the press, when Preston and Smith were suddenly told to prepare themselves for a trip, they anticipated a lynching and turned "pale as death itself and trembled like victims of palsy." Their apprehension was not entirely without cause. Two days later the cartoon donkey which voiced the sentiments of the *Tonopah Sun* appeared on the front page to prod readers with the words, "When a few of these anarchists stretch rope, then and not until then can we boast of our Western blood."[3]

Preston later insisted that the removal of himself and Smith to the state penitentiary occurred when the district judge finally consented to their attorneys' request to change their place of confinement so they would not be "murdered by slow torture in those dungeon like death-tanks." Realizing their presence was "provocative of trouble," the pair had requested incarceration first in Hawthorne instead of Goldfield, and then in the state penitentiary. In a pamphlet he later wrote, Preston bitterly described their confinement during those two weeks:

> The jail at Hawthorne was at the back and southwest corner of the Courthouse and being a part of the main building, and the two outer walls were about three feet thick, composed of brick and stone. The ceiling was high (about 15 feet) and the four windows were small and placed high up in the wall, probably 9 or 10 feet from the floor, thus making the jail room, although above ground, a veritable cellar. In this jail room was a row of cells, about eight in number, built of solid sheet steel, not the usual barred door and front effect. The individual cell was practically a sweat tank, the only ventilation being through several small holes in the roof of the tank, several other small holes over the door and a sort of wicket in the middle of the door which for Smith and Preston was kept closed most of the time, seldom being opened except when food was to be passed in. To get a clear idea of the ventilation or lack of ventilation of these tanks it must be remembered that these openings in the tanks let directly into the large cellar like jail room and only communicated indirectly or by a very circuitous route, with the outside. . . . It must be remembered too, that the jail was quite crowded which only made matters worse. . . .
>
> Bearing this condition in mind you may get some idea of the torture Smith and Preston suffered during two weeks of almost continuous confinement in these tanks, which were six by eight in dimensions and housed each two men at night. Some days they were permitted to take breakfast and the afternoon meal in the jail room which gave them a half hour each meal out of the tanks. Most days, however, they had to take meals in the tanks, thus making their confinement continuous throughout the day and night.

The effect of this treatment was a most striking running down of strength, health and mental stamina, all of which was, we have reason to believe, just the effect desired by the officers of the prosecution . . . one of the prosecuting officers was later heard to remark: "If we had those fellows (Smith and Preston) in our hands a few days longer neither of them would be able to testify in their own or anybody's behalf."

Preston claimed that their pallor and weakness when taken from jail were not due to fear of lynching as the press alleged; rather the law officers had "deliberately contrived to produce this condition by methods worthy of the inquisition, illegally and with malicious intent."[4] While the move to the state penitentiary may well have been requested, as Preston recalled, by the defense attorneys, its timing suggests that the authorities genuinely feared an escape attempt. Law enforcement officials would hardly have spent Easter Sunday escorting Preston and Smith to Carson if these fears had not been real and immediate. Preston clearly saw the questionable comforts of death row, where he was confined at close quarters with condemned murderers, as an improvement, yet the change was detrimental to his cause in at least one respect: he acknowledged that his confinement in Carson prevented "immediate communication," not only with his friends, but more importantly with his attorneys, now separated from him by a journey of more than 200 miles and sharply restricted in their efforts to prepare the case by a "shoe string" budget. Because jury selection for the Haywood trial was slated to commence at the end of April, the attention and resources the WFM would ordinarily have accorded to Preston and Smith were almost totally concentrated on the three union leaders and on the preliminary murder trial on an unrelated charge of Steve Adams, whose acquittal was important to the union because his serious legal predicament provided the prosecutors with the leverage by which they hoped to mold him into a corroborating witness for Orchard. These Idaho trials—Haywood's, Pettibone's, and Adams's, on two separate occasions—would so deplete the WFM treasury that the union would be unable even to pay Darrow his promised legal fee.[5]

While Preston and Smith remained in confinement, strife between the union and the mine owners and tension in the streets continued in Goldfield. Indeed in retrospect the *Goldfield Daily Tribune* saw the Silva shooting as the catalyst that set the events of that spring in motion.[6] Some perceived it as confirmation of their worst fears concerning union violence; others seized on it as a useful, even providential, incident that could be used to justify the destruction of the IWW, the shock that would serve to unite the long-divided mine owners. If any hoped the shooting would also turn union conservatives against the IWW, that hope was quickly dashed. The mines were shut down for two days to "allow" the miners to participate in an anti-IWW parade, but none materialized—no doubt to the chagrin of the mine owners. In a mass meeting on March 13, the miners voted 900 to 2 against the separation of the IWW and the WFM.

When the coroner's jury refrained on the same day from fixing the responsibility for Silva's death, an indignant meeting convened in the Montezuma Club that night. The belief had gained wide currency that, as historian Laura White later put it, the restaurant owner's demise was "a cold blooded murder and only the first of a series of outrages planned by a band of anarchists."[7] A bullet whistling out of the darkness near bank president John S. Cook the night after the shooting was seen as the second outrage, though no one was hurt and no union assassin crumpled in the nearby alley under Diamondfield Jack's answering volley of shots. Interested parties undoubtedly realized that in this climate of opinion a conviction certain to yield maximum publicity benefits to the union's opponents was likely if the Preston-Smith trial could be scheduled as quickly as possible. The rising public hysteria was already driving into Wingfield's legions many business and professional men who would not otherwise have condoned his policy of confrontation with the union.

On March 14 the Goldfield Mine Owners and Businessmen's Association (GMOBA) was organized in the Montezuma Club. Amid great enthusiasm, resolutions were passed in favor of closing down all mines and businesses until the IWW had been rooted out of Goldfield. On March 15 the temporary shutdown to encourage the abortive parade became a lockout; only saloons, barbershops, restaurants, and prounion establishments remained open. GMOBA's resolution declared "henceforth and forever" no one would be employed "who belongs to the outlaw organization known as the IWW"; to enforce this, mines and businesses would remain closed "for eternity" if necessary.[8] Just five days had passed since Morrie Preston shot John Silva.

Goldfield law enforcement officers endeavored throughout the trying weeks that followed to steer a careful course between GMOBA and the union. Censured in the *Sun* for his efforts to maintain neutrality, Constable Claude Inman responded that sitting on the fence was exactly the position he desired. Sheriff William A. Ingalls, by no means unsympathetic to the miners, reportedly appointed thirty prounion deputies when the trouble began, but GMOBA's executive committee offset this by appointing fifty from the group always referred to in the *Sun* as the "citizens" and undertaking to pay their expenses. In fact, "citizens" appears to be a misleading description of the deputies GMOBA was recruiting. White cites evidence that numerous ex-convicts were in this group, many with long records as "thugs" or holdup men.[9]

With this private army at their command, GMOBA indisputably controlled the city, and it grew difficult to discern where the mine owners' association ended and city governance began. GMOBA's executive committee remained in continuous session. Company guards were dispatched to patrol the streets and stationed at the entrances to public buildings and offices to forestall the anticipated assassination of the mine owners. Diamondfield Jack sped out of town on an urgent mission and returned with the tonneau of his auto stacked high with guns. Business ground to a halt. On March 19 the *Tonopah Sun* found the city tense and seething with "sensational rumors of every kind" and assured its readers that GMOBA stood ready to "act at the first indication of lawlessness."[10] It was not an assurance from which union men would draw much comfort.

Meanwhile Branson seemed to be assiduously striving in his own inimitable style to push the city over the brink. Beneath the headline "ANARCHISTS GROWING BOLDER AT GOLDFIELD," the next day's issue of the *Sun* featured an unsupported rumor that three scabs had disappeared in Goldfield, one murdered and two severely beaten. Though deputies set forth from the Montezuma Club in search of two "gangs" with prisoners, there was no one to be found—no doubt, the *Sun* suggested, because the bodies had been pitched into an old prospect hole. The newspaper added, "If the deputies had stumbled on that crowd of anarchists that night, the IWW men would never have been given a chance to talk. They would have been shot down like the dogs they are."[11] Branson generally used the term "anarchists" synonymously with IWW, well aware that America probably knew no harsher term of opprobrium during the first two decades of the twentieth century, which began with President McKinley's assassination by an anarchist in 1901 and saw recurrent bombings and assassinations attributed to anarchists.

Another of Branson's favorite themes appeared in the March 25 and 26 issues of the *Sun*. Here he accused the IWW of "methods worse than the Black Hand of Italy." Cards bearing a skull and crossbones and an order to leave town had, according to the *Sun,* been received by several non-IWW miners, one of the carpenters slated to testify for the state in the Preston-Smith trial, and also by "some of the brave men who have dared to assist Goldfield's citizens in their attempt to stamp out the corrupt anarchistic disease that was slowly eating away the heart of Nevada."[12]

There were sound reasons for the *Sun*'s renewed attacks. Despite the lockout, the deputy gunmen, and the intense pressure, the union appeared to be not only holding its own but also gaining ground, as was presently illustrated when Goldfield's unorganized miners voted to join the WFM and an attempt by conservative miners to establish a new union ended in failure. The *Sun* claimed the ability of the "wily agitator" St. John and his "fire eaters" to dominate miners' meetings had produced these unwelcome victories. A typical *Sun* cartoon depicted the WFM as a miner hauling a wagonload of IWW leaders cracking their whips over his bent and straining back; the cartoonist advised the miner to "jump the traces" while he could.[13]

On April 5, Vincent St. John, a .45 caliber shotgun protruding from his vest, was arrested for carrying concealed weapons, then disarmed and released. Constable Inman and Justice Solomon announced their intention to disarm everyone "not entitled to the privilege of carrying weapons, irrespective of position, wealth, or social standing." Other arrests ensued, and deputies soon confiscated so large a stack of armaments that storage space became a problem. Despite the law officers' declaration of neutrality, union men were the apparent objects of their attention, while GMOBA members, their supporters, and their hired gunmen became deputies with the right to carry arms.[14]

This warning to St. John coincided with a period of intense infighting between moderates and radicals within the union. The next day a mass meeting of miners convened by acting WFM national president Charles Mahoney voted 514 to 56 in favor of separating from the IWW. But an agreement was not yet in sight. On April 8 a committee informed the mine owners that the miners would insist on supporting IWW boycotts. The mine owners responded that this was unacceptable and held fast to the position Wingfield had enunciated in a press interview March 29: "If we back down on our policy now, we would show ourselves to be curs of the worst sort, and we are not that. Compromise be damned. The Goldfield mines will stay closed down until hell freezes over before we open them to let a lot of anarchists tell us how to run our property."[15]

The employers' intransigence apparently strengthened the radicals. When a meeting of the full WFM membership convened the next day, St. John leapt to his feet to speak against the employers' attempt to "kick out" the IWW, and even the conservative Mahoney concurred with him.

The miners then voted to nullify the separation from the IWW as an illegal act on the ground that there was no such union because the local had dropped its charter when it joined the miners' union.[16]

Two weeks later, with Goldfield veering ever closer to martial law and many union members suffering from the hardships of a prolonged lockout, the balance shifted once more. AFL organizer Grant Hamilton was gaining a more sympathetic hearing when he taunted the IWW, "You say you want all you produce in the city of Goldfield? You produced hell and you've got all of it."[17] By the time two hundred stands of arms for the formation of a militia arrived, St. John could no longer rally the votes behind the IWW, and the union sent its IWW charter back to national headquarters to be exchanged for one referring only to the WFM. On April 21 the WFM and the mine owners reached an agreement that signified the first defeat in Goldfield for the long-triumphant IWW. The union agreed not to support IWW boycotts and accepted a provision requiring a two-thirds strike vote. The only real compromise by employers was acceptance of the union's position that the link between the WFM and the IWW could not be totally severed as long as the two unions remained affiliated at the national level, a state of affairs expected to end at the next WFM convention (though it would in fact continue until 1908).

Walter Brown, president of WFM Local No. 220, and Mahoney refrained from comment and simply presented the agreement reached under their auspices to a mass meeting of miners convened in the ball park. Deputy sheriffs, their presence clearly underscoring the bitter alternative of military rule, surrounded the fence to prevent any non-members from entering; roadblocks manned by more deputies guarded all approaches. The only speech at the meeting was made by St. John, and it was a long and powerful diatribe against the agreement. The labor troubles were entirely the fault of the mine owners, said St. John, speaking in his usual simple, straight-from-the-shoulder style, and his followers should make no compromises with them. He argued that a two-thirds strike vote would be impossible to achieve and would bring Goldfield into perpetual captivity. The *Goldfield Daily Tribune* saw a veiled warning of union violence in his plea to send the mine owners a message: if Goldfield became a scab town, "they will find we have different cards up our sleeves to play." Opponents of the union had blamed St. John's persuasive powers and magnetic personality for blocking the earlier agreement. So many times he had carried the day, waiting patiently while his enemies tried to hiss him down, smiling, and in the end winning them over. But this time the cheers for St. John died away and the agreement was ratified. The eternity for which the mine owners had threatened to extend the lockout had lasted just thirty-eight days. Lindley Branson could write with satisfaction on the *Sun*'s editorial page, "the I.W.W. is dead."[18]

While the labor settlement at Goldfield moved through the final stage to ratification, Preston and Smith, accompanied by a full complement of deputies and the devoted Lillian Burton, set out on the train trip from Carson City to Hawthorne for the trial. Although Goldfield was by far the largest city in Esmeralda County and had recently won the designation of county seat, adequate courthouse facilities were not yet ready and legal business was still being conducted in Hawthorne, a little town near Walker Lake at the intersection of the freight roads from the old mining camps of Aurora, Candelaria, and Bodie. A glimpse of the town as it appeared to those converging for the trial in late April is included in a newspaper essay by special prosecutor Booth M. Malone. Rising in the morning at the Wooley house, where he was rooming, Malone stepped into the yard and found a desert paradise of flowers, tall, shady poplars, and blooming fruit trees—at least in contrast to the barren landscape he had just left behind in Goldfield:

> Turning to the right, I first saw a large and beautiful sheet of water which I afterwards learned to be Walker Lake. . . . Set midway between and surrounded on all sides by mountains, some of them snow capped and glistening in the morning sun on a sandy and sage brush plain, the village with its green foliage and lawns seemed like a little daisy in the desert. The lake reflected and threw over the town a soft and mellow light from the morning sun and gave it a rich and beautiful tinge of yellow that was indeed charming. I really stood entranced and thought it one of the most picturesque scenes I had ever beheld.[19]

Malone also took note of a "beautiful and toothsome" banquet "enlivened by music, song, and story" at Mrs. Arcum's "chinese home" during one of the trial's several tedious delays. Others, including the 140 prospective jurors summoned to Hawthorne, may have been less comfortably housed than the prestigious Malone. Accommodations were already at a premium, and beds would soon command high prices. The *Sun*'s cartoonist, only half in jest, drew two men sleeping under a bath towel on a crap table and captioned it, "The lawyers had suites in the haylofts so the reporters had to take over."[20]

Malone had been brought to Nevada from Denver as a special counsel, his fee reportedly paid by GMOBA, to bolster the talents of District

Attorney Albert Henry Swallow, his assistant, Emmett Walsh, and special prosecutor John Frank Douglas. Despite the frequent presence of corporation lawyers aiding elected officials in American labor cases, importing the likes of Malone was an unusual move in Goldfield, suggesting that the prosecution's case was in need of an infusion of legal talent from a highly distinguished western attorney. The background of the fifty-two-year-old Malone easily dwarfed that of the small-town lawyers in the courtroom—and the judge. After receiving his law degree from Albany Law School, Malone was admitted to practice before the U.S. Supreme Court and served as mayor of Beloit, Wisconsin, and later as Rock County district attorney, before moving to Denver in 1892. Following a stint as assistant district attorney, he was elected Denver district attorney in 1896 and became a district judge in 1901. He had stepped down from the bench less than six months before accepting the Preston-Smith case.

Although Malone was not yet ensconced in the union's legal demonology, and had even been praised by the WFM during his judgeship, his presence clearly signaled the mine owners' determination to secure a conviction with no possible margin for error and their lack of confidence in District Attorney Swallow. The district attorney's legal experience was not lengthy, having commenced five years earlier in Denver, where so many Goldfield attorneys had run their trial heats. Also, as a Democrat at a time and place where the Democrats had assumed a prolabor stance and were seeking to build a constituency among the miners, Swallow was not in the same partisan key as George Wingfield and other Republican notables in the mine owners' association, and Wingfield may have harbored apprehensions that the twenty-nine-year-old, Illinois-born prosecutor would be less zealous in prosecuting a union case than mindful of the sympathies of the miners who had voted him into office. If doubts of this nature lay behind the engaging of Judge Malone, a former president of the Colorado Republican State League, they would prove unfounded. Swallow, aided by Douglas, was to conduct his case brilliantly and zealously, with no more than occasional interjections from Malone. Only at the hour of the final argument would the famous Colorado attorney, whose prowess greatly alarmed the defense, at last break silence to consummate the prosecution's case.[21]

All things considered, it would appear that the union had more cause to doubt the competence and commitment of their attorneys than their opponents did. Although the great boom had attracted many outstanding legal talents to Goldfield and the able performance of two of them in subsequent union cases suggests that they would willingly have de-

fended Preston and Smith, the union instead turned to Patrick ("Patsy")
M. Bowler, a Tonopah attorney and an old-timer, and Frank J. Hangs,
an inauspiciously named WFM attorney from Colorado. In common
with many lawyers of the period, neither of the defense attorneys had
attended law school, or even graduated from college, though the dark,
heavy-set, forty-six-year-old Hangs was the more educated of the two,
having spent two and a half years at Denver University prior to his
admission to the bar in 1887. Both had held minor offices during their
long legal careers, Bowler as a district attorney before the great boom
transformed the central Nevada landscape and Hangs as a Denver justice
of the peace and a Cripple Creek city attorney.

Union men knew that Hangs could scarcely match the glittering
credentials of the prosecution team, but the defense of the WFM leadership had top priority. Before his summons to Goldfield, Hangs had been
working on the Haywood investigation in a subordinate capacity; a
Pinkerton informant later claimed the union attorney had tried to bribe
him to bear false witness on Haywood's behalf. Before his involvement
in the Haywood case, Hangs had played a prominent part in the 1903
Cripple Creek strike and reportedly was himself thrown in the bull pens
for his efforts to compel the state militia to observe the constitutional
rights of union men. Hangs, however, would later make clear that his
sympathy for Goldfield's union leaders was slight. He believed a
"tougher element" was in control of the union in Goldfield than in
Colorado, a group of men ready to override law and government
whenever they obstructed union power. He would take their case, but he
recoiled from their cause.[22]

In many ways, Bowler seemed the ideal complement to Hangs. After
making the overland journey west as a child in an ox-drawn wagon,
Bowler had worked as a buckaroo, then taught himself law. By the time
of his death he would enjoy a reputation for securing the freedom of
more murder clients than any other Nevada attorney of his time. Union
leaders doubtless believed that an old-timer like Bowler, who had been
practicing in the region twenty years before Goldfield was even a gleam
in a prospector's eye, would bring to the case the necessary connections
with the local establishment, would be more acceptable to a Nevada
judge and jury than an out-of-state attorney who had devoted himself to
radical causes, and would be in all ways the insider that outsiders like
themselves could never be. Also Bowler had shown himself willing and
able to buck the mine owners by successfully defending the accused in
Goldfield's first high-grading case nearly three years earlier. Willing he
was, and also idealist enough to defend many an impoverished but

innocent man without pay, yet it remained to be seen if the old vaquero schooled by the frontier understood how to do battle with the industrial juggernaut of the new age.[23]

None of Nevada's four district judges—perhaps none in the West—presided over a more diverse district than Frank Langan did. Comprising more than 10,000 square miles of territory, it included quiet and staid Carson City, the Nevada capital, the ranching communities in Douglas and Lyon counties, Goldfield and all the lesser mining camps of Esmeralda County, and the old Comstock region, now in a slump but still able to support a small population of miners. However, it was brawling, raucous Goldfield that occupied the lion's share of Judge Langan's time and would shortly lead to the appointment of two district judges for Goldfield alone and the restructuring of Langan's district without Esmeralda County.

Forty-one years old, heavy set, fair haired, with a short, thick mustache, Judge Langan was a native Nevadan and the son of an early pioneer on the Comstock, where he still lived with his wife and five children. He had received his LL.B. at twenty from Hastings Law School in San Francisco and immediately began two decades of law practice, interrupted only by a single term as assemblyman in the 1889 state legislature. In his electoral contests for district attorney on the Comstock, Langan had been defeated as often as he had won, a record which suggests political vulnerability, but he easily overwhelmed his Republican and Socialist opponents when he ran for district judge on the victorious Democrat-Silver ticket in 1906. Union men were led to believe that he would be more sympathetic to them than the incumbent Republican judge who had struck down the eight-hour law, and support from the Goldfield WFM may have played an important role in his victory. Although Langan had long experience as a prosecutor, having served as Storey County district attorney for two terms and also as assistant district attorney, at the time of the trial he had been on the bench for less than six months.[24]

The trial of Preston and Smith opened on April 19 with a sensational order from Judge Langan: "Mr. Sheriff, I want you to search every man who presents himself for admission to this court room, and if you find any weapons on him, bring him before the bar at once and I will see that he is severely punished." As deputy sheriffs searched spectators at the narrow door leading into the courtroom, a pile of revolvers of various sizes and descriptions began to accumulate. The *Goldfield Daily Tribune* reporter found excitement in the courthouse at "fever heat." So marked were the "lines of cleavage between friends and enemies of the accused men" that the judge barred both union men and members of the Montezuma Club from the proceedings, though it does not appear that this rule was effectively enforced. No violence would actually occur, except a spurt of gunfire from the darkness drumming into the sand near attorney Hangs's feet as he walked toward the Hawthorne jail one night to visit his clients and the jittery guards mistook his approach for an attempted jailbreak. But later events would suggest that someone would ponder the judge's anxieties and capitalize on them.

Preston and Smith were led into the jammed courtroom by a deputy sheriff. Unmoved by the stares of the crowd, Preston was almost overcome when he saw Lillian Burton, Zora Fischer, and Zora's four-year-old son, Louis. He caught the child and embraced him almost convulsively as they passed. When the prisoners were seated, Lillian leaned over Preston, affectionately stroking his forehead. Smith managed an occasional smile as the business of empaneling a jury proceeded, while Preston stared out the windows into the desert beyond.

As part of his effort to eliminate unfavorable jurors, attorney Bowler asked several talesmen if they were members of the Montezuma Club or had ever been entertained there. He also wanted to know whether the prospective juror harbored any prejudice regarding murders that followed labor troubles. Ten were excused because they admitted having already formed opinions on the case. A large crowd surged in the wake of the deputies when they led the accused men away at the end of the day.[25]

Preston later came to believe that "certain interested parties deliberately conspired to mislead possible jurors, and the people of the State at large" in a carefully planned and well-financed campaign of slander. He wrote: "not less than fifty men, fairly well known in the State, were hired to travel throughout the State at great expense, spreading false stories concerning the incidents of the shooting." The procedure was as follows:

> A hireling,—but unknown as such at the time,—would wander into a town and on meeting an acquaintance would remark that he had just come from Goldfield. The Goldfield affair being fresh in the public mind, the listener would naturally ask about the trouble there. Casually then, and confidentially, the paid agent would let it be known that he had been an eye-witness of the Silva shooting. After a little further mock mystery and simulated secretiveness he would say: "You know, my sympathies are with the Union, but that was such a cold-blooded affair, my testimony would be

against them, so I left." This would, of course, lead to further questions about the matter and the hired narrator, still casually and "by way of no harm," would conclude with the information that "this Preston fellow, who is an old-time dynamiter from Colorado, slipped into the restaurant and up behind Silva, and shot him twice before he knew what was up . . ."

This "confidential proof" that the prisoners were "old offenders," therefore clinched a state-wide snap judgment of the case. Here was a combination, backed by unlimited money, which it proved impossible to offset. . . . The revealer of this very effective scheme remarked in conclusion, "We knew we had the newspapers lined up and that they would undoubtedly go through with the plan, but this other method offered double assurance, and it was certainly worth the money for our purpose."

This boastful admission on the part of one of the participants, practically establishes the truth of the report that some of the Mine Owners contributed as high as $10,000 each to the fund. . . .[26]

Jury selection continued on Saturday with the defendants looking optimistic as they sat in court, Smith's black head characteristically tilted upward in a questioning attitude and considerably above the level of his short companion's blond one. Smith's wife, Alice, visited her husband at the noon recess and the period after adjournment but refrained from bringing her baby into the room while court was in session. The Montezuma Club and labor troubles continued to figure prominently in Bowler's questions. A "slight sensation" occurred in court when the defense attorney launched his first challenge against the acceptance of a juror on grounds of bias and Swallow resisted the challenge. Bowler protested that the prosecution might have the decency to wait until he had concluded his remarks and was sharply reproved by Judge Langan. It was not an auspicious omen.

Three more prospective jurors were excused because they did not believe in capital punishment, and the questioning wore on. Did the talesman consider that an organization had the right to boycott within proper limits? Did he think a restaurant owner had the right to assault a picket with a deadly weapon? Relying on a challenge for cause, Bowler attempted to oust a prospective juror who declared that he was prejudiced against Smith because the union man had attempted to organize his employees for the IWW, but Judge Langan denied the challenge. Although Bowler was able to reject the juror by using one of his limited number of peremptory challenges, the judge's ruling was the second sign, even before testimony began, that all did not bode well for the defense. The anticipated defense request for separate trials for the two defendants had not materialized, and it was now too late to enter it.

Those jurymen passed for cause but still subject to peremptory challenge were ordered sequestered by Judge Langan, a marked departure from normal legal procedure in that time and place.[27]

A surprise development that was to have a far-reaching effect on the trial rocketed into the news on the third day of jury selection, as the grand jury assembled in Hawthorne completed its task and rumors about secret indictments began to circulate. A similar story had gone the rounds in late March when Preston and Smith were indicted, and those inclined to place a sporting bet had found the odds two to one in favor of St. John's immediate arrest, but nothing had happened. This time, however, the rumormongers had made no mistake. Under Sheriff Bart Knight arrived in Goldfield on April 23 by the morning train with a pocketful of indictments. Deputies, their numbers bolstered by a host of men newly appointed for the occasion, moved quickly to pick up St. John and Ben Donnelly at Union Hall, Harry Jardine at his cabin, and A. J. Johnson in front of the Mohawk Saloon. Jerry Sexton was notified of his arrest in the office of a brokerage company where he was completing a deal, and requested a few minutes to finish his business. Dan Roudebush was out of the state. The *Tonopah Sun* noted with a sneer, "It is reported that at least fifty men skipped town yesterday fearing indictment or being called as witnesses."[28]

Although the arrests were carried out in great haste, the crowd of friends who gathered to laugh and joke with the union leaders as they waited under guard seemed in a jovial mood. When the prisoners were marched away to catch the train to Hawthorne, friends shouted "goodby, boys," as though they were "a bunch of picnickers." This lighthearted attitude was sharply rebuked in the *Tribune,* which laid the blame for Silva's death on an "inner circle" by whom Preston was "IN-STRUCTED TO KILL." Candidly acknowledging the true sources of the conspiracy case, the *Tribune* noted that the indictments had been filed in accordance with evidence "unearthed by the businessmen of Goldfield." Despite rumors that the miners' union would strike in protest against the indictment of their leaders, the WFM was apparently reluctant to take such action just when the long-awaited agreement had been reached. President Mahoney urged "conservatism in every case," and union members contented themselves with voting to obtain top legal talent to defend the indicted leaders.[29]

As the questioning of talesmen for the Preston-Smith trial continued on Monday, nearly the entire morning was spent on the examination of one prospective juror, a miner, concerning his views on the respective rights of capital and labor. By 3:00 that afternoon, thirteen peremptory challenges remained, and the press began voicing apprehensions that jury selection might consume several more days. It was well known that extreme care in jury selection often spelled the difference between victory and defeat when Goldfield public opinion was adverse to the defendant.

Nonetheless, by 11:15 the next morning, jury selection was suddenly complete, a development that cast some doubt on the judgment of the defense attorneys. Bowler and Hangs later claimed they had despaired of finding an unprejudiced jury because every prospective juror had already discussed the case. They even raised no objection when venire-man W. E. Steineck, a well-known mine operator, admitted with embarrassment that he had gone drinking with District Attorney Swallow. In the Haywood trial, by contrast, jury selection would grind on for a prolonged period and finally produce a jury consisting mostly of farmers, after the prosecution had rejected all union members and Socialists and Darrow had weeded out the businessmen with a ruthless efficiency that Haywood later likened to "killing snakes."[30] Bowler, unfortunately for his clients, was not one for killing snakes. The jury he pronounced acceptable contained a teamster from Sweetwater; a Goldfield real estate man; a Goldfield assayer; two mining men, one from Oro City and one from Mina; three miners, two from Aurora and one from Goldfield; and four ranchers, two from Sweetwater and two from the East Walker River. When court resumed after the lunch recess, all witnesses were sworn in and ordered excluded from the courtroom during the trial at the request of both the prosecution and the defense.[31]

The opening statement for the prosecution was made by special prosecutor John F. Douglas, a politician well known for his close connections with the local Republican establishment, which he would ably serve on several future occasions, and a future manager of the glamorous new Goldfield Hotel, completed the following year. A member of one of Nevada's earliest pioneer families, he had left the family ranch near Reno to attend the University of California, Berkeley, and read law in California. He arrived early at the Goldfield boom in February 1905. By the spring of 1906 Douglas had landed an appointment as Goldfield district attorney when political enemies forced the incumbent out of office, but Swallow defeated his effort to retain the coveted position in the November general election. His parallel career as manager of the original Goldfield Hotel had undergone a comparable setback when the hotel burned down that same autumn.[32]

Blond, clean-shaven, and youthful at thirty-two, with small monkey-like features, Douglas began his opening statement by describing the source of the difficulty between Silva and the IWW. He declared that the state would show that employees who left without notice had so hampered Silva's business that he had been forced to start docking their pay. Smith had called the strike following the former waitress's complaint, but Silva had nonetheless secured a cook and a waiter, both of whom Preston and Smith persuaded to come to Union Hall, where they were severely beaten. Defense attorney Bowler objected that this matter had nothing to do with the case, but Douglas explained that the state would prove a conspiracy to murder Silva, and the objection was overruled. That same night the defendants had met with others in Union Hall and conspired to murder Silva. Indeed Preston would have killed Silva a day sooner if he could have been enticed to the door of the restaurant. On the day of the shooting, the conspirators met again to spin their plot and to threaten the life of a well-known Goldfield citizen. Preston was chosen to commit the murder.

Shortly before the killing, Douglas continued, Preston and Smith were seen watching the restaurant, and Preston's remark about "getting the son of a bitch" had been overheard. Preston had commenced picketing. Finally, Silva went to the door and told Preston to go away and mind his own business. While the state acknowledged that Silva had a gun, the restaurant owner had held it behind him and made no move to use it. As Silva appeared in the door, said Douglas, "the cowardly assassin Preston fired at Silva, fatally wounding him, after which Preston ran to the corner, where he was joined by a number of his companions, who took him up to Miners' Union Hall." He was arrested the following day, after he learned that his identity was known. The state would also show that when Smith was arrested he asked the officer to protect him and inquired whether "the others" had also been arrested, showing the existence of a conspiracy to murder Silva. The prosecution would offer testimony revealing the presence of this conspiracy. This killing, Douglas concluded gravely, was one of the blackest crimes in the history of Nevada.

The union, in the person of Morrie Preston, stood accused of premeditated murder. It was now the state's task to prove it.[33]

IV

WITNESSES FOR THE PROSECUTION

Like a balky horse spurred to a gallop, the trial, once started, lunged forward with surprising speed. Douglas had made the prosecution's opening statement when court reconvened after lunch at 1:30; then came the witnesses. The first was a surveyor, who presented plats showing the layout and location of Silva's restaurant on Ramsey Street about seventy feet from Main Street. Dr. Bradford S. Galloway was next. With Dr. Delos A. Turner, he had attended Silva and taken him in a carriage to the hospital for treatment. He had remained until the patient died of "hemorrhage and gunshot wound" at about midnight, a little more than four hours after the shooting. Galloway said the fatal bullet had entered Silva's body on the left side between the seventh and eighth ribs and passed "slightly downward and backwards" through his stomach and the right lobe of his liver, grazing the top of his right kidney and lodging just under the skin in his back, about six inches from his spinal column. Dr. Galloway was unable to say whether the same bullet had also made the wound between the thumb and forefinger of Silva's left hand. Silva's clothing was torn, and the doctor had noticed an abrasion, possibly caused by a bullet, three to six inches long across Silva's chest in the vicinity of the stomach.

Bowler and Hangs were constantly on their feet objecting to the questions put to the doctor, being overruled, and requesting the exceptions on which they could base an appeal. "Give counsel the benefit of an exception," Judge Langan finally declared, in place of the customary "give counsel an exception." It was a formula that would grate on the nerves of the defense attorneys each time it was repeated throughout the trial and one in which WFM attorney Hilton saw clear evidence of judicial bias when he later reviewed the trial record:

> Counsel had a *right* to the exception. It was a constitutional right and its force ought not to be explained away by saying that even with the *"benefit of the exception,"* even when granting them all the grace they ask, still they are wrong and . . . guilty. . . . "We are trying these men, it is true, but their guilt," says the manner of the Court, "is so plain, that it is merely formal, and I am showing great patience, gentlemen of the jury, in letting them take up the time of the court with objections that you and I know are simply for delay, and yet I am magnanimously allowing the 'benefit of these exceptions.' "[1]

Despite Bowler's objections, Dr. Galloway was allowed to express his opinion that Silva was standing "sideways" rather than facing the man who shot him. It was not an image that accorded well with Preston's contention that he had shot in self-defense against a man who was threatening him.

Aside from Silva's wounds, both prosecution and defense were anxious to hear about Silva's dying declaration. When the doctor first told Silva he could only live a short time and asked him if he wanted to make a dying statement, Silva simply turned his head and said he didn't care. District Attorney Swallow and Constable Inman later put the question to him again. This time Silva responded that the man who shot him was "the walking delegate who took Smith's place, a short man." While confirming that this man's name was Preston, Silva denied that there had been any previous trouble between them. He told the district attorney that the walking delegates had been out in front of his restaurant interfering with his business and trying to keep people from coming inside. Bowler, apparently hoping to forestall histrionics on Silva's bereaved family by the prosecution during closing arguments, tried to determine during cross-examination whether Silva had mentioned any relatives. The doctor thought Silva had told someone, possibly Inman, that he had a wife in California, but he had been too busy caring for Silva in the operating room to pay much attention to the conversation.[2]

Dr. Galloway was followed by Mrs. Nellie Emery, a cook who had worked in the Nevada Restaurant and one of the few witnesses for the prosecution who belonged to the IWW. Because Emery had been present when the IWW business agents came to the Nevada Restaurant on several occasions to press the waitress's claims, her testimony linked them directly to Silva and showed Silva in the light most favorable to the prosecution, as a businessman standing up for his rights against the pressure tactics of a militant union. While Smith and Silva sat together on March 9, Mrs. Emery had heard Smith threaten to call out Silva's employees on strike; Silva had told him to go ahead, saying, "You no think I live?" On cross-examination Mrs. Emery declared that no hostility had been evident at the meeting between Silva and Preston earlier in the week. It was not an answer pleasing to defense attorney Bowler because he was anxious to elicit proof of Silva's violent feelings about the boycott to bolster Preston's claim of self-defense.[3]

William J. Muller, a waiter in Silva's restaurant, now moved forward to take the stand. Despite Bowler's objections, his testimony on an unrelated crime committed by Preston and Smith was admitted on the ground that it would prove the state's contention of conspiracy. Muller recounted in great detail that Preston had urged him to quit work at the Nevada Restaurant and persuaded him to come to Union Hall, where several men held him down while another struck him with the butt of a gun. As one man walked behind him covering him with a gun, Preston and others had then marched him out of Union Hall by a rear door and "down through the dark alleys and all the dark streets" into the desert two or three miles beyond the edge of town. Finally they had stopped, searched him for money, told him to keep going, and fired a couple of shots about two or three feet from him. Although Muller said he had been "led to believe I was not to see the sunrise," he did not seem to have been particularly frightened by these strong-arm tactics. He related that he "kept going for about five minutes" and then returned to Goldfield.

When Bowler moved to strike out Muller's testimony on the ground that it did not prove any allegations in the indictment or establish a conspiracy, Malone argued, "It is part and parcel of the same thing." The court denied the defense motion but conceded that the testimony did not show conspiracy and would be withdrawn from the jury "unless a continuous connection is shown." Bowler announced that he would reserve his cross-examination of Muller until that time, lest he jeopardize the right of the defense to their objections. In fact, he would never cross-examine Muller, and nothing would mitigate the damaging effects of the testimony that showed Preston and Smith terrorizing Silva's employee to force his compliance with union demands.[4]

Eloquent, confident, quick-witted, convincing, respected, and seemingly gifted with total recall of every detail, William Lovett Claiborne was the next witness for the state. Without him the prosecutors would have been compelled to confine their indictment to a murder charge against Preston alone, because the conspiracy charge against Smith and the entire union leadership rested almost solely on Claiborne's testimony. His appearance so early in the case as the fifth witness signaled a strategy of high dramatics. The bare minimum of witnesses had described the layout and location of the restaurant, the death of Silva, his altercation with Smith, and IWW terrorist tactics in action. With the early appearance of Claiborne, the ace in the prosecution's hand, Swallow hoped to indelibly impress the jury at the outset and all but settle the case on the first day of testimony.

The direct examination was conducted by Douglas. Under the prosecutor's questioning, Claiborne declared that he had arrived in Goldfield a month before the shooting and joined the IWW. He had been present in Union Hall on Saturday night, March 9. Bowler's objection to his testimony on the ground that, while it might establish conspiracy to assault Muller, it could not be related to a plot to murder Silva was overruled. The objection clearly suggested that the defense had no inkling of the direction the case was about to take. In Union Hall that night, between 11:00 and 3:30 in the morning, Claiborne had overheard a discussion among a group of union men that included the defendants, Walter Campbell, "Frank" Jardine, "John" Roudebush, and several others he identified as Vice, Sexton, Johnson, and Shoo Wall Pete, the driver of the brewery wagon. Campbell, who was "in some way very fractious," did most of the talking; he was writing names on a piece of paper while the others discussed which men would be the best choices for a party to kill Silva. Campbell asked if the other men in the group "would stick to do the work" and all assented except Shoo Wall Pete, who had departed. Asked if he would join the assassination squad or if he knew any of the men listed on Campbell's paper, Claiborne said that he was a stranger and did not know any of them. He took no further part in the conversation. Speaking of their failure to kill Silva on the previous evening, Smith said, "We would have got the son of a bitch if he had come to the door. I was looking in to the door, and he only got as far as the first table." Jardine suggested getting together the next day to "prepare the work right." Claiborne had gone home around 3:30 in the morning.

Claiborne now described the events of Sunday afternoon, March 10. At about 2:30 he returned to Union Hall and entered the office. Seventy-five to a hundred people were in the main hall, and Smith, Jardine, Campbell, Johnson, Sexton, Vice, and Donnelly eventually grouped themselves together. "Incensed over the proposition" that Diamondfield

Jack Davis remained alive, Johnson offered several new men $250 and "the moral and financial support of the lodge" to murder Davis. Johnson remarked that he himself had drawn a bead on Davis but when some people got in the way he was prevented from picking off his target. "Such men as Jack Davis," Claiborne heard Johnson say, "caused the trouble."

The group then adjourned to a smaller hall at the left of the main hall, where Campbell read two or three notes from St. John. In one note, St. John exhorted union members to stick together as the only way they could "win out in this trouble." He reminded them that "united we stand, divided we fall." Union men were told to deal "summarily" with any who opposed "our union and our wishes." The St. John note also contained the cryptic statement, "The red flag once waved would stop all trouble . . . the red flag need not wave more than once." The menacing red flag of Socialism to which Claiborne alluded was a vivid symbol that must have lingered in the minds of the jurors.

Claiborne continued. After some general remarks about the trouble in Goldfield and the need to compel Silva to keep his contract with the waitress, Johnson said Preston was "the man to do the work," and the rest concurred. At about 3:30 Preston came in. The others complimented him (presumably on his handling of Muller and his recent release from custody on the resulting charges) and inquired if he had seen St. John. About ten minutes after Preston's arrival, union president Roudebush came in with a package, which he unwrapped beside Claiborne. It contained two Colt automatic pistols and a box of cartridges. Roudebush asked Campbell, "What do you think of these? Don't you think these will do the work?"

When Attorney Douglas wanted to know if Claiborne had heard anything relating to the preparation of witnesses, Claiborne recalled hearing Smith tell Jardine, "Leave the men to me, leave my men to me, and I will take care of them." Asked by Johnson if he had his witnesses ready on the preceding evening when he failed in his effort to murder Silva, Smith confidently replied, "Yes, just leave that part to me. I always have my men on hand. My end of it will always be up." Had Preston said anything about witnesses, Douglas inquired? Yes, he said, "I want my friends here. I don't want no strangers here. I want men of my own kind." It was a point of particular importance to the state because it would discredit in advance anything the defense witnesses might say.[5]

According to the *Goldfield Daily Tribune,* Claiborne's revelations aroused an "immense sensation" in the courtroom. The prosecution's opening statement and the other witnesses who appeared that day were shunted aside in newspaper headlines by the electrifying news of Claiborne's story. Big, black letters across the front page of the *Tribune* read "STORY OF PLOT TO KILL," while subheadlines informed shocked readers of *"Two Hundred and Fifty Dollars for the Murder of Jack Davis"* and *"Atrocious Scheme to Assassinate Involving New Men Now Indicted." "Silva Would Have Been Potted Before Had He Shown Himself."* The *Sun* headline was *"Murderous Plot Is Revealed."*[6]

If Claiborne's disclosure created a sensation in the press, just one day after the surprise arrests of the union leadership, it also arrived as an unanticipated blow to the defense attorneys. In court the following morning, Bowler declared that he had been greatly surprised by Claiborne's story, and he requested a two-day continuance in order to secure additional witnesses in Goldfield to refute it. The prosecution protested on the ground that the indicted men, who would probably be called as witnesses, were already in the Hawthorne jail, clearly implying that prisoners were the only kind of people likely to testify for Preston and Smith. The prosecutors had undoubtedly planned the sudden shift, after the trial began, from the murder case the defense had obviously anticipated would hinge on the simple question of self-defense to a conspiracy case in which Silva's death was but the first installment in a union plot to murder the Goldfield elite. And spurring the trial onward at an uninterrupted gallop was part of the plan.[7]

In the Haywood trial, Clarence Darrow was greatly aided by the publication of key prosecution witness Harry Orchard's story in *Mc-Clure's Magazine* while jury selection was still in progress, a serious tactical error made in the hope of gaining favorable publicity for a confessed murderer. The prosecutors of Preston and Smith carefully avoided placing any such trump in Bowler's hands. It appears probable that the prosecution had deliberately suppressed the indictments of the union leaders at the end of March in order to avoid tipping Bowler off so he could prepare a stronger case. Indicting them after the Preston-Smith trial was already under way provided maximum advantage for the prosecution. Not only would Bowler be compelled to conduct his case on entirely new terrain, and to conduct it alone while Hangs was away scrambling for witnesses in Goldfield at the last minute, but also the necessary witnesses could hardly be located within two days, and that was all the time that remained before the defense must begin its presentation. Furthermore, the indictment of the union leaders, several of whom may previously have planned to testify on behalf of Preston and Smith, would undoubtedly cast doubt on their stories and strengthen Claiborne's. Would not their very indictment be taken as proof that the grand jury believed them guilty? All of them were now interested parties to the crime, men obliged to answer affirmatively when the prosecutors asked if they were charged with the crime of murder. Anything they might say on behalf of Preston and Smith would be weighed accordingly.

Besides aiding the prosecution, postponing the indictments of the union leaders until the day after the new contract was ratified also facilitated negotiations for the mine owners because it avoided jeopardizing the labor settlement by an inflammatory act certain to anger union members and strengthen the hand of the militants. From the mine owners' point of view, if all went well, the Preston-Smith trial might soon be followed by the conviction of higher targets, St. John and Roudebush, both of whom were held primarily responsible for blocking a settlement in early April, and their close lieutenants.

A cannier defense attorney would have anticipated the prosecution's strategy. The indictment of Smith had pointed in this direction. The rumors of additional indictments at the end of March had certainly suggested that the prosecution harbored a conspiracy theory and had produced some evidence to back it up, though not enough to proceed with the case. But Bowler had failed to read these signs and prepare for all eventualities. Now Judge Langan refused his request for a continuance, and the defense attorney was compelled to proceed immediately with the cross-examination of Claiborne and to proceed single-handedly with the case.

As Bowler reluctantly rose to begin the questioning, he was clearly at a loss. He managed to score some telling points, but his examination was foggy, diffuse, and often perfunctory, in contrast to the crisp, dramatic presentation by the prosecution. Many soft spots in Claiborne's testimony were not explored, and important points were obscured in the general miasma. The defense faced the most important task of the entire trial, the discrediting of the prosecution's key witness, yet Bowler made no serious effort to probe Claiborne's questionable background. After two purely rhetorical questions on whether Claiborne had been engaged by the mine owners to "join the WFM in order to act in the capacity of detective" or been "employed and paid to come here and give your evidence," the issue of Claiborne's possible connections with the mine owners was not further explored, and the laudatory description in the press of Claiborne as a graduate of three leading colleges, an ex-army officer, and "a member of one of the most prominent families of the South" remained fully intact. While Claiborne promised to produce his alleged diploma from Vanderbilt University and the discharge papers he had received after seven years as a lieutenant in the army, there is no evidence that he did in fact produce them, nor that the defense attorney pressed him further on these points (had Claiborne done so, as we shall see, his discharge papers would have told a very different story). Claiborne's assertion that although he was an attorney and not a laboring man, he had joined the IWW in order to get lumber hauled to the lot where he was building a house was accepted without any real challenge, as was his admission that he had not engaged in any business or profession during his three months in Goldfield.

Claiborne then declared that he had moved to Goldfield to improve his wife's health, an unusual motive in view of the harsh Goldfield climate, where summers were so hot that everyone with the means to do so took a long vacation in cooler climes, and where winters brought snow and icy winds. Early February, the time of Claiborne's arrival, had coincided with an unusually cold winter in which a record number of Goldfielders had died of pneumonia. Compounding the rigors of the climate, the boom had put housing at a premium, few reasonable accommodations were to be had at any price, and men were unrolling their blankets in the snow. Bowler's sarcastic queries, "Had you been previously informed of the climatic conditions at Goldfield?" and "You were then in search of a health resort where the climatic conditions would be suitable to your wife's health?" conveyed the suggestion that Goldfield was hardly the ideal spot for an ailing wife to convalesce.

After a few more desultory questions, which elicited the information that Claiborne had previously resided in Colorado, as well as in San Francisco, Bowler began a long inquiry on the physical layout of Union Hall. The aim of this extended exercise, it finally became clear, was to show that a dance lasting until 12:00 had been held in Union Hall on March 9, the night of the Muller fracas and the first of the two meetings that Claiborne had described. Claiborne had mentioned, however, that there was a social function before the meeting convened at 11:30 or 12:00, and the jurors may have believed he was only slightly mistaken about the hour. The point was lost in the bushes, as Bowler's questioning shuffled along, and far more critical questions were forever left behind. The most fascinating issue of all was never examined. In the words of WFM organizer Charles Tanner:

Suppose we do consider these men, working men, if you please, as desperate men. Are we also to consider them as a lot of idiots that would invite into their counsels a man whom they did not know and consult him as to the advisability of appointing a certain one among them to kill another party, and this man not even a working man, never having worked a day in the mine? The story is too ridiculous for anything and cannot be entertained by any reasonable person for a single moment.[8]

The defense attorney now scored a good point by suggesting that Preston and Smith could not have been present at the Sunday afternoon meeting Claiborne described because at that hour they were under arrest for the assault on Muller. Bowler then continued to plod over Claiborne's description of the meetings with slight results. Claiborne could not explain why notes from St. John should be read when the union leader was himself present in town. He nonetheless reiterated that Johnson and Rogers had said Silva should be killed, and he managed to repeatedly insert the suggestion, despite Bowler's fruitless attempts to confine his responses to Silva alone, that the death sentence pronounced on Silva was part of a wider plot to assassinate George Wingfield and other members of the GMOBA fraternity.

When court resumed the following morning, Claiborne continued to repeat his story under the proddings of a defense attorney who was displaying a particular interest in the names and even the physical descriptions of the conspirators. The time when Preston arrived at the Sunday afternoon conspirators' meeting was now placed considerably later, "right close to four," but Bowler did not press Claiborne on this contradiction. Now came the dramatic moment for which the defense had been preparing. Bowler announced that he had several witnesses he would like to have Claiborne identify in court. The state offering no objection, the sheriff and his deputies entered with five men who had been brought to jail the preceding night. Requested to point out each man and give his name, Claiborne identified Thomas Johnson (the towheaded man with the brown hat in his hand), Willis, Jardine, and Sexton. He said the fifth man had been in the party but he couldn't remember his name.

Bowler, probably with an air of triumph, now asked the five men to give their names. Belatedly the prosecutors realized their peril and rocketed into action. Only Johnson had given his name when Malone's quick objection that this was not the time for the defense to present rebuttal testimony was sustained over Bowler's protestation that the witnesses should give their names for purposes of identification. The moment of drama toward which Bowler had been driving with

monumental concentration had been deflated like a punctured balloon. The jurors may have suspected from Bowler's manner that someone in the group had been erroneously identified, but they had no way of being certain. The rules of evidence did not allow the defense to present its witnesses until the prosecution had completed its case. Much time and testimony would pass, and the jurors' opinions might well have irrevocably taken shape, by the time Bowler could place his witnesses on the stand one by one and demonstrate that Claiborne had been able to identify only one of them. In the antiunion press, the grand confrontation was played down and even falsified. The *Goldfield Daily Tribune* deprecatingly observed that Claiborne had correctly identified five of the eight men brought into court, though the defense was claiming he had made one error.[9]

The next witness, Thomas Bliss, took the stand for the single purpose of supplementing Claiborne's story. In his brief appearance, Bliss testified that as he watched from the corner of Main and Ramsey, he saw a group of men waiting in the street in front of the Hoffman Saloon. After the shooting, they surrounded Preston and walked together down Main Street to Union Hall. Bliss said he had overheard the men in the group, which included St. John, Donnelly, and Jardine, saying that Davis and Wingfield were "in their way more than anyone in Goldfield." Bliss had just traced the movements of the group under Douglas's guidance when the prosecutor suddenly announced that he would be recalled later for further questioning. With some reluctance, Judge Langan granted the motion. Bowler's by now customary motion to strike the witness's testimony as "incompetent, irrelevant, and immaterial" was countered by the state's argument that they expected to "show that one of the men was Joe Smith and the movements of the men in the conspiracy," and was overruled. Few of Bowler's objections were sustained.

On his first cross-examination, Bowler made only perfunctory inquiries on Bliss's background and gave every sign of accepting this highly questionable witness as the Utah mine owner he purported to be, just as he had accepted Claiborne. His main objective was to question Bliss closely on his movements in the street. On direct examination once more, Bliss resumed his interrupted story of the group's behavior. But nothing he said linked Smith to the others, and he later acknowledged on cross-examination that he had not seen Smith with the group. Although Bliss stuck to his story as Bowler took him over the street again, inch by inch, his memory suddenly faded when the defense attorney turned his attention to another matter. Bowler was curious why Bliss had not testified at the coroner's inquest. Bliss could not remember when he had

first informed the prosecution about what he had seen. Asked to whom
he had given his information, he said Diamondfield Jack Davis. When
Bowler slyly inquired whether Davis was connected with the prosecution, Bliss denied it. He said he had later given his information to
Douglas but remained unable to recall when that was. Bowler also
wondered why Bliss had been brought to Hawthorne twice to see
Preston, implying that the real reason was Bliss's inability to identify
Preston on his first try. Bliss explained that he had been asked to
make his second visit in order to see whether he could identify anyone else.[10]

Bliss was followed by a stronger and more authoritative witness, the
notorious Diamondfield Jack Davis. No longer the swaggering young
cowboy who had so nearly boasted his way to the gallows ten years
before, Davis was remembered by those who knew him in Goldfield as a
man of unassuming manner and unremarkable appearance who took
great pleasure in his formidable reputation as a gunman. He could
sometimes be seen at his own form of target practice, speeding across
the desert in his automobile, shooting jackrabbits. It was his habit, as
Bowler phrased it in a question to which the prosecution made spirited
objection, to go "up and down the streets in Goldfield armed with more
than one firearm." It may also have been his habit, as we learn from an
affidavit in the Gibson murder trial the following year, to inform
witnesses who intended to give evidence against his friends that he had a
notion to stamp their heads in the ground. Diamondfield Jack's notions
were always taken very seriously in Goldfield.

The gunman testified that he had been standing near the corner of
Ramsey and Main at the Cook Bank side when he heard the crack of
gunfire and looked over in time to see the flash of Preston's second shot
about 140 or 150 feet away. He watched Preston run to the telegraph
pole, where a "corral" of about a dozen men, including Roudebush, St.
John, Sexton, Vice, and Donnelly, surrounded the walking delegate and
accompanied him down Main Street to Union Hall in the manner
described by Bliss. Prior to the shooting, he saw Smith walking ahead of
the group. Davis said he had reason to notice these men "because I knew
they were a bunch of men I believed to be enemies of mine, and they had
made threats against me to some extent."

The prosecution now elicited from Davis the principal corroborating
testimony for the conspiracy revealed by Claiborne: Smith's alleged
remark at the time of his arrest. Davis, in his capacity as deputy sheriff,
had gone with three other men to Smith's home to arrest him on the night
of the shooting. As Davis and Smith walked down the hill together,
Smith had asked him, "Did you arrest the others?"

Bowler's cross-examination of Davis was conducted more aggressively and confidently than that of Claiborne or Bliss, possibly because Davis was not an unknown quantity to him. After taking Davis over the shooting and the "corral of men" once more without any real variation in his story, Bowler moved on to the arrest, and some additional details emerged. Smith had been in bed when Davis arrived but had come forth at Davis's call. Davis denied that he had at first insisted on taking Smith to jail without allowing him to dress, but he admitted grabbing Smith's friend Arthur Howell (Bowler had been momentarily unable to remember the man's name while framing his question) and telling him to sit down when Howell wanted to go along with Smith and "began to growl and continually growled." However, Davis absolutely denied pulling out his pistol and threatening to shoot Howell's head off—at least, "not in those words." He also denied that Smith's wife, with her baby in her arms, had come out and said, "Don't you kill that man in my house, he is a friend of ours," though he did remember her saying she didn't want trouble in the house.

As Smith and Davis descended the hill together, Smith had remarked that he was "unfortunate in belonging to a union that had gained the ill will of the people." Because a crowd of forty or fifty men had earlier been talking about a lynching, Davis, who righteously declared that he did not believe in lynching, ordered the other men to "scatter out so we would not be taken by surprise." Smith asked if Davis would protect him and was assured he would. When they had gone up the hill near the Watson house, Smith asked if the others were arrested. Davis had inquired who the others were, but Smith had given no reply.

To the query, "Did you not say on the way down to Mr. Smith after you had arrested him, and right in conjunction with the remark you made, that if his friends interfered you would shoot him or blow his head off, or words to that effect, that Preston had coughed his guts up?" Davis gave the qualified reply, "No, I don't think I did." Within moments this had stiffened to an absolute denial. Davis claimed he had not even known Preston's name at that time.

Bowler now turned to the witness's character and bias. Asked if it was "not a fact that you are an enemy of Mr. Smith's," Davis replied "not particularly" and denied having "any personal trouble that I know of" with Smith. Another facet of the bias issue which Bowler left completely untouched was Diamondfield Jack's relationship to the mine owners. The defense attorney may have lacked proof that Claiborne was a paid detective, he may not have learned the true identity of Bliss until later in the trial, but he undoubtedly shared what was then common knowledge in Goldfield—that Davis was Wingfield's personal bodyguard and that in the labor-management strife of late March he had served as virtual field commander of the Wingfield forces. Unless Bowler feared to open a Pandora's box of horror stories about IWW violence if he allowed the issues of Davis's relationship to Wingfield or Davis's clashes with the union to enter the trial, it was a serious omission.

Bowler, with a better sense of timing that he had previously displayed, then placed two telling questions near the end of his cross-examination, "Is it not a fact that you have been tried and convicted of murder in the state of Idaho?" Davis defiantly answered, "Sure." "And sentenced to be hung?" Bowler inquired, referring to Davis's conviction for the murder of two Mormon sheepherders in the days when he rode for the cattle outfit of John Sparks prior to Sparks's election as governor in 1902. Davis affirmed it.

With the next question, the prosecution's objection to this testimony as "incompetent and wholly immaterial" was sustained, and Bowler could proceed no farther in this direction. Although the defense attorney made no attempt to justify his line of inquiry, the record of the witness appeared a legitimate issue—at least it would always be treated as such when the record of a defense witness was at stake. To Bowler's final query, Davis admitted that he had no warrant for Smith's arrest, while the prosecution objected that no warrant was necessary for a crime of such magnitude.

During redirect examination, Douglas, for reasons obscure, did not bother to elicit the information that Davis had eventually been pardoned after his murder conviction. The sole purpose of his three brief questions was to indelibly fix in the minds of the jurors the prosecution's contention that Smith had asked Davis if the others had been arrested. On recross Bowler attempted without success to modify this point.[11]

There followed the tales of four carpenters, most of whom had been eating dinner in Silva's restaurant at the time of the shooting. Members of the AFL, rival to the IWW for the allegiance of Goldfield working men, they had not honored the IWW boycott. The first, Louis Dyer, related that as he stood talking in the street he had seen "a young fellow" peer around the corner several times. Smith had walked up to the young fellow and said, "You go down town and take the picket down, and I will get the son of a bitch." Smith then walked to the restaurant and back, remaining to talk to the other man awhile. It was then less than ten minutes before the shooting. Dramatically, Dyer identified the young man he had seen with Smith as Preston.

In the course of his cross-examination, Bowler took sarcastic note of the fact that Dyer had not testified before the coroner's jury. Having emphasized the point that the AFL was then "at war" with the IWW, Bowler, over Douglas's objection, propounded a rhetorical question on Dyer's attitude toward the accused men: "You would a little rather see them hung, would you not, than see them turned loose?" Dyer replied that if they were guilty he would and acknowledged that he did indeed hold "a fixed, settled, and positive opinion" as to their guilt. While Bowler succeeded in uncovering Dyer's hostility to the IWW, his questions allowed the witness to reawaken the issue of IWW terrorism. Dyer said he had been ordered to leave town by the IWW and had experienced "a terrible sensation" as a result. The sight of Smith stuck in his memory because it always aroused the feeling that he "naturally had to look out for myself," but he finally grew confused on whether he had seen Smith with the young fellow on Saturday or Sunday. Bowler's final questions emphasized the peculiar selectiveness of Dyer's memory and his hostility toward the IWW.[12]

The two succeeding carpenters, Joe Scott and Edward B. Green, told almost identical stories. Neither witness had observed the group of union leaders waiting in front of the Hoffman as they approached Silva's restaurant, nor had they seen any sign of Smith lurking at the corner. Neither had they seen a gun in Silva's hand as he advanced to the doorway while they were eating dinner inside the Nevada Restaurant, though Green related that when Silva earlier sat down at the table with them he had a gun wrapped in his apron so that the barrel protruded a couple of inches. Bowler wondered if Green hadn't found this a little "unusual," but Green said he "didn't think anything about it."[13]

Charles Hall, the next carpenter to take the stand, was a much stronger and more positive witness than Scott or Green, and his recollections of the events inside the Nevada Restaurant were at odds with theirs in most significant particulars. Hall asserted that the waiter, not Silva, had been handling a pistol at the table about ten minutes before the shooting. But he stated unequivocally that Silva had been holding a pistol in his right hand as he walked toward the door. Bowler, seizing this opportunity, pressed Hall until he admitted that he had failed to mention the gun before the coroner's jury, claiming that no one had inquired about it. He denied being interrogated by the prosecutors prior to the inquest. Nonetheless, Bowler propounded a question of critical interest to the defense: "Was there any effort made by any of the persons managing or conducting the inquest to conceal the fact that Silva at that time had a weapon upon him?" Hall denied this. The entire morning had been occupied by the examination of Hall and Green.[14]

As Hall arose from his chair, the defense could draw some comfort from the fact that the varying stories of these four carpenters had not materially strengthened the prosecution's case. Jurors might not be inclined to believe that the man Green and Scott said exhibited a gun to them and declared he would not allow the union to interfere with his business had walked to the door in a peaceful and amicable way. Better still, Hall had acknowledged that Silva held a gun. Up to this point, the gun had been glossed over in the prosecution's presentation to the point of invisibility. The public image of the shooting may well have been fixed by the front page drawing on the March 11 issue of the *Sun:* a dark, hunched sneak of a man with a black handlebar mustache shooting an unarmed Silva in the back. The accompanying story informed readers, "Just as darkness was mantling the camp in gloom . . . a stealthy hand opened the door of the restaurant, there was a flash and a report and Silva sank to the floor."

Constable Claude Inman, the last witness for the state, told a story on Silva's dying declaration that was substantially the same as Dr. Galloway's. When Inman asked Silva where his family was, the dying man had told him they were in Oakland. He had not said that he was married or given his relatives' address.

At 2:30 on Thursday afternoon, just two days after they began, the prosecutors rested their case. Bowler refused to the very end to cross-examine Muller, in the belief that the waiter's testimony should be stricken from the record. Judge Langan, however, ruled that Muller's testimony was admissible because, in conjunction with the accounts of other witnesses, it could establish conspiracy. Although the judge had denied Bowler's previous request for a continuance, he now agreed to adjourn until 9:00 the following morning, when the defense would begin its presentation. Only twelve witnesses had appeared for the prosecution,[15] and everything really rested on three men, Wingfield's bodyguard Diamondfield Jack Davis, the self-proclaimed Utah mine owner Thomas Bliss, and the eloquent, convincing, and mysterious blond stranger, recently arrived in Goldfield for his wife's health, William Claiborne.

V

WHOSE CONSPIRACY?

The defense attorneys began their presentation on April 26 with a clear and persuasive opening statement by Frank Hangs. The dark-haired, heavy-set attorney declared the defense would show that Preston had fired only in self-defense when Silva threatened his life. Preston had seen Silva rush to the kitchen, grab his gun, and hurry to the door with every intention of carrying out his often repeated threat against Preston. The evidence would verify that the fatal bullet could only have taken such a course if Silva stood in a crouching position with his gun in his right hand. Defense witnesses would prove that Silva had threatened Preston's life on many occasions and had even displayed the gun he intended to use for the deed. These threats had been made so often that Preston had every reason to believe his life was in danger on the evening of March 10.

As for the conspiracy, the defense would demonstrate that Claiborne's testimony was utterly false. They would present evidence that the accused men were not at the places Claiborne had indicated at the times he said he had heard them discuss their plans. The defense would show that Claiborne was not a man of good character; indeed his first act upon arriving in Goldfield had been to steal a piece of land by forceful means. If Attorney Hangs made any comment on those other two highly questionable witnesses and mainstays of the conspiracy theory, Davis and Bliss, the brief newspaper accounts of his remarks do not record it.[1]

Mrs. Elizabeth Alley, the first witness for the defense, had for some time been portrayed in the antiunion press as a veritable Madame

Defarge of union radicalism, recently fired from her position in the post office for union activities. A *Tonopah Sun* drawing of her, captioned "The I.W.W. Woman," showed a long face with full, curving lips and a hat of pheasant feathers atop upswept hair, giving her the appearance of a winged victory. On the night before the trial began, she had an altercation the press described as "tropical and spectacular" with J. Holman Buck, a newspaper editor and a past master of antiunion invective. She appeared on the veranda of Hawthorne's Nucleus Hotel just as Buck was declaring that certain labor leaders at Goldfield were getting the money while the common members of the organization were doing the work. "That's an infernal lie!" Elizabeth Alley interrupted. A spirited discussion ensued, to the edification of many bystanders, and Alley was by no means the loser.[2]

On taking the stand, Alley testified that while she was in Silva's restaurant two days before the shooting to see the cashier about buying a cabin, Preston had walked past in the street. Silva had become very excited and said, "If that man comes in here, I will blow his head off." She saw him make a motion to take a gun from his pocket. An objection by the prosecution prevented her from answering the question: from your knowledge of Silva's reputation in the community, "was he not considered a desperate, dangerous, and lawless man?"

Swallow's cross-examination undermined Alley's testimony by a device to be successfully used again and again with defense witnesses. Alley admitted under the district attorney's questioning that she had served as recording secretary of the IWW and was still a union member, though she attempted to mitigate this by volunteering the information that she had also belonged to the AFL. Swallow well knew that the jurors would develop the point on Alley's union affiliation in their own minds, recalling Claiborne's testimony on the preparation of witnesses and Preston's alleged request for union witnesses "of my own kind." Asked by the district attorney whether she took "quite an active interest" in the IWW, Alley defiantly replied, "I have always been interested in any organization that meant the betterment of the working class." On re-direct Alley said that she had told W. R. Dixon about Silva's threat and instructed him to communicate it to Preston.[3]

The proficiency with which Swallow dispatched the succeeding defense witnesses was a classic demonstration of the cross-examiner's art. Testimony by Margaret Heffernan, a waitress and a former partner of Silva's, concerning Silva's reputation as a violent and quarrelsome man was swiftly demolished by planting the idea that, in addition to her ties to the IWW, Heffernan harbored animosity against Silva as a result of the disagreement that had dissolved their partnership after five weeks. William Vangilder, the operator of a lunch counter in front of the Mohawk Saloon, who had quarreled with Silva over the payment of bills "pretty near every day" and sought Silva's arrest for assault, suffered the same fate as Heffernan on the witness stand, worsened somewhat by his admitted remark in the presence of prosecution witnesses that he had come to Hawthorne "for the almighty dollar." The prosecution, by adroit maneuver, was succeeding in twisting Silva's quarrels with the defense witnesses to discredit these witnesses. And while Bowler stood helplessly by, the testimony of a witness who had heard Silva threaten to shoot the picket in front of his door at 4:30 on Sunday afternoon was stricken from the record in accordance with the prosecutor's objection that the picket was neither Preston nor Smith.

The only one among these witnesses to survive the prosecutor's assault relatively intact was Charles Chambers, who had been present in the restaurant at the same time as Alley and corroborated her story. He had also heard Silva say he would blow Preston's head off if he came to the door. Chambers thought the restaurant owner was "a little excited," but after Alley left he began "joshing" Silva about the probable result of "talks of that kind." Silva again said he would blow Preston's head off, and added that he "had the goods to do it with," showing Chambers a gun that he kept in his pocket. Cross-examination revealed that Chambers had been a miner for twenty-five years and that he, too, was a union member.[4]

All these witnesses had been minor figures. When Vincent St. John rose to his feet later that morning, he was the first and the most famous union leader to take the stand for the defense. He wore a vest and a striped shirt, with no coat or tie, perhaps an implicit proletarian statement to be seen in contrast with the wing collars and bow ties of the prosecutors. His clean-shaven young face seemed unmarred by the many vicissitudes of his years as a miner and union organizer. He flatly denied writing the red flag note Claiborne claimed was read at the Sunday afternoon meeting of conspirators. He had no cause to write a letter, said St. John, having been present in Goldfield at the time. He also denied being part of the corral of men that Davis and Bliss had seen awaiting Preston in front of the Hoffman Saloon and protectively surrounding him after the shooting as he walked down the street to Union Hall.

On cross-examination, Swallow did not neglect to emphasize St. John's position in the IWW, his work as an organizer for the WFM over the past twelve years, and his previous arrests in Telluride and in Idaho. "Is it not a fact that you are commonly known as an agitator?" the district attorney demanded.

"That is what they designate me," St. John answered imperturbably. When Swallow inquired whether St. John was under arrest for Silva's murder, the witness was compelled to answer affirmatively. Asked if he was a member of "a political organization known as the IWW United," the witness replied, "I am a member of the IWW. It is not a political organization." (Indeed this was an article of faith with St. John, whose belief in industrial unionism rather than political activism would later lead to considerable friction with DeLeon and the anarchists.) He was a strong witness, but the district attorney nonetheless succeeded in finding an area of uncertainty in his story and damaging his credibility: doubt replaced his initial denials that he had gone down from Union Hall to hand something to the picket in front of Silva's restaurant following the Sunday afternoon meeting in Ladies' Aid Hall. Still probing, Swallow went on to wonder why St. John had remained at the cabin of his friend Tims that night instead of going home, with the suggestion sifting between the words that the witness had been hiding to avoid arrest. The answer he received cast the undeclared war between the union men and the mine owners into sharp relief. St. John said he had gone to Tims's cabin to do some writing and to get his rifle.

"I don't want to know that," the district attorney interjected sharply. "I want to know why you went to the cabin and remained there instead of going home."

He may not have wanted to know, but St. John told him anyway. On Sunday he had been warned repeatedly that Diamondfield Jack Davis and his men were coming to his place that night to run him out of town. Although Tims urged him to spend the night at the cabin, St. John insisted he "would hate to disappoint these parties if they came looking for me." Various union men then arrived with the information that Davis had enlarged his plans to make a broad sweep of the union leadership. St. John finally yielded to persuasion and sent his wife word that he would not be home that night. He had remained holed up at the Tims cabin with his rifle for a week. (Tims and another witness later took the stand to confirm his version of these events.)

In response to the query with which Swallow endeavored to make his implication clear, the witness said he had not known that Davis and his men sought his arrest, nor had he yet learned that Smith had been picked up. He had assumed, apparently, that another extralegal skirmish with the gunmen wearing deputies' badges was brewing and prepared to make a stand. The matter-of-fact way in which St. John related the evening's events suggested that he saw them as nothing more than ordinary incidents in the life of a union organizer.[5]

After the lunch recess, Bowler used his redirect examination of St. John for a gingerly attempt to defuse the issue of union radicalism that lay like an unexploded bomb beneath the surface of the case. The prosecutors had not heaped invective on the union radicals in their opening statement, relying instead on the imaginations of the jurors to paint in the fearsome reputations of the men the press sometimes termed "anarchistic slumgullions from foreign climes" in vivid colors, saving the rhetorical fire for their concluding arguments. Although he clearly anticipated the approaching blast, Bowler appeared to shrink from taking up the cause of union radicalism and making it his own. It was a dilemma that labor attorneys faced again and again, occasionally succeeded in avoiding, and sometimes resolved by detonating an explosion of their own. In the defense of Steve Adams, a preliminary to the Haywood trial, Darrow faced the issue squarely in words that almost applied better to Morrie Preston than to the man for whom he spoke them:

> It is not for him [Adams], an humble, almost unknown workman, that all the machinery of the state has been set in motion and all the mineowners of the West have been called to their aid. It is because back of all this there is a great issue of which this is but the beginning. Because out in the world is a great fight, a fight between capital and labor, of which this is but a manifestation up here in the hills. You know it; I know it; they know it. There is not a man so blind, there is not a person so prejudiced or bigoted, to believe that all this effort is being put forth to punish an unknown man for the murder of an unknown man. . . .[6]

A bold stroke of genius was needed to link Preston and the union he represented to the broader cause of labor, to break their isolation on the far left. Instead Bowler read the preamble to the WFM constitution, in a stiff and academic effort to demonstrate that a plot to murder Silva would have been contrary to the organization's constitution and bylaws. This exercise probably bored the jury to somnolence, and also produced one of the few touches of humor in a deadly serious case. Swallow, who had initially suggested that the entire constitution should be read rather than just a portion, changed his mind during the reading of the preamble and remarked that he thought it too long and would just as soon not listen to all of it. Bowler then attempted to shore up the weak points in St.

John's testimony. Under the attorney's guidance, St. John emphasized the extenuating circumstances of his Colorado and Idaho arrests and belatedly remembered, after "studying that proposition, thinking it over carefully," that he had gone out from Union Hall to give the picket in front of Silva's restaurant a pair of gloves to shield him from the bitter cold.

On recross-examination, Swallow moved swiftly to counter any ground St. John might have gained. The witness was compelled to admit that in Idaho he had used the name "John Vincent." Having thus suggested to the jury that a man who lied about his own name could hardly be relied on to tell the truth about anything, including the real contents of the mysterious package which might well have contained the murder weapon, the district attorney concluded by creating the impression that St. John was a fugitive from justice, fleeing to Idaho when warrants were issued for his arrest in Colorado. Bowler took up redirect once more to bring out the point that St. John had changed his name in order to get work after the mine owners put him on the black list. In his time, St. John had moved others with his eloquence, and would again. Now he stepped down from the stand, undone by a forgotten pair of gloves.[7]

Robert Elmer Vice, the twenty-eight-year-old, Iowa-born walking delegate and recording secretary for the miners' union and a member of the union committee that had negotiated the labor settlement less than a week earlier, was the next witness. Responding to Bowler's questions, Vice said he had attended the Saturday night dance in Union Hall till 11:45, then stopped at a restaurant on his way home to the cabin he shared with Dan Roudebush, where he found Roudebush asleep. He had attended no conspiratorial meeting, either that night or the following day. On Sunday afternoon he had gone home from Union Hall to have supper with some friends, a story later corroborated by his date, Maggie Gunn, and other witnesses. He had remained at the cabin with them during the entire time that Diamondfield Jack had placed him in the corral of men in front of the Hoffman Saloon. When Vice and his friends left the cabin, they had seen the crowd at the Nevada Restaurant in the wake of the shooting. Vice had then accompanied Maggie Gunn to her home. In an exchange which left Bowler looking decidedly foolish, Vice said Claiborne had been unable to remember his name when he was brought into court for identification, but he denied that Claiborne had applied his name to someone else. Swallow's cross-examination brought out the usual points by which he demolished the credibility of witnesses: Vice was a member of the WFM; he admitted having been in the Coeur d'Alene, which was much like hearing a Sioux warrior tell a cavalry officer that he had been present at the Bozeman Trail in 1866; his memory was a little too good to be true; he was himself under indictment for conspiring to murder Silva.[8]

Vice was followed by Harry Jardine, also a miner, also a union official, and also identified as one of the conspirators in Union Hall and the group in front of the Hoffman. Jardine related that when he closed Union Hall after the dance at 12:15, it was empty; he had then gone to sleep in the office. He absolutely denied that there had been any meeting in the hall at which Claiborne and the others had been present and plans laid to kill Silva. Attorney Hangs brought out the point that Claiborne had mistakenly identified Jardine as "Willis" in court.

It should have been a small triumph and a solid step toward discrediting Claiborne had Swallow not instantly risen to his feet to blot it out by eliciting the admission that Jardine had shaved his mustache since March 10. There was more: Jardine, too, had been in the Coeur d'Alene; he had known St. John in Colorado and had been friendly with Preston and Smith for some time, affirming that he worked with them "in a common cause"; he had taken the field as Nevada's first Socialist candidate for Congress the preceding fall. Last—but never least—he too had been arrested for conspiring to murder Silva.[9]

Had the prosecutor been in the habit of perusing the official journal of the WFM, as he undoubtedly was not, he would have known that the man before him was the author of many a burning manifesto urging unity for the One Big Union. In a recent missive, Jardine had condemned local newspaper editors as "mental prostitutes" for the mine owners and lashed into Tonopah's conservative union as a "shallow-brained painted woman, whose thoughts do not rise above her hips." Tonopah, wrote Jardine, has "tottered by the wayside, becoming satisfied with herself, and has become inoculated with the virus of money, hath become respectable—conventional respectability that boweth down to platitudes, phrases, and perfumed wind: fell in love with the flesh pots of Egypt, become worldly, become wise in her own conceit, hath become neglectful of our only child—the I.W.W." Jardine looked to the future salvation of this wayward one and the healing of the breach between moderates and radicals; "Get an axe," he advised:

> look up and around you and use your axe at the system that makes slaves of you, makes you old before you are young, makes jobites of you, puny, puling, puking, jobites wallowing around in the stench of your own vomit, that makes microscopical microbes of you with your nose to the grindstone of a job, your eyes blinded with the materialistic mud of an existence, your mind atrophied with the monotonous daily grind of toil.

Unite, brothers, under the banner of Industrial Unionism, "each for all and all for each," engineers and machinists, muckers, "masheen" men and helpers, all necessary labor, all useful to each other. Unite in every camp under "one union, one label, one enemy." Unite and forward to Economic Freedom.[10]

None of Jardine's ideological fervor had erupted on the stand, however. Perhaps the prosecutors planned to unfurl the red flag with greater effect during the examination of Smith and shied away from surfeit. Or perhaps Harry Jardine was simply an unknown quantity to them, just another union radical.

Of those Claiborne had placed in the conspiratorial meetings and the corral of men, Jerry Sexton, the next witness to come forward, had the strongest alibi because it in no way depended on the corroboration of friends or fellow union members. A mining engineer, Sexton had been verifiably at work on the night shift at the Review Lease from 11:00 onward. Sunday had been "change day," when the men moved to a new shift, and he had been at work in the mine from 3:00 in the afternoon until 11:00 at night. Hangs then struck a telling blow. Claiborne had erroneously identified Sexton in the courtroom as "Jardine." The defense could reasonably hope that this second provable error on Claiborne's part would suggest that his inability to identify Jardine was something more than confusion caused by the shaving of a mustache and cast doubt on his entire story.

Swallow's cross-examination failed to shake Sexton's testimony or damage his character. Sexton was vice president of the WFM, a fact that emerged, in the usual way, like a guilty secret on cross-examination and would probably have appeared less damaging if it had come out in response to a matter-of-fact question at the outset of direct examination. Swallow wondered if Sexton had ever worked in Burke, Idaho, or in the Coeur d'Alene, sounding code words intended to conjure images of union violence by reminding jurors of the bitter strife that had accompanied these union troubles, especially the infamous meeting in Burke, where union miners had voted to dynamite the Bunker Hill. If the witness had worked there, connecting him by inference with these bloody events would provide an extra bonus. In Sexton's case, the effect was probably minimal. A miner since the age of eleven, he had worked in the East, in Butte, and in Canada, but never in Idaho. Like the preceding defense witnesses, he was under indictment for Silva's murder.[11]

W. R. Dixon, a carpenter and the first witness to recount the shooting as it appeared from the sidewalk outside the restaurant, then told his story. On Sunday evening Dixon had walked over to Silva's restaurant to have his supper as usual when "I was accosted by the young man Preston, and he informed me that the house was unfair." Dixon, a WFM member, decided to have supper elsewhere when Preston gave him "the particulars." Preston then approached some other customers, as Dixon stood "thinking the matter over" and gazing through the windows into the restaurant, where Silva was sitting at a table. Dixon saw Silva glance toward the door and hurry into the kitchen "like a flash." Dixon warned Preston, "Look out, he's coming with a gun." Silva then stood in the doorway, "very excited, of course," pointing his gun at Preston and warning him "You go away, I kill you." Dixon "instantly ran away out of danger," heading toward the firebell at the end of the sidewalk. He heard two shots as he ran. Asked if he had fled as soon as he saw the gun, Dixon replied, "You bet I did." He was later surprised to learn that Silva, not Preston, was the one who had been shot.

On cross-examination Swallow mounted his usual effort to establish that Dixon was one of the union brotherhood and therefore not to be trusted. Nonetheless, Dixon was a vivid and convincing witness; his bluff, confident personality had injected a note of cheerfulness into the otherwise grim proceedings; and his testimony on Silva's rush to the door with the gun he pointed at Preston fully corroborated the defense version of events. The case for Morrie Preston was beginning to gather momentum.[12]

A. J. Johnson, a Goldfield miner for two years, was the next witness. He tried to cast some light on the doings of the mysterious Claiborne about two months previously when Johnson and others attempted to throw him off a lot where he was trying to establish squatter's rights. Claiborne had mouthed obscenities, which Johnson refused to repeat in court, and told him, "You white head, I will get you before I leave this town." A week later, Claiborne, with the aid of two women, had jumped another lot. Slight as it was, this squabbling over squatter's rights appeared to be the only scrap of evidence the defense had succeeded in uncovering about Claiborne.

Johnson said he had been at home in bed on Saturday night when Claiborne reported him at the conspirators' meeting and denied being present at Sunday's meeting either. About dusk he had gone to Union Hall, where he remained until the shots were fired. He had tried to make his way to the scene of the shooting, though people on the street shouted to him, "Go back, you're liable to get shot!"

During cross-examination, Swallow was eager to learn whether Johnson took "an active interest in union affairs." Johnson stolidly replied, "I am an ordinary member, the same as the rest of the 3,000 members." He admitted belonging to the carpenters' committee which notified AFL carpenters that they must join his union by a certain deadline in early March, but he denied using force. Swallow closed his questioning of Johnson with the ringing and dramatic series of questions and forced answers that had served him so well before. "You are under arrest at the present time, are you, Mr. Johnson?"

"Yes."

"Do you know with what crime you are charged?"

"Yes."

"What?"

"I am charged with murder."

"The murder of whom?"

"Of Silva."[13]

In R. M. ("Harry") Rogers, who had worked in the mines for fourteen years, lived in Goldfield since the camp's early days, and served as president of Local No. 220, the defense had a witness whose defiance still crackles through the pages of the transcript. His alibi for the Sunday meeting of conspirators was unshakable: he had been at work underground in the Mohawk Mine. That also ruled out his presence in the corral of men. Asked if he had been present at the Sunday meeting with Claiborne and others, Rogers asked, "Who is Mr. Claiborne?" Informed that Claiborne was the man who had identified him from the stand the previous day, Rogers indignantly replied, "Certainly not." It must have given Hangs considerable pleasure to inquire by what name Claiborne had identified Rogers and to receive the answer, "Jerry Sexton."

"Is your name Jerry Sexton?" Hangs inquired, savoring the moment.

"Not that I know of," said Rogers, and Hangs devised two more questions to underline the point. Rogers was the third member of the alleged conspirators' group that Claiborne had not identified accurately. Asked if he had ever held such a meeting with Claiborne, Rogers answered, "The only meeting I ever took part in were the regular meetings of the Miners' Union, which we have on Tuesday evenings."

Swallow's cross-examination established that Rogers had been a WFM member since 1899 and admitted to a very active interest in the union, which Swallow attempted to suggest extended to using strong-arm tactics against nonunion men. Rogers was also an avowed Socialist and, like many other witnesses, made no attempt to hide his friendship for Preston and Smith. "Well, if you will allow me," he said, "any member of the organization I am friendly with." Cross-examination closed with Swallow's usual ominous catechism on the witness's indictment for murder, after which court recessed until Saturday morning. By and large, the day had gone very well for the defense.[14]

It was now just a week since jury selection for the trial had begun. Preston and Smith were marched back to jail, and the spectators filed out of the crowded courtroom toward such diversions as an evening in Hawthorne afforded. If there was no crackling debate between Holman Buck and Elizabeth Alley to be observed and no invitation to a toothsome banquet at Mrs. Arcum's with the prosecutors, one could at least catch up on the news with the *Goldfield Daily Tribune,* for Hawthorne had no newspaper of its own. The *Tribune* reported that after the labor contract was ratified "the city awakened like the sleeping palace at the coming of the prince."[15] Goldfield's stockbrokers had reacted to the impending settlement with frenzy, more than 400,000 shares changing hands in the new exchange alone over the weekend. Within days, the pendulum was already swinging in reverse, and Monday's soaring prices wobbled downward. There was every sign, nonetheless, that the great boom was once more hurtling forward at full speed. So many people were streaming in that trains bound for Goldfield added extra coaches and passengers were required to make their reservations well in advance.

In the wider world beyond Goldfield, President Roosevelt had stirred up a hornet's nest by publicly referring to the union leaders indicted in Idaho as "undesirable citizens." This produced a deluge of letters from union men protesting that the president was misusing his office to influence the outcome of the trial. The pugnacious Roosevelt not only refused to qualify his stand, he amplified it: "They [Haywood, Moyer, and Debs] stand as the representatives of men who by their public utterances and manifestos, and by the utterances of newspapers they control, inspire bloodshed and violence. If this does not constitute undesirable citizenship, then there can never be undesirable citizens." Goldfielders would not have had much trouble in applying Roosevelt's remarks to Socialists and members of the IWW and WFM who were considerably closer at hand than Haywood, Moyer, and Debs—Preston and Smith belonged to all three categories—and would react with satisfaction or disgust, according to their various political persuasions. To Lillian Burton, if she read the paper that evening, it must have seemed as though the president himself was calling for Morrie's conviction.[16]

When trial proceedings resumed the next day, Ben Donnelly, the next miner to take the stand, declared that he had also been erroneously identified by Claiborne. The star witness for the prosecution had pointed him out in court as "Campbell." At the hour of the alleged conspirators' meeting on March 9, Donnelly said he was asleep in the cabin on Sundog Avenue that he shared with his three friends, Robaum, Kilkor, and Kurenbach. He had not been present at the other meeting either, nor in the corral of men in front of the Hoffman. He had attended a meeting in the Ladies' Aid room of Union Hall at about 2:00, along with St. John, Preston, and lawmen Knight and Inman. Afterward he had gone to the St. Louis Restaurant, returning at about 4:40 to the cabin, where he remained until dusk. He had then gone downtown with Kurenbach.

During his questioning of Donnelly, Swallow resorted, not for the first time, to the old legal trick sometimes known as taking the witness over the hurdles. If the witness could not remember at what hours he was asleep or in Union Hall on other days, why should March 9 and 10 be so remarkably clear in his memory? Swallow established that not only was Donnelly a WFM member but he belonged to the union leadership, having served as an officer on the Goldfield union's finance committee and as vice president of the Rhyolite local. (Although the point would not be raised during the trial, Donnelly's importance to GMOBA may have lain less in his union offices than in the fact that spies had fingered him as St. John's right-hand man.)[17]

The defense now brought John Kurenbach to the stand for the simple and limited purpose of confirming the alibi of his indicted cabin mate, Donnelly, but before he had finished, Kurenbach's testimony was to assume a terrible significance in the case. Swallow was unable to connect the witness with radicalism; Kurenbach had previously worked as a coal miner in West Virginia, Wyoming, Illinois, and Colorado—not in the Coeur d'Alene. Then Swallow suddenly whirled to fire an unexpected question at Kurenbach and succeeded in catching him in a serious contradiction. Having originally stated that after the shooting he did not see Preston until the next day, the witness hesitantly admitted before a hushed courtroom that Preston came to Union Hall and handed him the gun with which Silva had been shot. It was an artless lie, probably resulting from nothing more sinister than Bowler's recurrent failure to prepare his witnesses adequately and lay to rest Kurenbach's unfounded fear that he was incriminating Preston, but opponents of the union would attempt to use it to discredit the entire defense. On April 28, the day after the defendants themselves and numerous witnesses of greater importance than Kurenbach gave testimony, the headline of the *Goldfield Daily Tribune,* in letters nearly two inches high, was

"WITNESS FALSIFIES ON STAND." A subheadline read *Abortive Result of an Attempt to Save Preston from Complicity.* Many would undoubtedly take this to mean that Kurenbach's initial response had been planned by the defense. The ensuing report on the trial described how Kurenbach "was cleverly caught in the act of perjuring himself" by a stern prosecutor, made an "almost inaudible reply" when he realized his mistake, and then "slunk from the stand." Kurenbach was only one of many defense witnesses, but if the belief gained currency that the defendants and the witnesses on their behalf were perjuring themselves, no proof of innocence they presented could possibly be enough.[18]

The defense limped onward, lamed by this disaster. Fred Luxinger, a shingler in Goldfield and Rhyolite, was the next witness. He gave an account of the shooting as it appeared from outside the restaurant that dovetailed exactly with Dixon's story. As Luxinger walked toward Silva's restaurant that Sunday evening, Preston had come up to him and told him the place was unfair. They had discussed the matter. Preston presently accosted Dixon, then two other customers, one of whom entered while the other stayed outside talking to Preston. Inside the restaurant, Luxinger saw Silva rise quickly from the table and run into the kitchen. The restaurant owner then "rushed out" to the front door carrying "a big, black gun" in his right hand. Preston had "just stepped aside, stepped kind of back," saying something to the customer beside him. At Bowler's request, Luxinger illustrated Silva's actions as he stood in the doorway with the gun, waving his left hand, and said to Preston, "You go way, I kill you." As soon as Luxinger heard these words, he started to run. Two shots were fired almost instantly.

Despite efforts to discredit Luxinger along the usual lines, Swallow could uncover only one minor discrepancy: Luxinger had not seen Dixon ahead of him as he ran. Alone among all the witnesses in the trial, Luxinger belonged to both the WFM and the AFL. "Can you owe allegiance to both?" queried Swallow, implying that this was a man of some duplicity. Luxinger declared that he could. Like Dixon, he was a vivid and convincing witness, and he had seen Silva point his gun at Preston. The defense could reasonably hope that the image they presented of Silva's rush to the door with his gun, something which had so frightened both Dixon and Luxinger that they began to flee before any shots were fired, would lend strong support to Preston's plea of self-defense. One large question remained unanswered: if events at the restaurant had really happened as Dixon and Luxinger described them, where was John Silva's gun?[19]

The first of the defendants to take the stand was Joseph Smith. Preston believed their confinement in the tiny, dark, poorly ventilated Hawthorne jail before their removal to the state prison had been intended by the authorities to break them down mentally and physically, and it appeared that in Smith's case the ordeal may have taken a considerable toll. Smith was unable to recall—or calculate—the year of his birth, though he did know he was thirty-six years old. He could not remember in what year he had arrived in Goldfield, or how old he had been when he emigrated to the United States from Canada. He could not definitely state when he had first joined a labor organization. Several times he had to ask his lawyer to repeat a question. The poor impression Smith must have made on the jury was undoubtedly heightened by Bowler's curt and peremptory handling of his own client. He interrupted Smith, telling him to "leave that out" or admonishing him to "pay attention to my question," and by so doing spotlighted the accused man's dull-wittedness and uncertainty.

After stumbling over a few questions on his background, Smith described his movements during the fatal weekend. On the afternoon of March 9 he had been "in and out of the Hall, going to saloons, restaurants, and down to Silva's restaurant to put a picket on, and inspecting the house to see how the boycott was working." He had eaten supper at home with his wife around quarter past six and gone out once more on union business, returning home to his family and their guests, Arthur Howell and Mrs. Lowry, between 10:30 and 11:00 that night and remaining at home until the next morning. He denied attending any conspirators' meeting and said he had never seen Claiborne in Union Hall at any time.

Responding to Bowler's next questions, Smith denied every word and detail of the Sunday afternoon meeting. At 7:00 that evening Smith had been at home with his wife and several guests, not lurking at the corner near the Nevada Restaurant or awaiting Preston in a corral of men. Bowler then interrogated Smith on his arrest by Diamondfield Jack. "When he came to arrest me," said Smith, "he came outside and hollered, 'Smith! Smith! Smith!' and my wife said—"

"Leave that out, what your wife said," interrupted Bowler.

Smith eventually picked up the thread of his story, "Well, I went out after I seen Davis at the gate. He had a short gun and had it up to his shoulder and another sticking out at the side, and he said, 'Is your name Smith?' and I said, 'Yes,' and he said, 'We want you.' " A prolonged argument ensued, in which Smith endeavored to get Davis's permission to fetch his clothes or to allow his wife to bring them. Smith's friend

Arthur Howell (who subsequently corroborated his story on the stand) grew understandably concerned about what might happen to Smith in Davis's hands and asked permission to accompany them. Diamondfield Jack told him, "If you go to the foot of the hill, I will blow your brains out." When Howell started to put on his boots anyway, "Diamondfield Jack grabbed him by the hair, but his hair was too short."

"Mr. Smith, we don't care for that," Bowler irascibly cut in. "Did you finally leave the house with Jack Davis?"

Yes, they had left, but Smith denied calling on Davis for protection or asking him if the others had been arrested. He had, however, asked Davis the reason for his arrest. Davis had said "for a crime of murder." Smith said he told him "I was innocent and didn't know anything about it, but as he was an officer, I would go." They had gone down the hill, Davis holding Smith by the arm and the others talking among themselves, when Davis said to him, "Here, Smith, god damn son of a bitch, if any of your friends comes to your assistance, I will kill you."

"What was the occasion of his making that remark to you?" asked Bowler.

"I don't know," said Smith dully. "He apparently was afraid of my friends coming to my assistance."

In random fashion, Bowler's questions now backtracked to Smith's movements on Sunday afternoon. Smith thought, though he was not sure, that he had said something to Preston about relieving the picket in front of the Nevada Restaurant after eight hours, but he had said it on Sunday morning, not Sunday afternoon. He had seen Preston when the two of them were released from jail around 4:45 after their arrest for the Muller assault and they had walked to Union Hall together. He had not been standing near the Hoffman immediately prior to the shooting, and until he was discharged from prison late that night, he had known "only what was told me" about Silva's death.

As Bowler's questioning of Smith gradually wound down, little had been done to advance the cause of the defense. Too much time had been spent in flat denials of the statements made by prosecution witnesses, too little in developing Smith's own story. Bowler's method of leap-frogging back and forth over time created confusion instead of presenting a clear, chronological picture of Smith's movements, and buried the strongest part, Smith's vivid account of his arrest by Davis, in the midst of his testimony. The prosecuting attorneys, watching nearby, had undoubtedly noted that Smith's memory was very poor and he was not quick-witted. With a witness like this, the red flag of St. John's cryptic note could be waved with theatrical effect.

The district attorney rose to his feet. No one who had seen the near contempt with which Bowler had treated his own client could doubt, as the wing-collared figure turned his stern, accusing gaze on the defendant, that Swallow was about to make hash of Joseph Smith. He did exactly that. After a few innocuous introductory questions, Swallow inexorably proceeded to wring the last drop of juice from Smith's radical beliefs. Smith, a member of labor organizations for some thirteen years, acknowledged that he had "always taken a great interest in the labor cause" and been "very active in it," but when Swallow asked him, "Don't you believe that this world is divided into the laboring class and capitalists?" Smith answered, "I don't understand." It was only a temporary refuge. Compelled by the rules of evidence to answer complicated questions with a simple "yes" or "no," Smith had no choice but to respond affirmatively to the inflammatory catechism that quickly followed. Yes, he believed "there is such a thing as the labor class," and the capitalist class. Asked if he believed "that we are engaged in a warfare," he would say only, "I believe there is two classes." Yes, he believed their interests were "diametrically opposed." Yes, he believed "there is no interest between the employer and employee." Yes, he believed that "we are engaged in international warfare." Yes, he believed "labor must constantly struggle to free itself from the capitalists or the greed of the capitalists." He had been a union officer for about two years.

With the full dimensions of Smith's radicalism unveiled, Swallow moved to consider the Muller assault, which would occupy a disproportionate part of the cross interrogatory. Smith eventually acknowledged that "there was trouble" after they entered Union Hall but could not recall whether Muller had been struck and was unable to give the names of those present. Now, for the time being, Swallow moved away from the topic. He would return to it, for maximum effect, at the close of his examination.

Ever since Silva first came to Goldfield, Smith had known him, but Smith could not recall just when that was. Silva had joined the IWW a few months after its inception and paid his first dues to Smith. Asked if he remembered discussing a dispute with Silva over those dues, Smith replied with a flash of spirit, "No, sir, I talk my business in the Hall."

Although he remembered calling out the help after he visited Silva with the waitress, Smith was unable to recall the hour or even the day that he had placed the picket at the Nevada Restaurant, nor could he recollect the names of any of the pickets. Swallow, taking this opportunity to cast doubt on one of the strongest defense witnesses, inquired whether one of the pickets was named Luxinger. Smith denied it. At no time would the prosecution present evidence to show that Luxinger was really an IWW picket rather than the casual patron of Silva's restaurant he claimed to be. But the seed of an idea had been planted.

The one blessing conferred by Smith's poor memory was that it offered Swallow no opportunity for taking him over the hurdles. Under sharp questioning by the district attorney, he struggled uncertainly to remember the times of his arrest for the Muller assault and his subsequent release from jail. (Bowler had unfortunately neglected to bring forward sheriff's deputies or other disinterested witnesses to clarify these points.) Smith could not state definitely how far the Hall was from the jail, nor could he name the friends who had accompanied him on the walk back. Reaching Union Hall, Smith had remained to talk with those in the office, while Preston left almost immediately. "Discussing your jail experience and what you were charged with, were you not?" inquired Swallow.

"I don't know as I did," said Smith. Leaving the Hall, he had gone to the Frisco Restaurant on business, stopped at the Northern Saloon for a drink with a friend, and proceeded to the Palace Saloon "just looking around to see if there was any new applications." Again returning to the Hall, Smith filed the new applications for union membership with the secretary and stayed until around 6:00. Swallow then questioned him intensively on the route he followed as he walked home. He had not seen Davis, whom he said he knew well, between his release from jail and 7:00. The news that Silva had been shot reached him around 7:30 or 8:00. At this point, court adjourned for the noon recess.

When Douglas took over Smith's cross-examination that afternoon, he ascertained that Smith had learned of the shooting from a neighbor he encountered as he started out from his house with Hoey. After the man remarked that no one knew who was responsible, Smith decided he had better go home; "We had a boycott on the restaurant, and if they didn't know, I might be blamed." It was a damaging admission, and Douglas quickly closed in. Had Smith not stated on direct examination that he had not left home on Sunday night after dinner until his arrest? "Why did you think, Mr. Smith, that you would be accused of the murder?"

"Because I was carrying a boycott on that house."

"Was there any personal hostility between you and Silva that was known to anybody by which you might infer that you would be accused of the murder?"

Smith explained that among the AFL carpenters who boarded at Silva's "there was considerable animosity toward me" as an IWW member.

Douglas now moved to the stinging question: "Now, Mr. Smith, is it not rather a peculiar circumstance that you claimed to have been conducting a peaceable boycott against John Silva's restaurant and that you should infer from the shooting that you might be accused of having something to do with his murder?"

When Bowler's objection that this called for the witness's opinion was overruled, Smith's answer sharply highlighted the union warfare in Goldfield. He said that the members of the carpenters' union had been threatening to "run me out of town" and "break my face." Douglas well knew the jurors would wonder whether Smith's admitted fear that he was a suspect instead related to the conspiracy he was so eager to deny. The quarrel with the carpenters led, by logical steps, to an intensive series of questions on the Muller assault. The defense, no doubt believing that the longer Smith remained on the stand the deeper he would sink into the quagmire, made no effort to repair the damage by redirect examination.[20]

After several minor witnesses took the stand in quick succession, more than two-thirds of the testimony was complete, but the defense still had not succeeded in laying to rest the problem so common in labor cases—the credibility of defense witnesses. In the Haywood trial, for example, the prosecution would attempt to capitalize on these recurrent, suspicions by declaring that anyone who contradicted Harry Orchard was "a person interested as a party to this conspiracy"; Darrow, armed with ample union funds for investigation and a gifted lawyer's awareness of the absolute necessity of disinterested testimony, would produce defense witnesses from all walks of life, a good many of whom were neither WFM members nor friends of the defendants.[21] In Goldfield the problem of credibility was equally pressing. The only people able to corroborate the alibis of the principal figures in the case were their friends and union associates. Even the passersby in the street, in the near vicinity of Union Hall and in a town where WFM-IWW membership was large, were likely to be union men. Much of the testimony for the defense might therefore be discredited. The defense contention that Silva had advanced to the restaurant doorway armed and in a threatening way was probably established, thanks above all to prosecution witness Charles Hall, whose lack of bias on this point could not be doubted. The fact that Claiborne had been unable to identify more than one of the alleged conspirators and that Sexton and Rogers, both of whom were working in the mines, had strong alibis, might discredit his testimony. The main task remaining for the defense was to undermine, weaken, and destroy the credibility of the conspiracy story.

VI

PRESTON TAKES THE STAND

Just as the prosecution's case hinged on Claiborne, sole witness to the
conspiracy, that of the defense ultimately centered on the chief pro-
tagonist, Morrie Preston. Regardless of other testimony, the jury's
decision on whether he was an innocent young man or a union assassin
was bound to depend on the impression that Preston himself created.
The timing of his appearance, if Bowler had planned it at all, did little to
enhance that impression. Dixon and Luxinger, the only defense witnesses whose testimony bore directly on Preston's confrontation with
Silva and two of the strongest witnesses the defense produced, should
logically have appeared immediately before Preston or directly afterward, instead of being distanced from him by numerous other witnesses.
It could only be hoped that the jury still bore the accounts of these two
men clearly in mind and would realize how well they jibed with Preston's story.

As he seated himself, Preston's youthful appearance, which made
him seem younger than his twenty-four years and sometimes led other
witnesses to call him the "young fellow," his short stature, and his open
Irish features must have made him look like anything but the union
assassin the prosecution had portrayed. Yet there may have been something disquieting about his wild, staring gray eyes. In response to
Bowler's preliminary questions, Preston described his movements on
March 9 and March 10. He said that on the night of March 9 he had been
at home and in bed in the little one-room tent on North Bellevue Street
that he shared with William Jurgens. On Sunday afternoon at 2:00 he

had waited about half an hour in the Union Hall office for a man who failed to appear. He then encountered St. John and Donnelly at the bottom of the stairs on his way to the meeting in Ladies' Aid Hall. The meeting adjourned as soon as he arrived, but he lingered for ten or fifteen minutes.

After the meeting, he departed for the Hermitage Saloon corner of Main and Crook streets, where he encountered Smith and Constable Inman and was arrested for the Muller assault. He guessed that it might have been 4:15 or 4:30 (somewhat earlier than Smith had thought) when he was released from jail and walked back to Union Hall with Smith and Inman. He next proceeded with Inman to the Palace Saloon in search of the justice of the peace in order to reclaim the union record books taken from his pockets at the time of his arrest. He judged it was then about 5:00.

He presently returned to the Union Hall office, where he copied some union records before setting out for home. On reaching the corner of Ramsey and Main, he thought about the picket at the Nevada Restaurant: "I went down and gave him a word of encouragement and said, 'It looks good,' or something to that effect, that his work and our work was effective, at least it looked that way to me." Bowler wondered what work that was. "In notifying people that the Nevada Restaurant was unfair," said Preston. Was that "by violence or force"? Preston said "by persuasion" and affirmed that he meant "by peaceable means." After a moment's word with the picket, Preston again started home, only to remember that he had an errand at the Rand Restaurant. Reaching the Rand, he decided on the spur of the moment that he would instead pause for supper at the Jones Cafe on Main Street. After supper he noticed that there was no longer a picket in front of the Nevada Restaurant and took the station himself, accosting Silva's customers to explain that the place was unfair.

Douglas cut in with an objection, and Preston eventually continued his story. Either Dixon or Luxinger had then arrived outside the restaurant. "And while we were standing there the partner of Mr. Silva came into the room where Mr. Silva was sitting at the table . . . exhibiting a revolver, holding it over the table over the head of Mr. Silva in plain view, and said something and smiled, and put it to his side and walked back into the kitchen." (This man was waiter Paul Schultz, and Preston's words were supported by the recollections of prosecution witness Charles Hall, who claimed the waiter, not Silva, was the one who exhibited a gun while the carpenters sat at the table.) Although Schultz had not testified, Preston had recognized him among the prosecution witnesses called into court and placed under the rule. While talking to two other customers, Preston's attention was attracted by a "commotion" inside the restaurant. He saw Silva get up from the table and run into the kitchen. How had he gone? "He went hurriedly."

After indicating on the restaurant plan his own position and those of the others, Preston went on. He saw Silva take down the revolver hanging from a nail in the kitchen. As the restaurant owner approached, Preston backed toward the edge of the sidewalk and took out his own revolver. Reaching the door, Silva "made a motion like this, he says, 'Go on. I kill you,' and just as he said that, he said, 'Go on. I kill you. You mind your own business,' and drew his gun up that way. And as he did I reached my gun around and pulled the trigger of the revolver and shot." He fired twice.

"Then what did you do? Where did you go?" asked Bowler.

"I turned and ran toward Main Street. I put the revolver in my pocket. I did not run fast, but at first I was on a run. Then I assumed a fast walk, and then I turned the corner and walked along Main Street to Miners' Union Hall, went upstairs, and said to the first party I saw, and said, 'Here, I have shot a man. Take this.' I said this to Kurenbach. At first he resisted, and [I] practically forced the revolver on him. I ran through the Hall and got to the back door and walked downstairs. I walked hurriedly through the whole town . . . to Miners' Union Hospital. I went around the wall and into the room into a cellar or basement in one sense of the word—well, it was a room under the kitchen. The ground slopes there . . . I sat in there. I knew the place. I had been working there. There was a cot, and I sat on that cot, and I thought of what had happened. . . ." As he spoke, his head bent forward and his voice slid to a higher pitch while he struggled for self-control.

"We object to his thoughts. It is not admissible," Douglas interjected sarcastically. "We don't care what he thought afterwards. He should have thought before." Judge Langan told Preston to state what he did, not what he thought.

"What I did, I sat down and wept. I cried. I cried because I had shot a human being," said Preston. Suddenly he broke down and wept. This demonstration opened the floodgates of emotion. Lillian Burton and Zora Fischer, watching in the courtroom, also burst into tears. So did Smith. The prosecution protested at such an exhibition in the presence of the jury, and Judge Langan suggested that Preston and the others should attempt to control their feelings. At length, Preston pulled himself together and continued his story in a flat, dull monotone. He said that after he became quiet that night he went to bed in the little cabin for patients with illnesses that could not be treated in the wards.

Bowler used his final questions to emphasize that Preston had felt imperiled by Silva. Preston again told how Silva had stood in the door, threatened to kill him, and raised his revolver. He affirmed that he had believed his life was in danger. Silva's tone had been positive: "His voice was such that I was convinced that he would carry out his threats." Preston affirmed that prior to the shooting he had been advised of Silva's previous threats to kill him but gave no details. (Both the defense and the prosecution had omitted asking Dixon whether he had in fact relayed to Preston the threat overheard by Alley.) At the close of Bowler's examination, it was clear that Preston had made a better witness than Smith had. Even the *Sun* saw the "boy dupe" as one of the best witnesses in the case. Yet, as Douglas rose to his feet to take his turn, much depended on how well Preston would hold up under his interrogation.

Douglas began with some innocuous questions on Preston's early employment in Goldfield. Suddenly Bowler rose to his feet in haste and said to the prosecuting attorney, "I have forgotten something in this examination. Will you allow me to interrupt you?"

Douglas gave his permission, no doubt well aware that any afterthoughts Bowler wanted to interject at this stage would not damage the prosecution's case and might even enhance it. When Bowler asked his client if he had been present at the conspiratorial meetings described by Claiborne, if he had made the statements Claiborne attributed to him, and if he had walked down the street surrounded by a corral of men, the jurors probably attached no more importance to his denials than his own attorney had obviously attached to them when he so nearly neglected to include them in the record. Astonishingly, Bowler had forgotten about the Claiborne meetings.

Douglas returned to his inquiries about the previous autumn, and Preston told of nursing at the hospital until he was elected the union's business agent on December 28. Douglas wondered what his duties were in that position. "To get new members, to look into any reports that were made about any conditions, see that the members of the union lived up to their obligations to the union, and attend to any trouble that might arise insofar as I was able," said Preston.

At this point Douglas's early affability began to drop away. "Was it part of your duties to compel non-union workers in the town of Goldfield to join the union?" he asked.

"It was my duty to see that men who were not members of the union joined the union if I could do so by peaceable means," answered Preston.

"And if you could not do so without physical force, was it part of your duty to run them out of town by force?" demanded Douglas still more sharply. Preston denied it.

Douglas now inquired for what cause Preston had been arrested on Sunday afternoon. When Hangs's objection was predictably overruled, Preston answered that he had been arrested for assault with a deadly weapon with intent to kill "if I remember rightly." Douglas then proceeded to dwell once more, as he had done in his examination of Smith, on the Muller assault. Preston denied accompanying Muller out of the Hall, or even knowing what had happened to him. Judge Langan eventually sustained Hangs's objection to one of these questions on the ground that it assumed the conversations with Preston related by Muller had actually taken place, but in the course of the brief legal wrangle this entailed, Douglas beamed a clear signal to the jury: "We don't expect this witness will admit any of these things alleged in the indictment." This prejudicial statement was allowed to stand without reprimand by Judge Langan.

Much more on the Muller assault ensued before Douglas turned to a new subject. He wondered if Preston had a gun in his possession on March 10. Preston affirmed it. The gun had been taken from him at his Sunday afternoon arrest and had not been returned. The gun in his pocket as he stood in front of the Nevada Restaurant was also his, an Iver Johnson .38 self-action automatic that he had owned for about two years. Douglas wanted to know why Preston had obtained the gun.

"I had reason to think my life was in danger," said Preston.

Douglas pressed him to state the reasons, and Preston's answer, like a brief flash of lightning on a dark night, momentarily illuminated the tension in Goldfield that March. On the Wednesday before the shooting, said Preston, "there was considerable agitation." He had walked home alone that night, and someone had pointed a gun in his stomach. "I went ahead, and every man I met on that street on my way home had a gun in his hand. I thought it was time for me to have one." He had not felt secure with his old gun. Douglas continued to make much of Preston's two guns, in order to imply that a man not engaged in acts of clandestine violence to enforce the union's will would hardly require them.

The prosecuting attorney next inquired about the cause of the trouble with Silva. Preston's answer indicated that the waitress's complaint which immediately preceded the boycott was the union's second problem with Silva. "Sometime about February" a girl who was an IWW member complained that Silva had withheld her pay. When Preston went to investigate, Silva spoke of his rule on withholding one day's pay from employees who left without notice. "I told him we did not recognize those rules, that when a member of our union worked for a day's wages, he or she was entitled to have the day's wages. And I told him that unless he paid the girl we would have to call the help out, and he said, 'Go ahead, go ahead.' " The union, however, had allowed the matter to drop because the girl was going away to Los Angeles. Asked if "it was a principle of yours that no employer could oppose a rule of your union in that regard," Preston answered affirmatively.

Early in the week preceding the shooting, the union secretary left Preston a note telling him to investigate the complaint of a woman who said Silva had docked her pay. Preston went to the restaurant—he would later describe it in his writings as "a little, poorly kept beanery of the 'poodle-dog' type"—to find out if she was the same woman who had previously complained. Unable to accomplish anything, he let the matter drop. On Saturday "the young lady appeared on the scene" and reiterated her complaint. Silva refused to pay her when Preston again went to see him, and Preston felt certain he would not budge "unless action was taken." (Preston would later assert that the union had agreed to allow Silva his twenty-four-hour-notice rule provided this particular complaint was settled, but negotiations had broken down following Silva's refusal.) After Smith returned to the office with the announcement that he had called out Silva's employees, Preston inquired no further into the matter.

Moving forward to the scene of the shooting, Douglas wanted to know if Preston had testified that Silva approached the front door "very rapidly." Preston, mindful of the pitfalls of the law, replied carefully, "My testimony was that he approached this door hurriedly." He said Silva's gun had been "in plain view" to him from the time the restaurant owner left the kitchen until he reached the door, but he was not certain whether his own gun had been in sight of Silva. (Here it should be noted that Preston may have damaged his credibility by slightly overstating his case, for he himself later acknowledged that Silva held his gun behind while approaching, as Hall believed, and only pointed it at him in the doorway.)

Caught up in the rapid momentum of his own questions, Douglas pressed steadily toward his goal. In the exchange that ensued, Preston stuck to his story without contradiction. Douglas, dwelling with detailed questions on the moment when Preston fired his gun, must have vividly impressed the jurors' minds with the pitiful image of the dying man who "struggled back" as if "grabbing his chest" between the first and second shots, as Preston was compelled to describe it in his own words.

At the close of this painful reminiscence came the questions the prosecution undoubtedly anticipated would trip a witness with Preston's inclination to reveal his thoughts. Preston affirmed that he had been told that Silva had threatened to shoot him. Now came the clincher, and it did not fail in its intended effect: "Why didn't you go away from the front of his place of business?" Bowler gamely tried to forestall his client's answer on the ground that the question called for a conclusion of the witness and was swiftly overruled. There was nothing he could do to prevent the airing of Preston's conclusions.

"In the first place I didn't think of his having made the threat, that was not in my mind," said Preston uncomfortably. "When he came towards the door I did not think he would shoot. I did not think he would try to. I was of the opinion that he would try to make a bluff."

"So far as you know, was there anything but a bluff?"

"So far as I now know, so far as I know now—" Preston stumbled confusedly, and the question was reread. He answered, "I don't know."

"You mean to say then, Mr. Preston, that in spite of the fact that you had been warned that he made threats against you, that when he appeared in the door of the kitchen you did not think anything about the threats he had made?"

"I did not."

"You believed, did you not, Mr. Preston, that you were under the bann [sic] of a conspiracy—" Bowler swiftly interjected an objection which cut off Douglas's question at that point. It hardly mattered. The jurors had heard Preston himself acknowledge that he thought Silva was only bluffing. The cross-examination of Morrie Preston was over.

On redirect examination, Bowler tried, with notable lack of success, to recoup the lost ground by developing the idea that Preston had abruptly changed his mind and believed his life was in danger as Silva stood in the doorway, but the questioning was quickly terminated when the court sustained an objection by the state on the ground that Bowler had already examined the witness on this subject.

During the recross interrogatory, Douglas directed a single rhetorical question to the accused man for pure dramatic effect: "Mr. Preston, when you entered Miners' Union Hall and handed the gun to Mr. John Kurenbach, did you not say, 'Here, take this gun. I killed that dago son of a bitch'?" Preston of course denied it.[1]

With the close of Preston's testimony at 4:00, Bowler, who had four more witnesses en route from Goldfield, asked for and received an adjournment until Monday, April 29. However, the resumption of the defense presentation on Monday was not to be, because one of those strange accidents that can unpredictably alter the course of a trial would intervene. Juror W. B. Skinner, a Goldfield real estate man, came down with mumps. His physician announced in court on Monday that Skinner was too weak and dizzy to resume his duties before Saturday. Although some observers predicted a mistrial, Judge Langan, with the consent of both the prosecution and the defense, ordered the case to be continued until the following Monday, May 6, when court would resume in Goldfield. The jury would remain sequestered in Hawthorne until Skinner was well enough to travel.

Whether Juror Skinner's mumps had any effect on the case is a matter of conjecture. The defendants probably gained moral support from the move to Goldfield. While they had originally requested a change of venue because their most implacable enemies were centered in Goldfield and the antiunion press had spared no effort to inflame public opinion against them, Goldfield was also the stronghold of their union friends. In no other county seat in Nevada, not in the old mining towns of the Comstock era where the WFM and the IWW were still scratching for a handhold, surely not in the ranching centers where union radicals were hated and feared, could Preston and Smith hope for as warm a reception as they would receive in Goldfield. The character of the crowd in the courtroom would markedly change. They would be among friends.

The effects of this ten-day interlude on the jurors may not have been inconsequential. Judge Langan adjured them not to discuss the case, not to permit anyone to discuss it in their presence, and not to form any opinion until the case was submitted. After the trial it was revealed that Deputy Sheriff Jones had disregarded this admonition. Allen Jarvis, one of the three miners on the jury, later said that Jones had remarked in the presence of the jurors that "in Pennsylvania when the Molly Maguires were so bad, a number of them were taken out and strung up, and the same thing would be done here in Nevada." Speaking of a May Day celebration—it must then have been around the first of May, International Labor Day—Jones had said that "the flag would fly over the court house, and that nobody would dare to pull it down or trample it, and that there would be no red flag floating over it either, and that nothing of that kind would be attempted or permitted in his presence."[2] Again, the red flag.

If the jurors' opinions, consciously or unconsciously, began to take shape during this unusual interlude, the process probably did not work to the benefit of the defense. The prosecution's case was already complete, but only twenty-four of the forty-two defense witnesses had appeared at this point. The prosecution's contention, resting on only a handful of major witnesses, was simple and clear, while the defense's effort to disprove that contention was a lengthy and complicated one, which depended on mustering a large number of witnesses to contradict one detail or another and cumulatively discredit the prosecution. This necessary dependence on details could not have benefited from the interlude in which some were bound to fade from memory. The case still held two major surprise developments in store, both favorable to the defense, but if the jurors' opinions had already begun to jell, these surprises would explode with diminished effect. Although the interlude gave the defense some needed time to gather witnesses to contradict Claiborne's surprise testimony, it was pure bad luck for them that the last evidence the jurors heard before this extended intermission did not relate to one of Claiborne's erroneous identifications or to Luxinger racing down the street in the belief that Silva was about to shoot. It was Preston, fumbling to explain his seemingly contradictory behavior. What rang in their ears was Douglas's resounding question whether Preston had told Kurenbach, "Here, take this gun. I killed that dago son of a bitch." Despite the judge's admonition to resist forming opinions, it would have been difficult for the jurors not to ask themselves during the next ten days whether Preston did.

May is, by many measures, the loveliest month in Goldfield. Summer means dust and blistering heat; autumn brings no flaming foliage to the treeless desert; winter masks the pastel hues of the hills in snow. But May is the warmth that comes between the bitter cold and the scorching heat, the time when dawns are soft and rosy on the Malapai mesa west of the city and the sun's warmth is welcome. Nights are still nippy, but daytime temperatures often hover in the sixties and seventies. Wildflowers tint the eastern hills, creamy white blossoms burst from the shaggy, ungainly Joshua palms, and the wild creatures of the desert come to life after the cold winter. In this time of warmth and beauty, in Goldfield's fifth spring, jurors, attorneys, deputies, prisoners, and witnesses set out to continue the trial. The first contingent of thirty or forty, mostly witnesses, reached the railroad station at Thorne only to find a four-hour delay stretching before them and no restaurant or saloon at hand. Diamondfield Jack, with a lordly gesture of beneficence, commandeered a shipment of canned goods destined for Hawthorne and treated the crowd to a feast of canned peaches, crackers, and coffee. More delay was in store. The group finally boarded the train, only to be laid over for a full twelve hours at Mina by an accident farther down the line. A good burro could have made better time than the railroad.

A few days later prisoners and lawmen followed. Although the sheriff originally intended to place St. John and the other indicted union leaders under guard at a secret location because the stone jail was bursting with high graders, he finally decided to squeeze everyone inside. The jurors, having brought their bedding along, made themselves as comfortable as possible in the temporary courtroom inside a wooden building, its exterior covered with pebble dash and gaily decorated in yellow and red, at the corner of Main and Gold.[3]

When court convened once more on May 6, Judge Langan temporarily excluded the jury from the room to make a grave announcement. He had received a threatening letter. Dated Goldfield, May 5, and scrawled in an erratic hand with curiously enlarged h's, the letter read: "Dear Judge. there are two of our boys now being trid in your court and i want to tell you now that if you hang them, or send them up for life you will die for it you will be *killed* like a *dog* [here the writer sketched a childish skull and crossbones]. *POISON BEWARE* for every man of ours you kill or send up to the pen. *we* will kill one of you for every hair in the man's head of ours you kill Jack Davis Claborne Bliss Wingfield and lot more [illegible] traitor of [son?] of a [bitch?] Claborne we will get him soon Take warning all. DEATH."

Frank Hangs at once issued a statement condemning the "cowardly" and "unwarranted" act and asserting, as legal protocol demanded, that his clients had been treated with "the utmost fairness" by Judge Langan. President Brown of the Goldfield WFM immediately dispatched a letter to Judge Langan. The union "is not in sympathy with, nor does it approve such infamous action. We brand the writer of the letter as an enemy of organized labor, and express the hope that the writer may be discovered and summarily dealt with. We have every confidence in you, and know that you will give the defendants a square deal, and that is all they are entitled to." The Esmeralda County commissioners offered a $1,000 reward for evidence leading to the apprehension of the writer. Claiborne allowed it to be known that he too had received several threatening letters, the latest of which addressed him as "you white-headed Swede, you son of a bitch" and "you traitor" and warned him to get out of town and "not testify any more against our boys" or "the black hand will sure get you." According to Claiborne, the letter concluded, "Death is too good for you."

Judge Langan declared from the bench that he would "do my duty as I see it in the law," regardless of threats, and expressed hearty appreciation to the miners' union for their supportive letter. Preston and Smith were led into court, wearing new clothes and looking more cheerful than in Hawthorne. Because the necessary courtroom furniture had not yet arrived from the old county seat, the trial was postponed another day.[4]

Who had written this anonymous letter? Lindley Branson, editor of the *Tonopah Sun,* had no doubts. "The talk that the letter was not written by sympathizers of Preston and Smith is rot," the *Sun*'s editorial column declared:

> Haven't scores of such letters, with skulls and crossbones, been received by friends of law and order at Goldfield for weeks? Have the people forgotten that all through the late labor trouble at that city such written threats were of more than daily occurrence? No denials of their authorship were made then and nobody for a moment doubted or thought that they came from any other source than the I.W.W. Whether from individual members or the conspiracy as a whole is not material. The sympathy of the I.W.W. is with such methods. The leaders of the gang of bandits openly advocate anarchistic ideas. Murder and assassination, according to their own boasts, are their chief stock in trade and the burden of their public and private talk.[5]

The *Goldfield Daily Tribune,* sharing Branson's view that the letter had been written in the disguised hand of a woman, was slightly more cautious: "Why it is that this band of cowards expects to accomplish a beneficial purpose by inditing such a letter, passes ordinary intelligence. Surely no good can result to the prisoners on trial. On the contrary, prejudice against them arises as a pure matter of course."[6] As the *Tribune* indirectly suggested, so counterproductive was this threat that IWW members believed the letter had been written by their opponents in an effort to discredit their cause. Threatening letters, which Orchard, under McParland's tutelage, claimed the WFM planned to dispatch to its enemies after the Steunenberg assassination, loomed similarly large in the Haywood trial and may have been evolving into conventional weapons for the opponents of the radical unions.[7]

While promising to do everything in their power to apprehend the perpetrator, law enforcement officials in Goldfield viewed the letter with dubious eyes and refused to ascribe it to the IWW. Sheriff Ingalls and Constable Inman believed the letter's author was a crank—in Inman's view, one seeking to prolong the labor troubles and no friend of Preston and Smith. "I can not conceive," said Ingalls, "how anyone having the interest of labor at heart could be so supremely foolish as to write such a letter as this. It is prejudicial to public opinion and can not serve any good end." Inman expressed certainty that the miners' union had nothing whatever to do with the matter.[8]

What effect the letter exerted on the Preston-Smith trial is difficult to gauge. The jurors were not supposed to know about it, though some supporters of the defense believed, with good reason, that the letter had been written for the purpose of influencing them.[9] The crowds in the Goldfield courtroom during the remainder of the trial, largely union supporters, showed no hostility to the defendants. While Judge Langan's rulings grew no more adverse to the accused men than they had been before he received the letter, the possibility that he was subliminally affected by it during the composition of his charge to the jury cannot be ruled out. In a wider sense, the effects of the letter could only be, as Sheriff Ingalls had rightly noted, "prejudicial to public opinion." The Nevada supreme court justices who would hear the appeals of Preston and Smith in the event of their conviction would probably read of the outrage and react adversely, as would the members of the parole board. The Nevada public was likely to be persuaded that union members were in truth the dangerous anarchists portrayed by their opponents. The rumors the *Sun* had been circulating for some time on threatening letters to prosecution witness Dyer and others would seem to be confirmed. The anonymous letter to Judge Langan may well have been one more way the shooting of John Silva could be used to discredit and destroy the radical unions, a transparently illogical move for the union but an extremely clever one for its opponents.

When court at last convened on May 7, with juror Skinner ready to carry on, Preston and Smith were marched into court, handcuffed as usual, their manacles a clear cue to the jurors that these were dangerous men. Deputy sheriffs ostentatiously guarded the jurors and the judge. Before trial proceedings resumed, an angry Judge Langan once more excluded the jury from the room while he denounced the letter.

The first witness to appear for the defense after this long hiatus was a housewife named Mary McKune, and few in the courtroom audience could have guessed that she was about to give testimony potentially devastating to the prosecution. Mrs. McKune said that before moving to Goldfield in October she had been acquainted in Price, Utah, with the prosecution witness who gave his name as Bliss. "I know of him for years," she said. "He lived in the same town." His name had been Maxwell in those days. On March 10 from sometime in the afternoon until 8:00, at the hours when Bliss said he had been observing the corral of men, he had been at her house on Fifth Avenue in Goldfield. Bowler had no more to ask of Mrs. McKune.

Cross-examination commenced with Attorney Douglas inquiring about the occupations of the McKunes. Mrs. McKune said that she kept house for her husband. He was now tending bar in Beatty, a job he had taken three weeks earlier, after a stint as watchman for the railroad. Douglas next wanted to know "the occasion" of Bliss's presence in the McKune house.

The answer led him onto thin ice and suggested that in this un-educated, stolid woman he was encountering one of the most dangerous witnesses of the trial. "When he came to town he was broke, and he knew my husband," said Mary McKune. In response to the next question, she added that Bliss "said he was broke and did not have anything to buy anything to eat with."

Edging swiftly away from this unsatisfactory image of the prosecution witness who had represented himself as a Utah mine owner, Douglas began an effort to discredit the witness by his time-tested formula. Surprisingly, he was stymied. Neither Mrs. McKune nor her husband belonged to any labor organization. Asked if the Palace Saloon where her husband tended bar was a dance hall, Mrs. McKune indignantly replied, "No, sir, it is not." How had she known it was 8:00 when Bliss left her house on March 10? "I looked at the clock," said Mrs. McKune with exquisite simplicity. What had called her attention to the clock? When her husband told her he would be home in an hour, she had looked at the clock. On Monday Bliss had returned to the McKune house and remained "pretty near all day," leaving after supper. He afterward boarded with the McKunes until he left for the trial in Hawthorne on April 29. His partner, Frank Branch, also received a subpoena to appear (interestingly, Branch had not testified). On none of these points was Douglas, despite his best efforts, able to confuse Mrs. McKune or catch her in a contradiction. She did, however, elaborate a little. Bliss had ceased to board with her: "When he got money, he found another place."

How did she know? "It looks to me that way," said Mrs. McKune. "He told me he was going to get paid and would give me some money." He had sent ten dollars along by Frank Branch before he went to the trial. Even the *Sun* was obliged to acknowledge that "cross examination did not shake the witness to any visible extent."

After an inconsequential redirect examination, Mrs. McKune stepped down from the stand, leaving one of the larger mysteries in Bowler's conduct of the case behind her. Her testimony had suggested that Bliss was not really where he said he was on March 10 and that he was using a name that was not his own. Questions from the prosecution, not the defense, had elicited the information that he was apparently broke for weeks. Mrs. McKune may have had a good deal more to tell. Better yet, Bliss could be recalled and queried. Already, with brief questions of a standard variety, they had learned that he was dull-witted and easily tripped, lacking Claiborne's nimble mind, and there was every likelihood that he would stumble into damaging admissions now that the defense had some real ammunition in hand. Where and for what had someone paid the "Utah mine owner" who had been mooching meals from the McKunes for weeks on the strength of their acquaintance in Price? No further witnesses dealing with the true identity and past activities of Bliss were introduced. For a few moments, while Mrs. McKune was on the stand, Bowler had the chance to crack the prosecution's case wide open. We cannot know how loudly the name she had revealed (Maxwell) or the place (Price) resonated in the minds of the jurors or whether there were any among them who put the name and the place together and guessed what McKune had come so near to telling them: the witness for the prosecution was really a gunfighter from Butch Cassidy's Wild Bunch.[10]

Two witnesses then took the stand to corroborate Jerry Sexton's alibi, though confusion over "change day," the day of the week on which miners on the graveyard shift moved to the afternoon shift, somewhat detracted from their testimony. Bowler had obviously neglected to prepare them so that their memories were refreshed and their thoughts in order by the time they took the stand, and even their answers to initial and predictable questions were weakened by their fumbling through the drawers of memory for misplaced items. The pertinent comment of trial lawyer Louis Nizer is all too applicable here: "A lawyer who will put his witness on the stand without thorough preparation disserves his client, his profession, and the truth."[11]

Two of the succeeding witnesses were part of a defense effort to prove that the conspiratorial meeting Claiborne purported to have observed on Saturday night could not possibly have taken place during or after the dance in Union Hall. The defense attorneys were often unable to elicit the definite and positive answers they sought,[12] but the testimony suggested that Claiborne was probably mistaken about the time of the conspirators' conclave, as he had also indisputably been mistaken about the identity of several of the men present.

The defense next began to present witnesses who would cast doubt on the corral of men Diamondfield Jack and Bliss said they had seen surround Preston immediately after the shooting. James Brown, an IWW bartender, and A. W. Lanterman, a miner, had both seen Preston walk up the street to Union Hall unaccompanied. However, Douglas gleaned an unexpected bonus from Lanterman during cross-examination. By the time the prosecutor asked whether there was anything "particular about Mr. Preston or his actions that attracted you toward him," Lanterman seemed nettled by the doubts cast upon his veracity, and he began to volunteer convincing details. He answered, "No, he had a grin on his face."

"Looked as though he was well pleased?" inquired Douglas, the more deeply to impress this unpleasant image on the minds of the jurors.

"I don't know as he was," said Lanterman uncomfortably.

"That would indicate pleasure on a man's face?" Douglas queried.

"It was a sickly looking smile," said Lanterman.[13]

As the next witness, Sam Tregonning, rose to take the stand, fireworks could be expected, for during the past month this short, heavy-set figure with the dark mustache had emerged as a major focus of invective in the antiunion press. A former employee at the bottling works, he had recently taken the place of Preston and Smith as walking delegate for the union; he was now a "curbstone broker." The *Sun* claimed that prior to his arrival in Goldfield in 1904 he had worked for the Salvation Army in Chicago, where he had acquired his skill in verbal exhortation, before making off with another man's wife and being fired for conduct unbecoming a Christian. The *Sun* also accused him of hiring out his services to a Goldfield stockbroker and providing tips gained from his inside knowledge of the labor situation (similar charges had been leveled against St. John). Salvation Army reject or not—and, given the source, the story may well have been a fabrication—Tregonning was unquestionably a fiery personality. This was evident at a meeting, well guarded by armed deputies, at which a visiting organizer who was attempting to create a rival conservative union called upon the IWW to debate and Tregonning rose eagerly to meet the challenge. Apparently it was an insincere one, for deputies immediately dragged him away. In an even more explosive affair, headlines declared "TREGONNING ARRESTED FOR DESECRATING FLAG AND CONSTITUTION." The article accused the English-born Tregonning of "making his living bulldozing and hoodwinking honest American miners." Mention was also made of "the red flag of anarchy, which is the only one seen hanging in Union Hall."[14]

A *Sun* article three days later expanded these charges against Tregonning and Goldfield law enforcement officials. Tregonning had served as ringleader and made "treasonable" speeches at a meeting in Columbia where a speaker had shocked public opinion by insulting the flag. In the midst of a big crowd in front of Union Hall on Saturday night, the *Sun* asserted, Tregonning had shouted, "God damn the stars and stripes! To hell with the Constitution." Arrested for this offense, he was released without authorization a few moments later by Bart Knight, "an I.W.W. deputy."[15] The real reason for the *Sun*'s campaign against Tregonning was probably the editor's belief that he was one of the IWW's most influential members, indeed the one largely responsible for the WFM-IWW merger in Goldfield. The moderate positions Tregonning had sometimes adopted on union matters in no way softened Branson's attitude. Tregonning of course denied the *Sun*'s charge of playing the stock market and offered $100 in gold to anyone who could prove otherwise. Law enforcement officials declared that Tregonning had never been appointed a deputy, while noting that he was as eligible for the post as any other man.

If Tregonning was visibly ruffled by the *Sun*'s reportage, Constable Inman was furious. On April 18 he sued the *Sun* for $10,000 in damages for "malicious statements and lies detrimental to my character." He also issued a public statement with the heading "Twenty-nine lines and almost as many lies" that declared, among many other things, "Has there been any one individual that has done as much to aggravate strained relations between labor and capital as that same Tonopah Sun? It is my firm and honest belief, and the belief of the vast majority, that the Tonopah Sun is the worst and by far the greatest of all agitators." Inman went on to suggest that Branson ought to have been jailed long since.[16]

The newspapers do not reveal what became of Inman's suit; no doubt he dropped it when his temper cooled and Branson publicly acknowledged his error. Tregonning's alleged inflammatory statement, according to Inman, was actually a snatch of conversation overheard when Tregonning was describing the London bread riots to a group of men. The miners' union moved swiftly to nullify its enemies' efforts to portray it as unpatriotic. The stars and stripes flew proudly over Union Hall, and many miners began wearing American flag pins.

After the prosecution withdrew an initial objection to Tregonning's appearance, he testified, under Bowler's guidance, that he was sitting in the secretary's office in Union Hall when he heard two shots. He "jumped up and ran downstairs," passing Preston in the street. Preston was alone; St. John and the others were nowhere to be seen.

Cross-examination commenced. After strongly emphasizing, in his usual way, the curious circumstance that the witness could name only three of the men he had seen on the street that evening, Douglas began to bear down on the curbstone broker with unusual force. "You are very much interested, are you not, Mr. Tregonning, in this trial?"

"No sir, not any more than any other case."

"Wouldn't your friendship and personal acquaintance with the defendants elicit more interest in you than an ordinary case in which the principals were not your friends?"

"No sir, absolutely not."

"Mr. Tregonning, are you the man that attended a meeting of the miners at Columbia at the behest of one Mr. Toplitz and when the American flag was mentioned, you said, 'To hell with the flag, damn the Constitution'?"

Bowler's objection to this on the ground that it was not cross-examination was sustained, but Douglas managed to wave the red flag before the jury and, in effect, to disqualify Tregonning because he was a radical. "We believe this is competent testimony as tending to show the condition of the witness's mind . . ." Douglas explained. "We believe it is relevant to show this man's mind in order that the jurors may know how much weight to give to his testimony. If his attitude toward the flag is such as indicated *then his taking an oath is a point that the jury should take into consideration.*"

Tregonning, with a defiant flash of the fire that made him such a controversial figure, cut in to say that he would like to answer. "I never made no such statement," he said. "Mr. Nichols will take an affidavit on it."

"Did you make a statement similar to that?" Douglas demanded.

"No sir, I love the flag."

"Are you the man that was arrested on the sidewalk somewhere in the neighborhood of Miners' Union Hall because of inflammatory utterances you made with reference to what ought to be done to clear up the labor situation here?"[17]

Bowler's objection to this line of questioning was sustained, and the cross-examination of Sam Tregonning was over. Neither this alleged anarchist firebrand nor any other defense witness in the case had made a radical statement of any kind. The closest the prosecution had come to eliciting the confessions of a radical had been the admissions laboriously dredged from Smith about his concurrence with the IWW credo on class conflict. Still, Douglas had not wasted his time. He had used Tregonning to implant a suspicion in the minds of the jurors that the oaths of unpatriotic union radicals could not be trusted.

When the trial resumed after lunch, the defense effort to discredit the testimony of Diamondfield Jack took a new twist. A. J. Whitkop, a miner in the Atlanta, came forward to say he had been in the Hoffman House when he heard the shots and ran over to Silva's restaurant. Returning to the Hoffman, he saw Diamondfield Jack, with whom he "had a contract" that evening. At this point, the defense was compelled by an objection from the prosecutors to recall Davis to the stand in order to lay the proper foundation for Whitkop's evidence. Whitkop then testified that Diamondfield Jack had asked him where the shooting occurred and afterward departed by a side door. (This, of course, conflicted with Davis's story that he had seen the flash of gunfire about 150 feet away from him and watched Preston run to the telegraph pole, where a corral of men surrounded him.)

The prosecutors then moved in on Whitkop. The witness declared he "wouldn't say positive" who else was in the saloon and decided after further questioning that Davis had made his appearance no more than a minute after the shooting. Whitkop did not know Preston or Smith, though he was a union member. On reading about Diamondfield Jack's testimony in the newspaper, he had told union president Brown about his encounter with Davis. Whitkop's story was subsequently fortified by the testimony of a cook who recalled seeing Diamondfield Jack standing by the fire hydrant on Columbia Street east of Main at the time of the shooting (this, of course, conflicted with Davis's story that he had been on the corner of Ramsey and Main).[18]

One of the final defense witnesses was a carpenter to whom Silva had related his problem with the union. When Silva allowed that he meant to conduct his business in his own way, the carpenter had remarked, "The first thing you know, you will have one of these fellows walking up to your door and you will lose your trade." Silva had said that if they came to his door he would kill them. Blocked from pursuing his usual themes of friendship with the accused or membership in the radical unions with one of Silva's AFL boarders, Douglas tried to cast doubt on the carpenter by homing in on his inability to recall whether the conversation had occurred two days before the shooting or three. The witness declared, "To tell the truth, I have been trying to forget about the case."[19]

C. S. Johnson, a miner and a brother of the indicted A. J. Johnson, took the stand to affirm that during the contretemps over lot jumping he had heard Claiborne threaten his brother, "You tow-headed son of a bitch, I will get you yet. I will make you leave this town." C. S. Johnson was so intent on confirming his brother's alibi that he said he had been in front of the Cook Bank when questioned on his whereabouts on March 9. Reminded by Hangs that the question referred to *Saturday* night, Johnson at first did not know, then guessed he was at home. He eventually decided that he had reached home before 11:00, finding his brother already there. These uncertainties and the overeagerness that led him to blurt out his account of Sunday evening in the wrong place can hardly have done much to establish an alibi for A. J. Johnson and suggested that the defense attorneys had again failed to prepare their witness adequately, even though he was a witness they regarded as critically important to their case. C. S. Johnson said that perhaps three men were visible in front of the Hoffman from the corner of Ramsey and Main where he was standing at the time of the shooting, but Diamondfield Jack was nowhere in sight.

Douglas's cross-examination proceeded to take Johnson over the most extensive series of hurdles he had yet devised, in an effort to weaken his statement that there were only three men outside the Hoffman by showing that he could not always remember how many he had seen at other spots or at other times or on other days—thus destroying his credibility. How many men were on the Exploration building corner? How many in front of the Texas Saloon? How many near the Nixon building? At the corner of Hall and Main, "how many would that be?" Did he know any of them? How many in front of the State Bank and Trust building? What time had he gone downtown on March 12, two days after the shooting? Couldn't he say approximately? How many men were in front of the Palace Saloon? Had he seen some? Well, had he seen any men there or not? Where was he coming from? "In a case where there is a shooting, a man's attention would be attracted more than any other time," C. S. Johnson finally protested.

Bowler used his redirect to make just one point: Johnson had not seen a corral of men in front of the Hoffman saloon.[20] In his opening statement, Hangs had promised that Claiborne would be discredited by his demonstrable malice toward the Johnsons. Douglas had therefore given C. S. Johnson his particular attention, with the usual devastating results. The proof of Claiborne's malice unfortunately depended on the word of an indicted man and his badly confused brother.

VII

THE VERDICT

With C. S. Johnson's departure from the stand, the defense attorneys completed their presentation. Those Goldfielders who had insisted day after day that the defense was certain to subpoena Wingfield and other leading mine operators were at last obliged to admit they had been far off the track. Confronting the formidable Wingfield was a bold and risky strategy far beyond the range of Bowler and Hangs. With these and other possibilities forever foreclosed to the defense, the prosecution moved once more to center stage.

Prosecution rebuttal commenced by recalling Smith. Douglas had just one question to put to him: had he asked Davis in the presence of Sam Calvin, "Did you arrest the others?" Bowler protested that Smith had already testified on this but was once again overruled. When Smith began to answer that he had not made the remark attributed to him, the prosecutor interrupted. Bowler protested that his client should be allowed to speak: "I humbly beseech the court to allow him to explain his answer." That Bowler was reduced to humbly beseeching the court instead of making his stand on legal grounds was perhaps an indication that he believed his position hopeless. Although Smith was eventually allowed to repeat his earlier answer, the prosecution had succeeded in placing the damning words "Did you arrest the others?" once more in the forefront of the case.[1] Yet this was to be the last real setback for the defense, even though the rebuttal process compelled them to fight a defensive battle on terrain not of their own choosing. The difficulties that had weighed against them all along the way would at last be shunted aside in the eleventh hour. Fighting their last round in a final burst of mettlesome vigor born of desperation, their every punch struck home.

When the prosecution recalled Nellie Emery, the last of several who testified that Silva was well known to be a peaceful, quiet man, the defense effort to prove that he was quite the reverse sped forward with a rush. Mrs. Emery affirmed that Silva had gone after a carpenter named Saunders with a knife, though she could not recall if he had threatened to kill his partner, Margaret Heffernan. Bowler did not neglect to also inquire whether Silva had followed Lewis Trooy around Goldfield threatening to kill him, until these persecutions landed him in jail. When Douglas, on redirect, asked Mrs. Emery to explain "the difficulty" between Silva and Saunders, the answer could not have been a better one for the defense if they had dictated it themselves. Mrs. Emery said that when Saunders had attempted to collect a bill, which Silva refused to pay, Saunders nailed the front door of the restaurant shut. Then "John comes into the kitchen for a knife, and said, 'I kill him.'" Mrs. Emery had tried to persuade him to have Saunders arrested instead. At this point, Douglas hurriedly brought her tale to a halt.[2]

Endeavoring to revert to the more fruitful theme of "the others," the prosecution next brought forward Sam Calvin to state that he had accompanied Davis during Smith's arrest and overheard Smith's words. Curiously, as Bowler brought out during his interrogatory, Calvin had then "dropped back" and had overheard no other remarks. Charles Hall then returned to the stand to give a reprise of his earlier evidence, with the defense attorneys fruitlessly protesting that Hall had already testified on these matters, but the court upheld the prosecution's argument that they could not anticipate Preston's contention of self-defense and the evidence was now essential.[3]

As Paul Schultz, the often mentioned waiter in the Nevada Restaurant, came forward, over defense objections that his testimony was inadmissible because it was not rebuttal and should have been included in the prosecution's case in chief, the defense obviously had no clue to the significance of this witness. Ironically, the man they sought so strenuously to exclude would prove far more valuable to the defense than to the prosecution. Schultz confirmed Hall's statement that Silva held the gun behind him, clearly the sole purpose for which the prosecution had so belatedly brought him to the stand. But his last words on direct contained something odd and suggestive. He was positive of the way Silva had held the gun, he said, because he was watching it: "It was my gun." In later accounts of the confrontation, Preston was to claim that Silva had attempted to shoot him and had only been prevented from doing so by an inability to operate the gun. Preston had not testified on this point, however, perhaps because he had not then understood Silva's difficulties with the gun. Now a vital clue had emerged: perhaps Silva had pulled the trigger without raising the safety catch on the Colt .38 automatic because he was unfamiliar with a gun not belonging to him. The trial's first day in Goldfield, a day which began with the surprise testimony of Mary McKune, now ended with Schultz's elliptical remark for all to ponder.

Bowler's initial questions the next morning elicited the information that Schultz was a new arrival in Goldfield and had not begun working at Silva's until March 10. He said he had turned the pistol over to Constable Inman, and Bowler now asked the sheriff to produce it as evidence. The attorney's excitement must have been mounting as he inquired whether Schultz had seen Silva with a pistol in his hand prior to the shooting. The state's objection, proffered in a rare utterance by the prestigious Malone, that this was not cross-examination was sustained. Bowler's objections and requests for exceptions had often appeared tired, desultory, and formal, but this time his response resounded with righteous indignation. Since the prosecution had introduced Schultz and he had testified to Silva's possession of the gun and his position in the door, "we are entitled to an exhaustive, thorough, and searching cross examination, and by the ruling of the court we are deprived of a fair and impartial trial."

Lacking the resourcefulness to circumvent the obstacle in his path and arrive at the same spot by another route, Bowler questioned Schultz on Silva's position in the doorway and his own actions after picking the gun up from the spot where it had fallen beneath one of the tables after the shooting. Schultz replied, "I didn't intend to tell. The next day I told it was my gun." The prosecution's request to have this revealing answer stricken as unresponsive was granted. Schultz said he placed the gun on the kitchen shelf a while, then put it in his pocket and brought it home. Prosecution objections to this line of questioning were sustained, with Bowler once again vigorously protesting that his clients were being deprived of a fair trial. The questioning continued. Schultz admitted that he had told the "chief of police" (probably Inman) about the gun on the day of the inquest. Many in that courtroom, not excluding the jurors, must have wondered whether the prosecutors had initially planned to suppress the evidence on this gun in order to strengthen their case. It was suddenly clear that the prosecution had known long before Preston's indictment that Silva was armed but had not placed the gun in evidence. Only one of the prosecution witnesses, Hall, had even acknowledged its existence, and he had not mentioned it in his testimony before the grand jury. Throughout the pretrial period, the antiunion press had described Silva as "an unarmed man," and no one in an official capacity had undertaken to disabuse the public of that notion.

Bowler's closing questions were devoted to Schultz's record. Most reluctantly, after numerous attempts to escape the question, Schultz acknowledged that he had recently been convicted of larceny. Redirect was solely devoted to a successful effort to enable Schultz to remove this onus by explaining that his conviction had resulted from a minor dispute over the purchase of a lunch wagon. After two more rebuttal witnesses took their turns,[4] the evidence was complete, and it was time for the final summations.

On the afternoon of May 8, Douglas opened for the state with a vituperative attack on the character and patriotism of the defendants and the witnesses for the defense. Elizabeth Alley was a "notorious female anarchist" whose testimony should have no effect on any honest man. Sam Tregonning had given sworn testimony with a lie in his heart when he said he loved the flag; every citizen knew that Tregonning hated the very sight of the flag and was a leader in lawless anarchy. St. John was an "arch agitator, the man to whom more want and suffering, most destitute families, could be charged than to any other man in the state of Nevada." Preston and Smith themselves were part and parcel of a band of bloody-minded anarchists who "waved aloft the red flag of anarchy while they trampled the stars and stripes in the dust." As he spoke, the *Sun* reported:

> Douglas repeatedly turned to where Preston and Smith sat behind their attorneys and, shaking his hands in their very faces, declared them to be assassins of the lowest type. So strong did the attorney become in his denunciation that at times the whole court sat amazed at the unrestricted liberty he gave his tongue. Guilty or innocent of the grave charge against them, the defendants appeared to be the least disturbed of any in the room by the burning words of the attorney. Smith sat with his head tilted back a bit, in characteristic attitude, and his black beady eyes gave no sign of feeling as the hot wrath of the attorney was poured out on the heads of himself and his companion. Preston at times took his eyes off of the man who repeatedly declared him to be a cold-blooded killer of men to gain his own ends, and let his glance wander in a half abstracted way over the court. Both men were calmly chewing gum throughout the whole afternoon.[5]

Past shock? Beyond anger? Fatalistic? Resigned? Controlled? We only know that Preston and Smith sat imperturbably and listened as from afar while Douglas waved the red flag and raked them with invective. "The red flag must wave but once," St. John was supposed to have written in the note quoted by Claiborne; the *Sun* had described this flag in a recent editorial as "the flag that waves over the revolutionaries and nihilists of Russia, the members of the Black Hand of Italy, and the I.W.W." Now the red flag billowed fully unfurled over the prosecution's case. The testimony of Mary McKune, the strange concealment of Paul Schultz's gun, the inability of Claiborne to identify several conspirators—all the evidence that might have loomed so large was being enveloped in its brilliant, mesmerizing folds.

Frank Hangs, as he rose in the waning afternoon to make the opening statement for the defense, appeared genuinely shocked by Douglas's remarks. The prosecutor, said Hangs, had allowed his personal spite to dominate his utterances, and this must not pass unchallenged. Hangs found such vituperation not only wrong but also self-defeating. His own presentation was calm and unemotional, though laced with many satiric comments on Douglas. He turned to the conspiracy, calling it a complete fabrication. Claiborne, Davis, and Bliss had lied from first to last, and the defense had met and overwhelmed every point in their stories. As he began to examine the shooting, Hangs argued that the defense had demonstrated that Silva was a man of hot and ungovernable temper who had more than once threatened Preston's life. Using the plat to illustrate how Silva had stood in the doorway, Hangs contended that it was a physical fact that in order for the bullet to have taken the course that it did, Silva must have raised his gun hand. Suddenly—and belatedly—his listeners must have seen the significance of the intensive questioning of Dr. Galloway and the defense attorneys' lively interest in the condition of the door casing. (Preston himself believed that his first shot had struck Silva in the abdomen and the second had gone wild, lodging in the doorjamb above the restaurant owner's head.) In his final remarks, Hangs tried to counteract the emotional effect of the red flag by reminding the jurors of their duty. If they believed any part of the testimony the defense had offered, if they were true to themselves and to their trust, if they expected to be able to look their God in the face, they must find Preston guilty of no more than justifiable homicide.[6]

When Hangs ended his appeal, court recessed until the following morning. Attorneys for both sides were no doubt hard at work that night in an effort to deflect the missiles already launched by the opposition, but the prosecutors had a special advantage. Judge Langan had furnished them with a copy of the instructions he would give to the jury, and this was a great aid in preparing their final argument. No copy of the instructions was supplied to the defense.[7]

The defense's objections to the instructions submitted to the court by the state constituted the first order of business when the trial convened the following morning, but Judge Langan postponed resolving these issues until later. The defense believed the timing was calculated to their maximum disadvantage. Not only had they received no advance copy, but also, if the final decision on the instructions was not to be reached after the completion of all closing arguments, it should have been done before any closing arguments began, so the defense would have an equal opportunity to shape its plea in the direction the instructions demanded and comment on them.[8] This was a chance that Bowler and Hangs would not receive.

As Bowler launched into the emotional appeal to the jury that marked the last stand for the defense, his task was an unusually difficult one: he must distill a mass of testimony from many witnesses, all of whom had contributed something on a bewildering variety of minor points, into a single statement that was simple, clear, and dramatic; he must select the strongest points in his case and bear down hard on them, instead of frittering away his time explaining weaknesses; he must compensate in these final moments for his own recurrent failures and speak for the dull-witted Smith and the poorly prepared Preston more eloquently than they had succeeded in speaking for themselves; perhaps most important of all, he must deflate the issue of union radicalism. It was a formidable assignment.

Bowler began by attacking Douglas's prejudicial remarks, as Hangs had done the day before. With an old-fashioned touch of gallantry toward Elizabeth Alley, the defense attorney declared that he "blushed that man born of woman" should heap such abuse on the fair sex. He edged toward the red flag, observing that the union to which the defendants belonged was "an organization instituted for the most laudable purposes" and that Preston's picketing had been peaceful. He abstained, however, from confronting the issue of radicalism more squarely. Perhaps he hoped to shift the battle to another arena, where discourse on the evidence would tacitly rebuke Douglas; perhaps his uncomfortable silence issued from his own inner conflict on the union and an absurd hope that the issue might yet dwindle away if he ignored it. Another Darrow was needed to send a denunciation of the moneyed opposition ringing through the courtroom, to shape belief by the sheer power of his own conviction. A short time later in Idaho the great attorney would tell the jurors, "I speak for the poor, the weak, for the weary, for that long line of men, who, in darkness and despair have born the labors of the human race," and win Bill Haywood's acquittal.[9] In Goldfield that morning in May, the bony, aging frontier lawyer before the court seemed far less certain for whom he spoke.

Bowler next shifted to the scene of the shooting, describing Silva as a pusillanimous and vindictive character of the kind who had to be killing someone if he was not himself killed. He dramatically described the wild excitement of Silva's rush with a gun toward the front door to drive Preston away. Then, just as momentum began to build, with one of the abrupt shifts that had characterized his approach throughout the case, Bowler suddenly dropped the shooting and began to talk about the conspiracy, which he called a "base fabrication" existing only in the minds of Claiborne, Bliss, and the other witnesses for the prosecution. Claiborne's angry declaration to Johnson, "I'll get you, you tow-headed son of a bitch," and his effort to place Johnson in the forefront of his conspiracy yarn, as the man who had attempted to kill Diamondfield Jack and had offered money to any union member who would pick him off, revealed that the whole story was a malicious concoction tailored to satisfy Claiborne's personal grudges. After pointing out discrepancies in the testimony of Davis and Bliss, he observed that the conspiracy was indeed a base plot, not by the defendants, but on the part of the witnesses for the state. It was a trenchant point.

Now Bowler made a backward leap to the shooting. He dwelled long on the technical argument earlier outlined by Hangs. He recited Preston's testimony on the shooting, ending with the declaration that any man would be justified in shooting in self-defense under such circumstances. He strongly stressed the evidence of defense witnesses who had heard Silva threaten Preston prior to the day of the shooting. Once more he emphasized, as had Hangs, that Preston and the other union men had the legal right to conduct a boycott. Any American had this right; he challenged the state to show one law to the contrary. He read the indictment of Smith to the jury, argued that the state had failed to prove any of these charges, and demanded Smith's release as right. He warned the jury against the persuasive powers of Judge Malone, whose closing argument would undoubtedly be a "dangerous weapon" likely to shake their conclusions. He urged them to stand fast. In a final angry thrust at Douglas, he said, "It's filthy lucre behind the case that stimulated counsel to the tirade of abuse and vituperation made yesterday." Dramatically, he reminded the jurors of the magnitude of their duty and placed the case in their hands. With the final formality of thanking the court for its courtesy and consideration, the defense of Morrie Preston and Joseph Smith was over.[10] After Bowler completed his argument, and before the noon recess, the last contested provisions in the court's instructions were settled.

Bowler's final argument had occupied the morning; as Judge Booth Malone, so long a silent presence, at last arose after the lunch recess in the warm, sunny May afternoon to make the final address for the state, it quickly became clear that Bowler had good cause for his apprehensions concerning the effectiveness of Malone. This was a man of unprepossessing appearance. He wore a dark suit and a bow tie. The short mustache, the wavy forelock, the dark semicircular brows above bulging, bespectacled eyes would have better served a vaudeville comedian than a former judge of great reputation, but Bowler knew better than to underestimate him. If Douglas's dramatic fulminations, against a background of prolonged antiunion agitation in the press, had fired the blood of the jurors and created a disposition to convict, Judge Malone would now assure them that it was legally correct to do so—indeed it was their public duty. Dignified, eloquent, mature, renowned for his legal learning, Malone was a figure exuding paternal wisdom. Indeed his experience on the bench was far lengthier than Judge Langan's. In contrast to Bowler's vehement emotion, he spoke calmly and evenly, paying his respects to judge and jury and beginning with a plain statement of the case. Here was a man of wisdom and dignity, who spoke so simply, without cheap appeals to sentiment, a man of such authority that he at once inspired trust. The "dangerous weapon" against whom Bowler had fruitlessly tried to steel the jurors was whistling toward its target.

Witness by witness, Malone compared and recited the facts "in a masterly way," as the *Sun* admiringly described it. "The evidence took on form and substance under his skillful handling. The case for the state became a tangible thing instead of a mass of confused utterances." Malone dwelt, "with insistent force," on the fact that Silva had been shot by Preston as the premeditated result of a plot to commit murder. Accordingly, Preston's plea of self-defense was an absolutely untenable theory.[11]

Malone passed lightly over the testimony of Claiborne, tacitly acknowledging the weakness of this portion of the case. Instead he fell back on Davis. Since no one save Davis, the accused Smith, and possibly Calvin, had been present at the time Davis claimed Smith had asked whether "the others" had been arrested, the defense had been unable to disprove this incriminating remark. Nor, since the defense attorneys had already spoken their last word, would they receive an opportunity to point out that the remark was now logically inconsistent, a single wall left standing when they had demolished the edifice of the conspiracy theory. If no conspiratorial meeting were held—and they had cast serious doubt on Claiborne—then there was no plot and no "others" about whom Smith would inquire. In Preston's angry words, "Take away the evidence of this perjured tool of the powers that be in the State of Nevada and there is nothing left; there is no corroborative testimony." Malone, however, bore down with telling effect on Smith's incriminating remark: "What does this mean? What can it mean but that there was a deliberate plot afoot to take the life of John Silva, a plot in which both of these defendants were concerned, of which they were a part? What then becomes of the self defense plea of Preston?"[12]

Malone next undertook to demolish the technical argument so emphasized by both defense attorneys—that Silva must have held his gun in a threatening manner for the bullet to take such a course. Knowing their witnesses were likely to be disbelieved, the defense attorneys had sought to impress the jury through objective evidence, but this hope buckled under Malone's assault. The first shot, declared Malone, had passed across Silva's body leaving the bruiselike crease Dr. Galloway had described. Silva must therefore have been standing sideways with his gun held behind him as Hall had testified.

In Judge Malone's final remarks, the red flag was once more unfurled. He reminded the jurors that the issue before them was not merely the guilt of Preston and Smith but also Nevada's future. The peace and prosperity of the state in the years to come depended on wiping out the band of agitators to which the accused men belonged. A conviction would convince outside investors that their money would be safe in Nevada and bring prosperous times to the state. In solemn tones he told the jury that the future of the great state of Nevada rested in their hands. The defense swiftly objected to this "reprehensible inflammatory utterance," but Judge Langan declined to rebuke Malone for his remarks.[13] As the defense attorneys recognized, it was a cruelly effective argument in a state where the revived prosperity brought by new mining discoveries was just beginning, capital was still scarce enough to make the moods and whims of outside investors a matter of constant anxiety in the press, and Goldfield mining stocks were already ebbing into the doldrums once more, after the burst of frenetic activity that accompanied the labor settlement. Preston thought Malone's appeal to the jury amounted to this:

> To you who are in the real estate business, if you want values to keep up you must convict these men, otherwise capital will not invest here, the mines will close and Goldfield will be no more. To you who have homes here, to you who have places of business here, to you who expect to work here, to you who are all tied up here, I say a conviction must be had or the prosperity of Goldfield is at an end; your property will be worthless. In other words he cleverly and craftily pitted the interests and property rights of the jurors against the innocence and liberty of the defendants, making it appear to the jurors that if they did not convict it would cost them practically all they had in Goldfield.[14]

Moreover, the ranchers on the jury were likely to remember the starving eighties and nineties, when Nevada's population dwindled and the state government struggled as hard as the homesteader to make ends meet. To the survivors of those desperate years, Malone could safely surmise, prosperity shone like the promised land, at last attained after nearly a generation of hardship and not to be weighed lightly.

With his last words to the jury, Malone set aside his rational approach to stir emotion by the pitiful spectacle of the mortally wounded John Silva. "What was the last thought of this dying man as he lay there, gentlemen of the jury?" he demanded. "It was for his wife and poor orphan children." Morrie Preston listened in bitter silence, but these words would long rankle, for he knew, as Malone and Judge Langan also surely knew, that no evidence had been presented that Silva had either wife or child.[15]

Judge Langan had no doubt devoted considerable time to the composition of his instructions, being fully aware of the excited attention they would arouse in this, the most famous case of his brief judicial career. Instructions are intended to summarize the evidence and elucidate the law; yet Judge Langan would also have been cognizant of the powerful influence they could exert on the outcome of the trial, for in cases hinging on self-defense the instructions often made the difference between conviction and acquittal. This was especially true in Nevada because it was one of the states requiring written instructions that could be taken along by the jury for reference during their deliberations. The jurors' recollections of witnesses or closing arguments might be confused or contradictory, but the instructions could be reread in the jury room and often proved critically important.

While some judges liked to preface their instructions with sonorities on the grandeur of the Anglo-Saxon legal system and exhortations to the jury on impartiality and the solemnity of their task, Judge Langan's commenced dryly and abruptly with no such rhetorical preliminaries. To aid the jury in their task of deciding whether Preston and Smith had murdered Silva "wilfully, feloniously . . . and with malice afore-thought," Judge Langan defined first and second degree murder. He went on to explain that manslaughter meant an unlawful killing in the "sudden heat of passion" without malice or premeditation; voluntary manslaughter required either a "serious and highly provoking injury . . . sufficient to excite an irresistible passion in a reasonable person" or an attempt to commit such an injury. "Words, actions or gestures, however grievous" or inflammatory were insufficient unless accompanied by an assault. Bowler and Hangs, as they listened, believed that including manslaughter in the instructions harmed their clients' chances of acquittal. Preston and Smith, accused of murder resulting from conspiracy, were either guilty as charged of murder in the first degree or they were innocent. The judge, by adding this irrelevant explication of manslaughter, was really providing the jurors with alternate options, should they wish to punish the accused radicals severely but shy from seeing them hang.[16]

Judge Langan went on to explain the law on self-defense. "If the danger was not imminent and there was reasonable opportunity to escape it was the duty of the defendant to escape and decline any conflict. If he had such reasonable opportunity, the conflict was not necessary and therefore not justifiable." Langan's elucidations continued, eventually arriving at another point of critical interest to the defense. "Preston," said the judge, "seeks to justify or excuse the killing of the said John Silva on the ground of threats alleged to have been made against the said Preston"; this could not "avail, justify or excuse" the killing, unless Silva showed an intention to harm Preston at the time of the killing. If Preston "had a reasonable apprehension" at the time of the shooting that Silva intended to assault him, he had a right to defend himself. Bowler and Hangs sat helplessly by, believing that Judge Langan was misstating the statute in a way that would harm their client. They knew that they had never sought to *justify* the killing on the basis of threats. This evidence was only meant to show Silva's probable intent and Preston's reasons for believing himself in danger. By coupling "menaces" with threats, the judge seemed to be telling the jury that an overt act, Silva's rush to the door with gun in hand, was without legal significance in Preston's plea of self-defense. They knew this was not the law. Significantly, no mention had been made of the legal provision that the right of self-defense extended even to the taking of life if necessary.[17]

Judge Langan now turned to Smith, advising the jury that an accessory to murder was one who, whether present or not, aided or abetted in the crime. For both defendants to be found guilty, the evidence must prove beyond reasonable doubt that they acted in concert, yet it need not be proven that they met and agreed to commit the crime. "Such concert of action may be proven by circumstances." If Smith was an accessory, "that is all the law requires to make them both equally guilty."

Reasonable doubt was then defined and the jury adjured that when they entertained a reasonable doubt on the degree of a defendant's guilt, he could only be convicted on the lowest of these degrees. Next came the stereotypical charge to the jury to evaluate the testimony of witnesses carefully and arrive at their verdict "without fear, favor or affection, bias or prejudice, or sympathy." It would have been a common enough instruction had it not commenced with the observation that Preston and Smith had testified on their own behalf, and therefore implied that the caution to be on guard against willful false swearing applied especially to them.[18]

This final charge was followed by the instructions requested by the prosecution and approved by the judge. The fourth to be granted judicial approval must have stirred the apprehension of Bowler and Hangs: "The court instructs the Jury that a party charged with an unlawful or deadly assault upon another can not avail himself of the claim of necessary self defense if the necessity for such defense was brought on by his own deliberate wrongful act." Bowler had emphasized in his closing argument that Preston's presence picketing the restaurant in a peaceful manner was fully in accordance with law, and the attorney would attempt to bring this out once more when his own turn to request instructions arrived. But, in an era when the union activities so long suppressed by law were just beginning to be recognized as legal, would the jury believe the judge was advising them that Preston's presence outside the restaurant was a "deliberate wrongful act" that vitiated his plea of self-defense?[19]

The sixth instruction bore no apparent relation to any evidence presented in the case. The jury was informed that "one who is feloniously assailed in his own home or place of business is not bound to retreat even though by so doing he might secure his own safety, but he may arm himself and stand his ground and take his assailant's life, if it becomes necessary, and this homicide is justifiable." Since Preston had not been feloniously assailed while defending hearth and home, this piece of legal information could only confuse the jurors or lead them to suppose that the judge meant picketing was defined by law as felonious assault against Silva's place of business and this vindicated the restaurant owner's attack on Preston.[20]

The shadow of the gallows lay across the state's instructions numbered seven and fourteen: if the jurors believed Preston "sought the deceased and provoked or brought on the difficulty . . . by an unlawful act of his committed at the time, or that the defendant voluntarily and of his own free will entered into the difficulty, then there is no self defense in the case, and the jury can not acquit on that ground; and in such case it makes no difference how imminent the defendant's real or apparent peril may have become during the conflict"; the fourteenth concluded "when one believes himself about to be attacked . . . it is his duty to avoid the attack, if it is in his power to do so, a right to self defense does not arise until he had done everything in his power to avoid this necessity." Under these charges, later to be termed by Bowler and Hangs "a monstrous misstatement of the law," the legal right of self-defense had been whittled away. How could the jury now acquit Preston, after being told that it was impossible to do so if he had voluntarily "entered into the difficulty," as they were likely to assume that he had done when he took up the picket's duties? While Nevada's statute required that the deceased must be the assailant for the murderer to invoke self-defense, the law nowhere obliged him to avoid the conflict. A man thus threatened, the defense attorneys would later write, "has the power to desert his family, leave his home, commit a sacrifice of all his worldly belongings—must he do all this to avoid the necessity? Pshaw! what nonsense . . . he is not required to go out and dig a grave for himself and crawl into it to avoid the necessity."[21]

Now it was the defense attorneys' turn to request additional instructions, and it would lead them into several angry altercations with Judge Langan. Instructions were affirmed which stated that the danger must be weighed from the defendant's point of view, that he was not compelled to flee before he could justify homicide, and that his testimony was to be received like that of any other witness; the attorneys could only hope that they had succeeded in correcting earlier contradictory instructions on these points. Four instructions were refused, three of them further amplifying the right of self-defense. Judge Langan accepted an instruction affirming Preston's right to picket in a peaceful manner but added to it the modification: it is "equally true" that Silva had the right to enforce such rules as he thought fit for the conduct of his business and no one "had any right to unlawfully interfere with him, or his business, or to make any unlawful attempt, or do any unlawful act to compel him to change such rules." The defense attorneys protested these decisions in vain. They saw only too well that Judge Langan's "modification" had completely altered the meaning of their instruction to suggest that Preston had committed an "unlawful act" of interference with Silva's business. But some comfort could still be drawn from the belief that if their clients were found guilty, Judge Langan's prejudice against them would provide a clear-cut issue on which to base their appeal. With the judge's instructions in hand, the jury retired.[22]

"GOLDFIELD RED-HANDED MURDERERS CONVICTED BY JURY LAST NIGHT AT 10:30," read the headlines in the *Sun* the next day. "ANARCHY DISMAYED." In the early hours of the evening, most spectators had drifted away from the courtroom in the belief that both sides had presented strong arguments and some time would pass before agreement could be reached. The jury went out for supper, then returned to heated debate. The argument inside the jury room was clearly audible above the street noises, and the voices of the people waiting outside sank to whispers. Suddenly, after five hours of wrangling, a peremptory summons arrived from the jury. Deputy sheriffs scurried over the city in search of the judge and the attorneys. A crowd gathered. Preston and Smith were marched into the room, looking haggard in the harsh glare of the electric lights. Smith feigned an attitude of sleepy indifference; Preston, by contrast, was alert and trembling with anxiety. The verdict was read: Preston was guilty of second degree murder and recommended to the mercy of the court; Smith was guilty of manslaughter, with no recommendation of mercy. *Sun* reporter K. L. Simpson thought "Preston appeared to be on the verge of tears as the full meaning of the verdict dawned upon him, but Joe Smith . . . glared at the clerk with brazen affrontery, not a feature showing aught but cold, hard defiance."[23]

It was later learned that on the first ballot seven jurors had favored Preston's conviction for first degree murder, three had voted for second degree murder, and two for acquittal. Allen Jarvis, one of the three miners on the jury, was among the latter. Had even one of the jurors favoring acquittal held out, as supporters of the prosecution so obviously feared and as so often happened among Goldfield's stubborn, independent jurors, the result would have been a hung jury. The prosecution's case might well have crumbled during a second trial. Still, the one unyielding barrier to a verdict of first degree murder and the death sentence that almost certainly would have accompanied it was Allen Jarvis. A compromise was reached after four or five ballots; the two who favored acquittal faltered in their convictions, and the seven who had favored first degree from the start moderated their stance, when it became clear that no amount of argument could budge Jarvis from his refusal to go along with this verdict; juror Alex E. Bettles, a mining man, convinced Jarvis that Judge Langan had instructed the jury to agree on a verdict; the verdict of murder in the second degree was at last agreed on, with separate balloting on Smith. Smith's conviction for manslaughter, a crime committed in the heat of passion and totally inapplicable to a conspirator charged as an accessory, was a legal monstrosity begotten by Judge Langan's misleading instructions.[24]

The press applauded the verdict. The *Sun* termed it "AN AGREE-ABLE SURPRISE," while expressing disappointment that the jury had not fixed the penalty at death. Editor Branson used the occasion to level a final blast at the two prisoners:

> [Smith's] daily life was steeped and boiled down with deliberate and cruelly planned murder of men who had the manhood to stand out and say they believed in law and order and would protect their rights under the constitution. And when John Silva was shot down for standing guard over his property rights the cowardly, red-handed assassins set up the shameless and cur-like plea of self defense.[25]

The verdict left Preston shattered. To understand his outrage, it is necessary to bear in mind that the judicial processing of homicide cases on the frontier was very different from today's practices. Goldfield was a frontier boomtown, and in these towns a murder conviction was the rare exception, as careful research on the trans-Sierra mining camps has demonstrated. A murder conviction following an affray in which both participants were armed with guns and presumed by their peers to have a fighting chance was an even greater rarity. An awareness of these probabilities may have influenced the withholding of Schultz and other signs that the prosecutors were not only downplaying Silva's gun but may have also dallied with the idea of denying its existence before they decided to build their case on the conspiracy theory. Although Goldfield had seen its share of homicides, acquittal was so great a likelihood that on one of these occasions involving an affray with firearms the district attorney did not even bother to appear in court.[26] Still, the anomaly of Preston's conviction in the context of his times led many of his union supporters to believe that his motion for a new trial would be granted or his appeal would easily be won, and the case the *Industrial Union Bulletin,* organ of the IWW, called "about the rankest frame-up ever made in the West" would soon be overturned.[27]

To help accomplish this result, another Colorado attorney arrived in town shortly after the verdict. He was the WFM's consummate troubleshooter, the same attorney who was to mount the final effort to save the life of Joe Hill eight years later, when Stegner sketched him at sixty-four: "a graying man, frail and pot bellied, with a cool fighter's face oddly out of character with his sagging sedentary body. His eyes were pouched like a hound's. From above sagging lower lids the hazel irises looked out with a remote and uninterested air that matched the frowning thrust of his face no better than his face matched his body."[28] Judge Orrin Nelson Hilton was the best, after Darrow, that the WFM could give, though it was already too late when they gave him. A New Englander in background and a westerner by choice, Hilton was born in Lowell, Massachusetts, and educated at Bates College, Maine, where he received his LL.D. He had then migrated to Colorado by way of Michigan, where he became a county judge in the 1880s. As editor of the tenth edition of Wharton's classic treatise on criminal evidence, he was hobbled by none of the deficiencies of education and experience that had immobilized Bowler and Hangs while Malone looped legalistic circles around them. He had apparently arrived on behalf of his old client St. John, but he would soon take over the legal effort for Preston and Smith.

Hilton began raining verbal punches at the bench as soon as he entered the courtroom on May 23. He accused one of the witnesses for the prosecution of writing the threatening letter to Judge Langan and communicating it to the jury with the express intention of influencing them. The matter demanded a court order for immediate investigation. "If it should be done," Hilton declared darkly, "I'll warrant that the cowardly deed could be brought home to the scoundrel that wrote it." Thanks to Jarvis, the attorneys had definite knowledge that the jurors had known about the letter during their deliberations. It was but one of the many dirty tricks used in the prosecution's effort to secure the conviction of Preston and Smith, he charged. Hilton also sought a separate trial for St. John and denounced conditions at the Goldfield jail. Just outside the jail door, a large and growing pile of manure from the adjoining livery stable sent redolent fumes throughout the single three- by fifteen-foot cell, seething with vermin, where the union leaders were confined with up to three other prisoners, sometimes including women. Hilton called the jail a place "unfit to keep swine." Judge Langan responded that the prisoners had been offered the option of the state penitentiary, and he made no move to order an investigation of the threatening letter.[29]

Meantime Bowler and Hangs entered motions to win a new trial for their clients and to halt the judgment. A large crowd, including Lillian

Burton and Alice Smith, gathered in the courtroom. Preston and Smith, both looking well and listening attentively, appeared to have taken heart during the interval since the verdict. On behalf of Smith alone, Hangs entered a motion for a new trial; he argued that Smith had been charged as an accessory before the fact. The crime of manslaughter for which he was convicted did not admit of this charge, because it pertained to killing without malice and could not be applied to an accessory before the fact who was not present. His client was therefore either guilty of murder in the first degree or innocent of any offense whatever.

In the motion filed on behalf of both defendants, Hangs contended that the prosecutors were guilty of misconduct because they had made false statements which prejudiced the jurors against the accused men. One glaring example was Malone's moving rhetoric about Silva's bereaved widow and orphan children, their existence unsupported by any evidence in the trial. Another was the exhortation to the jury to convict the defendants as a stimulus to investment in Nevada, regardless of their guilt or innocence. Hangs also argued that the admission of Muller's testimony as proof of conspiracy was a judicial error because the Muller assault occurred before the purported conspiracy began. The dark, heavy-set attorney once more attacked the credibility of Claiborne. Could anyone seriously believe that he would have failed to inform the law officers if he had really heard murder plotted in Union Hall? This man's testimony could not possibly be credited and should not have figured in the case in any way. Hangs then registered his objections to Judge Langan's instructions, contending that they had served to prejudice the jurors against his clients. He concluded his three-hour argument by filing several depositions in support of his motions: Jarvis's statement, more witnesses confirming the whereabouts of Diamondfield Jack, and a statement by M. H. Corson, who said that the day after Silva's death Hall told him that Silva had been in a terrible rage just before the shooting and had said he would kill the men who were boycotting him. According to Corson, Hall said he expected his evidence to clear Preston and Smith, but when Corson later asked him whether he had testified on these matters, Hall asked him not to say anything about it. Apart from Jarvis's statement, the court would be unlikely to give much weight to witnesses who had failed to appear at the trial and submit themselves to cross-examination.[30]

The next day Hilton entered an affidavit by St. John requesting a change of venue. Malone then commenced his argument against the defense motions. He first dealt with the contention that Smith could not legally be found guilty of voluntary manslaughter: the law recognized no essential distinction between accessories and principals; the testimony of Dyer had placed Smith at the scene of the crime getting the picket out of the way while Preston killed Silva; if the judge's instructions had led to a verdict of manslaughter instead of first degree murder, Smith hardly had cause to complain. Malone denied making misstatements to the jury. Although he had mentioned Silva's family, as the dying man himself had done, he had also cautioned the jury not to decide the case on sympathy. Malone continued his justifications. The admission of Muller's testimony was entirely proper because it showed that Muller had been threatened with death by Preston, beaten, and run out of town, despite the defense's contention that the boycott of the Nevada Restaurant had been peacefully and legally conducted. The evidence in the depositions submitted by the defense was simply cumulative, not grounds for granting a new trial. Malone submitted a deposition of his own from Deputy Sheriff Jones, who denied that he had made the remarks attributed to him by Jarvis. The attorney then aimed a shaft at Jarvis, observing that he was generally understood to be the juror who prevented a verdict of first degree murder against Preston. Malone closed with a declaration that the judge's instructions had been perfectly comprehensive and had covered all matters refused to the defense as separate instructions—a final verbal bow to Judge Langan.

Bowler then rose to make the final argument for the defense in his usual seesaw style. This was an angry Bowler, still fired by the indignation that overcame him in the final stages of the trial, a Bowler who despite his age and long experience—perhaps because of them— sounded vaguely amazed at the course of jurisprudence in this case. "We have no bouquets to throw at the court," he announced. "We stand here flatfooted and demand what we consider are our rights." He went on to say that the case was a "comedy of errors" tried in a community so enraged against the defendants that jury selection had been seriously hampered. In a gibe at Malone and Douglas, he noted that regularly elected prosecuting officers had been crowded out by private attorneys hired by the mine owners. Bowler then sailed into the instructions Judge Langan had denied to the defendants or altered by his own additions, especially the critical instruction on the right of self-defense. This was followed by a lengthy exposition lasting until the noon recess on the legality of strikes and boycotts. After lunch Bowler took up the cudgels once more on the matter of instructions. In conclusion, he reiterated an argument earlier advanced by Hangs that Judge Langan had committed highly prejudicial errors when he admitted Muller's testimony on an unrelated crime and allowed the prosecutors to cross-examine his clients on the subject. (Within a month Muller was to receive a commission as a deputy sheriff.) Judge Langan declared that he would rule on the motions Monday morning, May 27.[31]

When Monday morning arrived, a large crowd of men stood outside the courtroom clamoring for admission. The only women present were Lillian Burton and Alice Smith, who silently took her place beside her husband. Preston's initial nervousness subsided as he sat talking to Lillian while he waited for proceedings to begin. To the surprise of no one, Judge Langan denied the motions for arrest of judgment and a new trial. The defense had probably anticipated this, knowing that the judge was unlikely to find fault with his own instructions and that the new evidence they had presented was scanty, and instead counted on winning their appeal to the Nevada supreme court. The motion on Smith's behalf was denied on the basis of Malone's argument that the law made no distinction between principals and accessories before the fact. As to the motions on behalf of both men, declared Judge Langan, he had concluded after careful consideration that his own instructions were "complete in every particular," indeed "harmonious in every particular, and not misleading or contradictory in any respect." He dismissed the new evidence as insufficient and discounted the Jarvis deposition because it was contradicted by Jones. As he pronounced sentence on the two prisoners, who rose to their feet and stood calmly before him, Judge Langan confined himself to a brief and somber reprimand:

> The crime involved the taking of a human life, a crime the highest known to law. John Silva's life was taken unnecessarily. The conflict could easily have been avoided and the trouble amicably settled, but you thought otherwise, and Silva died. You must now suffer the penalty for the heinous crime you committed. The whole superstructure of our government is founded upon law and order, and in order to maintain that government the laws at all hazards must be respected and obeyed. Human life is too sacred and precious to be sacrificed unwarrantedly. I feel it my duty, in view of the recommendation of the jury . . . not to confine you, M. R. Preston, in the state prison for the remainder of your natural life, which it would be my sworn duty to do under the law and the evidence in this case, were not such recommendation made.[32]

Smith received the maximum sentence of ten years. Preston was sentenced to twenty-five, the usual penalty for second degree murder in that time and place. There were tears in the eyes of both men as they left the courthouse, but Preston managed a smile for Lillian.

VIII

BURNT OFFERINGS

Judge Langan's denial of the motions for a new trial was not entirely unexpected, and the defense attorneys still had grounds for optimism as they began preparing their briefs for the appeal to the Nevada supreme court. Presently Hilton appeared in court once more on behalf of the indicted union leaders, spouting sensational charges and castigating Malone as a hireling of the mining magnates ("the coin of United States Senator Nixon was jingling in the pockets of Judge Malone"). He succeeded in getting the union leaders admitted to bail. The amount was set high at $10,000 apiece, but St. John and two others were able to post it immediately. When the annual WFM convention assembled at Denver in June, St. John—no doubt an unwelcome presence—and Rogers were able to take their places in the Goldfield delegation. In a cheery note dashed off to Smith at the penitentiary, St. John observed, "We expect a hot time here and we may not get fooled," and signed off, "Well so long Joe be a good kid and we will have you back with us before long both of you. Yours for the Republic of Labor in our time."[1] Smith was in good spirits as he wrote a reply to his "Comrade & Brother": "Yours of the 9th to hand and contents noted and were glad to hear from you. We are still Pluging along at the same old stand and getting along nicely, We are thinking very strongly of buying the place. Well John we hope things will come yours up there tell baby Rogers to cheer up it may not be true. We got a letter from Jerry [Sexton?] and we heard he had a little wage Slave come to his home. Well this [is] all for this time give our best regards to the boys and tell them to dig in hoping to hear from you soon I am yours for the working class."[2]

At the behest of the Goldfield delegation, led by Rogers, one of the WFM convention's first acts was to pass a resolution expressing the union's belief that Preston and Smith were the innocent "victims of a conspiracy" and pledging a united effort to win their freedom.[3]

Also in June, Goldfield's radical Socialists of the St. John faction intensified the endeavor to launch their own newspaper, *Nevada Workman,* by appealing to all WFM members to buy shares. The newspaper's announced objective was "to counteract the false and malicious lies with which the press of our state has inflamed the minds of the people against our Brothers Preston and Smith." With the convicted men still seeking redress and the union leaders still awaiting trial for conspiracy, a newspaper to refute the "misrepresentations and slanders of our capitalist press" was "an imperative necessity." Yet less than six months after the appearance of its first issue on August 17, *Nevada Workman* expired without fulfilling its founders' hopes for a newspaper powerful and persuasive enough to nullify Branson's *Tonopah Sun.*[4] Instead of winning the hearts and minds of the people, Goldfield's union men were becoming ever more embattled, ever more feared, and ever more isolated.

Summer brought another labor dispute and another victory for the mine owners. On July 18, incipient trouble over the hiring of watchmen was averted by the mine owners, but the miners' discontent was not so readily defused when Senator Nixon announced on August 17 that a change room would be opened at the Mohawk Mine to stop high grading, numerous court cases having failed to exert a deterrent effect. By August 18 the miners' union had officially sanctioned a wildcat walkout called by miners in the Mohawk. Arbitration on the change room controversy began on August 21, with each side rejecting the other's proposals, but direct negotiations finally broke the stalemate, and the miners resumed work September 8. The WFM agreed to accept the change rooms, while Goldfield Con undertook to remedy objectionable features and to reinstate all former employees.[5]

As the WFM surrendered yet another fortification in Goldfield and strove to regroup its lines, the effort by the national unions to arouse the rank and file in support of Preston and Smith intensified. The report of the General Executive Board to the IWW national convention of 1907 sought to place the case in the context of the class struggle and to wring full propaganda value from it. The Haywood case was won, though Moyer and Pettibone were not yet free, the clashes at Wheatland and Spokane were still in the future, and during this temporary lull, Preston and Smith loomed very large in the IWW report:

Goldfield was the storm center; it was there where the forces of capitalism clashed in bitter conflict with the army of labor. Extermination of every IWW supporter was the object. . . . Fellow workers we must not weaken in our endeavor to constantly hold up the crimes of the capitalist class and their hired hessians and tools to the workers of the land. . . . Preston and Smith will be set free if everyone is resolved to do his duty in the propaganda among our fellow men.[6]

If the *Sun* and the interests it represented had inflated Preston and Smith out of all proportion as dangerous criminal anarchists, the IWW was equally willing to add them to its roster of the blessed martyrs.

In November yet another Preston and Smith defense committee, this one based in Goldfield, announced that despite the "nefarious design" of the capitalists, the charges against St. John and the other union leaders had been dismissed. Fellow workers were urged to come to the rescue once again, and those who had already done so received thanks. At least some locals responded: the Greenwood, British Columbia, WFM local, always one of the most vocal and militant, passed a resolution in language of the purplest hue extending "heartfelt sympathy to Bros. Preston and Smith, the afflicted and helpless burnt offerings of the sacrificial orgies of a blood thirsty capitalist brood of vampires, who fatten on the life-blood of the long suffering toiler."[7] Throughout this period much criticism was being voiced against the WFM for its failure to aid Preston and Smith and the union leaders. The WFM responded defensively in the annual report that the Federation had "defrayed the legal expense" for "the six other brothers" and engaged an "able attorney," Hilton, for Preston and Smith.[8]

Preston himself had no fault to find with the WFM, though he repudiated some of the defense committees operating in his name. When it was all over, he expressed the deepest gratitude to the miners' union for "constant efforts exerted to secure my release, the heavy tax they endured to support me financially, and the ready sanction and support" they had granted him. His gratitude to the IWW was clearly of a lesser order and centered on "the self-imposed restraint they practiced through respect for my unwarranted condition."[9] By the fall of 1907, Preston had undoubtedly seen enough of the judicial process to know that the triumphant claim that worker agitation had freed Haywood was a pipe-dream of power by the powerless. He would have learned that resolutions celebrating him as a burnt offering to capitalist vampires would never unlock the doors of the state penitentiary, and perhaps would not have minded much that his cause had failed to kindle the imaginations of the rank and file, despite repeated exhortations to duty by the union leaders. Preston clearly had little taste for providing living proof of the crimes of the capitalist class. The IWW could serve him best with silence. He knew by then that what he really needed was a good lawyer.

November brought a famous visitor bearing optimistic assurances— Big Bill Haywood, sent by the WFM national executive board to work for the release of Preston and Smith. "The boys in the penitentiary were glad of my coming," Haywood recalled. "I told them that I felt the chances were good for a pardon." In addition to visiting Governor Sparks and the supreme court justices, he paid a call on Attorney General Stoddard, who "spoke favorably about endorsing a parole."[10]

Yet beneath the surface civility of Haywood's reception by Nevada officials, the downfall of the Goldfield miners' union was already under way. Just as the shooting of Silva was later seen as the catalyst setting off a chain of events that culminated in the first major defeat for the union, the final liquidation of the union commenced symbolically with the shooting on November 5 of Vincent St. John. His assailant, Paddy Mullaney, was another veteran of Cripple Creek, but the same ideological chasm that separated the WFM from the IWW on the national level divided the Mullaney group of Socialists committed to a militant industrial union from St. John's revolutionary syndicalist faction, and the two men were reportedly engaged in a struggle for dominance within the local union. Mullaney, who held no formal position in the union, or took a prominent part in union affairs, or even attended recent meetings, was evidently a behind-the-scenes operator. Friction between Mullaney and St. John over alleged illegal voting methods had developed during the last union election, in which Charles McKinnon, Haywood's brother-in-law, had defeated a more conservative candidate for the union presidency. The situation was exacerbated when Mullaney's group defeated St. John's effort to have the Goldfield WFM declare a sympathy strike in support of the striking WFM local at Bishop, a development widely thought to signify that the radicals' influence was waning within the union. Tempers grew so hot that each man threatened the life of the other, and both, in the *Goldfield Chronicle*'s phrase, began "going armed in anticipation of a mortal struggle."[11]

That struggle arrived when St. John and Mullaney stood earnestly conversing in front of the Palm Restaurant late one afternoon. The two men grew more and more excited. Suddenly Mullaney whipped out a revolver and began shooting at St. John, striking him twice in the left wrist and once in the upper right arm. As the bullets whistled past, the crowd scattered, some throwing themselves to the ground and others dashing for cover. One of the flying bullets narrowly missed District Attorney Swallow as he walked past in the street. Other passersby were not so lucky: one received a bullet in the abdomen, and a miner with a large family sustained a wound that necessitated amputating his leg. St. John made a run for Sheriff Ingalls's office in the Palace Saloon but sank to the street, weak from loss of blood, in front of the Hermitage Saloon. While the excited crowd surged around the wounded and deputies hastened forth, Mullaney walked quietly away; the press called him "the coolest man on the street." These injuries were to leave St. John crippled for life. He presently departed from Goldfield to receive medical treatment in Chicago and to become secretary and general organizer of the IWW at the national level. Mullaney was soon out on bail, allegedly furnished by prominent members of the Goldfield Citizens' Alliance. The press later indicated that "for some reason" he was never prosecuted for assault—evidently a shooting spree was not a crime if one of the victims was the Saint. Mullaney remained in Goldfield until May 1908. Then, upon returning to his old haunts in Cripple Creek, he suddenly went so violently insane that four men could scarcely restrain him.[12]

On November 14, 1907, less than two weeks after the shooting, Goldfield Con announced that the miners must accept half their pay in scrip, a decision the company ascribed to bank failures and the smelters' inability to pay cash for gold ore in the wake of the October financial panic. Two days later came another fiat from Goldfield Con: all scrip would be issued through Goldfield's only bank, the John S. Cook, in which Nixon and Wingfield held the controlling interest. The issue of scrip, or "worthless paper," as many miners called it, instantly erased all divisions between conservatives and radicals within the union. After extended deliberations with the belligerent mine operators' association, the miners' union voted overwhelmingly to reject scrip unless its future monetary redemption was guaranteed, and then went on to approve a strike on the following morning, November 27, by unanimous vote.[13]

This was not a decision in which the radical union leaders played any discernible part. St. John, incapacitated by his wounds, was unable to take an active role; Donnelly had departed for Utah during the summer; Roudebush had never returned from his journey to California; Jardine, militant to the end, had headed for Galveston in October and would later surface in Globe. Goldfield was out of bounds for all because the charges against them had been dropped on condition that they leave the city. It had apparently been decided that the evidence was too weak to proceed with the prosecutions, but the conspiracy indictments none-theless served to expel in advance of the crisis the radical leaders who might have rallied union resistance.[14]

Production plummeted to nothing during the strike. The siege began with the mine owners bent on total eradication of the WFM and IWW. The local press, the AFL, and most businessmen supported their efforts. Sympathy for the strikers was muted, for the depression in which the nation floundered in the wake of the October panic had not left Gold-field unaffected. Even here, in the spot local boosters proudly de-scribed as "the greatest gold camp in the world," the wolf lurked at the door.

On December 2 the mine owners issued a declaration of war: all former agreements with WFM Local No. 220 were canceled. No out-rage was registered in the press, though if the WFM had abrogated its agreements, a storm of accusations concerning the illegality of such acts would undoubtedly have followed. The mine owners justified their cancellation by asserting that the union had not taken a two-thirds secret vote. Yet the union had followed the procedure set forth in the April agreement, where a secret vote was not stipulated. When union presi-dent McKinnon sought negotiations to settle the dispute, the mine owners evasively responded that they were unable to get a committee together.[15]

On the same day, a committee of mine owners, including Wingfield, met with Governor Sparks under the guise of selecting a smelter site, the real purpose of their visit a well-guarded secret. Although billed in his last election as "the peacemaker" beneath whose stewardship "the reign of musketry" was not required, Sparks proved entirely willing to play the part assigned to him in the mine owners' scenario. Indeed in the spring they had been compelled to restrain him from rash action at a time when they were not yet ready for a full-scale confrontation with the union. Upon receiving a coded telegram from the mine owners, Sparks wired President Roosevelt on December 5 that "domestic violence and unlawful combinations and conspiracies" existed in Goldfield. Roosevelt's response was swift. On December 6 three companies of the Twenty-second Infantry under the command of Colonel Alfred Reynolds arrived from San Francisco. The Preston-Smith case loomed large in the governor's public justification. Sparks told the Goldfield press that "to prevent a repetition of what happened last spring" he had requested the troops: "Why, you had a man shot down in cold blood here in your town during the times of March and April, and things were run so highhanded that certainly they would have been repeated and enlarged upon at this time if the military were not present."[16]

The governor's move, which was supported by Nevada's congressional delegation, as well as the mine owners, outraged many Goldfield citizens. The miners, caught completely by surprise, appeared too stunned to react. The mine owners then implemented their plans to eradicate the union while under the protection of federal troops. On December 9 they established a card system, illegal under Nevada law, and reduced wages to four dollars a day for all skilled labor. In the letter the mine owners issued to the press in an attempt to win public support, the Preston-Smith case was cited as one of the primary vindications for their policy of coercion: "Citizens and merchants of the camp who have dared to protest against or even disapprove these [union] outrages have been threatened, boycotted, beaten up and even murdered." The shooting of Silva "in cold blood" was the only proof cited for these allegations.[17]

Although the mine owners may have anticipated on the basis of a spy's report that the WFM's silent majority would return to work, few men were willing to sign their "yellow dog" contracts. It made no difference. Wingfield and other operators soon recruited nonunion labor from surrounding states. The mine owners declared that they were not fighting organized labor and stood willing to employ AFL workers and those WFM members who repudiated their leadership. These were the same mine owners who had declared during the spring lockout in Goldfield that they had no quarrel with the WFM and sought only the separation of decent WFM miners from the radical IWW. The union's March warning to scabs, "The object of the Mine Owners' association is to smash the Western Federation of Miners . . . your turn next. . . . An injury to one is an injury to all," now seemed prophetic. Too late the mine owners' strategy of divide and conquer emerged in sharp relief. The nonunion labor importation tactic was so extensive and successful during the depression that WFM Local No. 220 would be driven underground by the spring of 1908.[18]

President Roosevelt, whose relations with labor had been somewhat touchy since the "undesirable citizens" controversy, began to entertain some second thoughts on the dispatch of troops to Goldfield. After Secretary of State Elihu Root telegraphed Governor Sparks that the evidence to date did not support his contention of "domestic violence," Roosevelt sent three federal representatives to Goldfield to investigate.

The Roosevelt Commission, consisting of Lawrence O. Murray, assistant secretary of commerce, Herbert Knox Smith, commissioner of corporations, and Charles P. Neill, commissioner of labor, arrived December 15 and immediately began a full-scale investigation. In their statement to the commission, the mine owners testified that troops were necessary because the union's "tyranny" in dealing with businessmen had become unbearable. The principal proof cited was that a union delegate had called Silva to the door of his restaurant as darkness fell and shot him down "in cold blood." No doubt the commission accepted this as fact, in view of the conviction of Preston and Smith, but on probing mine owner allegations that the union had deported seven hundred of its opponents, the commissioners could find evidence for the deportations of only twenty men over a two-year period, and these had resulted not from current disputes but from old grievances imported from Cripple Creek. The commission's report concluded:

> We find no evidence that any condition then existed not easily controlled by the local authorities. Neither immediately preceding nor since the arrival of troops has there been any particular disorder, but immediately after arrival of troops mine owners announced reduction of wages from $5 to $4, and positively refused employment to all men who do not agree to renounce in writing the local union, although a law of Nevada prohibits such requirement.
>
> So far as can be learned no county officer was consulted by [the] governor previous to calling for troops. All still resent his action and consider it was unnecessary.[19]

After reading the report December 20, President Roosevelt decided to evacuate the troops.

Governor Sparks, however, insisted that the troops had forestalled violence and pressed for their continued presence. By this time the President was visibly annoyed. He sent Sparks an ultimatum: he would give orders for the troops to remain only if the Nevada governor called a special session of the state legislature to authorize a state police force. Sparks immediately capitulated and called the session. In February, after the legislature had enacted a state police bill over the strong protests of union labor throughout the state, the state police began replacing the infantry. All federal troops had departed by March 7.[20]

Besides implementing an open-shop policy and relying on executive and legislative support to crush the union, the mine owners also utilized the courts to obtain their objectives. On March 6, 1908, Goldfield Con won an overwhelming victory in its injunction suit against the miners' union; once again the Preston-Smith case had proved useful, enabling Goldfield Con to charge the union in its complaint with "the murder of innocent persons." In the decision, the union was labeled a conspirator and found guilty of illegal acts of picketing. The court also invalidated the 1903 Nevada statute prohibiting the card system, observing that an employer had a constitutional right to reject business relations with anyone "and it is immaterial what his reasons are, whether good or bad, well or ill founded, or entirely trivial and whimsical." On April 3 the miners' strike was called off by a vote of 90 to 25. The small number of members voting, in a union that had once numbered more than three thousand, only emphasized the devastation of Local No. 220 during the previous four months.[21] It had taken little more than a year, after the shooting of John Silva, to destroy the One Big Union in Goldfield.

In retrospect, and in view of the radicals' formidable reputation and burning rhetoric, the decline and fall of the union in Goldfield was remarkably free of violence. While some fisticuffs, intimidation, and deportations took place, no destruction of property occurred. The only serious casualties during a long period of labor confrontation, beginning with the strike in December 1906 and culminating in the destruction of the union, were Silva and the three men wounded by Mullaney, whose outburst may have been the product of mental instability. None of these shootings occurred in direct confrontations between the union and the mine owners. The Mullaney–St. John affair was an internecine union quarrel between rival factions (at least it appears so on the basis of the available evidence). Even Silva's death had taken place in a twilight zone of interunion quarreling: although the restaurant owner was patron-ized by the AFL and some believed the mine owners had urged him to resist the IWW, Preston saw the union's dispute with Silva as a minor affair with no such ramifications; it is also important to bear in mind that Silva was a former IWW member and that he had indisputably employed IWW help until the boycott was declared the day before the shooting.[22] The old image of IWW and WFM members as men of violence, heirs to the Molly Maguires, dynamiters, murderers, criminal agitators, clings to them to this day, yet careful examination of events in Goldfield has uncovered no evidence of significant acts of violence by the union.

Why had a union with so strong and militant a reputation crumbled so quickly? The national leaders of the WFM, as well as several later historians, believed that the union had been mortally wounded by the prolonged quarrel between radicals and conservatives within its ranks and laid its downfall at the radicals' door, even though the radical leaders had been removed from the scene. *Miners' Magazine* observed: "The Goldfield miners' union until a year ago was looked upon as the most powerful and aggressive local union in the Western Federation of Miners. No. 220 was complete master of the industrial situation in Goldfield until the reptile of disruption crawled like a serpent into the local union."[23]

It seems clear today that even a conservative and cautious WFM purged of the radicals would have been unacceptable to the mine owners. Indeed the positions advocated by the radicals had been consistently rejected by the union's conservative majority from the April agreement through the proposed sympathy strike in October, but even this record of moderate behavior failed to soften the implacable opposition of the mine owners. If anything, the events of 1907 suggest the ineffectiveness of union conservatism. Perhaps the Goldfield miners' union, despite the rhetorical flamboyance of its leaders, was never so strong and militant as its reputation—or as St. John later liked to recall it. Although propitious circumstances during the leasing era had allowed the union to gain strength and win reasonable wages, and although the IWW had thoroughly organized town workers, the union had capitulated in every labor dispute with the mine owners since the 1906 strike.[24] The presence of the radicals, however ineffectual, may have affected the outcome primarily by producing a negative public reaction to the union and a continuing fear among politicians that the radicals might gain influence at any time. This nullified the benefits to the union's public image that might otherwise have accrued from its conservative behavior.

The call for federal troops was a coup that depended on support from Nevada's high officials and the state's voters, presently to register their approval in a referendum on the state police bill. Any attempt to crush the union by a special force of local deputies was an uncertain proposition, in view of the Goldfield law officers' policy of neutrality, and might well have been met with armed resistance by the union on the Colorado model. Federal troops were therefore the most desirable alternative for the mine owners because Nevada had no state police force. The 1907 legislature had taken no action on Governor Sparks's recommendation to organize a state militia, a measure opposed by labor because the force could be used against the unions. The only move to establish state police power came three days after the Silva shooting when the conservative senate hastily passed a state warden bill which afterward expired in the assembly judiciary committee without reaching the floor. The session ended in late March before the Preston-Smith trial

began.[25] During the period that separated these legislative rebuffs from the arrival of federal troops and the passage of a state police bill by the 1908 special session, an alteration in public attitudes had apparently taken place throughout the state. Labor had been isolated from former allies, a point soon to be demonstrated by popular vote when the new state police bill won ten of fourteen counties in a 1908 statewide referendum. While voter turnout on referendum issues is generally lower than the vote on public offices, the turnout on the police bill referendum was more than 20 percent higher than any other referendum in the decade from 1902 to 1912, indicating the strong degree of popular interest generated by the issue.[26] There is consequently some cause to believe that public support for suppressing the unions by state force had been gained through an effective publicity campaign of negative symbolism not dissimilar to the efforts of modern political action committees. The possibility arises that it was the position of the members of the Roosevelt Commission as outsiders who had not been subjected to months of emotional indoctrination by the local press that enabled them to arrive at a conclusion favorable to the WFM on the basis of the evidence alone.

In the highly symbolic world of public relations, so tenuously anchored to events in Goldfield, the Silva shooting had played a central role because it was the only violent incident the mine owners could point to from all those months of bloodless tension to prove their allegations that the revolutionary threats of the Bloody Sunday celebration were turning into realities. Time and again newspaper stories and editorials had hammered home the theme that crushing the union had been necessary because it was an organization dedicated to violence, the principal verification for which was the "hellish work" of Preston and Smith. If Preston had been acquitted on grounds of self-defense after the usual pattern of a frontier homicide, this necessary piece of proof would have been lost; instead his conviction and the opportunity to publicize the union conspiracy story during the trial had served the larger purpose of psychologically separating labor from supporting groups throughout the state (in accordance with the general pattern observed by historian Melvyn Dubofsky) as well as providing the immediate means to expel the radical union leaders from Goldfield. "The Mine Owners exploited the killing of Silva to the world to prove that the union men . . . were a bunch of desperadoes who would stop at nothing to accomplish their ends," observed Fred Clough, a former president of No. 220.[27] In the spring of 1908, the Preston-Smith case still retained a certain residual significance as continuing justification for the mine owners' coercive acts.

In the same month that the last emasculated remnants of the Goldfield union forswore the strike, the Nevada supreme court arrived at a decision on the Preston-Smith appeal. Two briefs had been submitted on their behalf, one by Hilton and the other by Bowler and Hangs. Both elucidated at greater length and in more polished style most of the points that had been made in the motions to win a new trial and to set aside the verdict: the inadmissibility of Muller's testimony; Judge Langan's prejudice, especially as revealed in his instructions; the false and prejudicial statements of Douglas and Malone; the total inapplicability of the verdict to the charge against Smith; Preston's right of self-defense.[28]

All these were compelling points of law, leaving good reason to hope for a favorable outcome. To take one issue alone, the continuing influence at all levels of the widespread belief in the right to self-defense in an armed confrontation is aptly illustrated by the successful appeal in the Sterling P. ("Slim") Grimmett case. This was prosecuted in Goldfield in 1910 and presented several analogous features to Preston's affray, without, of course, the ideological overtones of the Preston-Smith case. Slim Grimmett and Edward Baker were professional gamblers at a hotel saloon in Mina. Baker (like Silva) was known for his violent temper and had made numerous threats against Grimmett, of which the latter was aware. Grimmett, however, did not avoid Baker; he armed himself and confronted Baker (like Preston). When Grimmett demanded payment of a debt, Baker (like Silva) became enraged. He attacked Grimmett with a pool cue but was restrained by saloon patrons. Noticing that Grimmett's hand had slipped into his pocket for his gun, Baker began rummaging through the drawers behind the bar for a gun. Grimmett fired the first shot while Baker's back was turned. Baker returned his fire, missing, and was fatally shot by Grimmett's second bullet. Although Grimmett's plea of self-defense was less compelling than Preston's because his unarmed victim's back was turned when he fired the first shot, he was convicted of manslaughter, not second degree murder, and received a sentence of six years. This verdict was quickly reversed by the Nevada supreme court, composed of the same justices who heard the Preston-Smith appeal. The court declared: a man in Grimmett's predicament "need not flee but has the right to stand his ground and slay his adversary."[29] By rights, Morrie Preston had every reason to hope for such a verdict.

Preston believed that "great popular excitement and prejudice" had prevented him from receiving a fair trial. He later wrote, "Nine out of ten men in Goldfield at that time, except they were union men, would have been exonerated from all blame."[30] Yet the supreme court justices sat in

Columbia Mountain looms in the background of this 1907 Goldfield panorama. The white, two-story building at center left (see arrow) is Miners' Union Hall. The Nevada Restaurant was located on Ramsey Street above and to the left of the hall. (Nevada Historical Society)

At the end of the "Bloody Sunday" parade on January 20, 1907, a large crowd gathered in front of Miners' Union Hall to hear speeches by St. John, Preston, and other union officials on the balcony. (Nevada State Museum)

This typical Arthur Buel cartoon of the IWW personified (*Tonopah Daily Sun,* March 30, 1907) bears scant resemblance to IWW leader Vincent St. John as Buel sketched him for the *Sun* during the Preston-Smith trial (April 29, 1907).

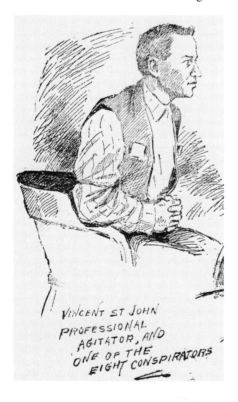

Silva's "assassination" (*Tonopah Daily Sun,* March 11, 1907).

George Wingfield. (Nevada Historical Society)

William Claiborne. (Richard Johnston Collection)

"Diamondfield" Jack Davis. (Nevada Historical Society)

Morrie Preston and Joseph Smith in their Nevada State Prison identification photos. (Nevada State Division of Archives and Records)

Goldfield May 5 1907

Judge Frank Langan

Dear Judge.

there are two of our boys now being tried in your court and I want to tell you now that if you hang them, or send them up for life you will die for it you will be killed like a dog & Poison Beware

for every man of ours you kill or send up to the pen. We will kill one of you for every hair in the mans head of ours you kill Jack Davis Claborne. Bliss Maxfield and lot more that traitor of ... of a ... Claborne we will get him soon Take warning all ... DEATH:

This threatening letter to Judge Langan was reproduced in the *Goldfield Daily Tribune* of May 7, 1907. Comparing it with a photocopy of a 1922 note from Claiborne to the Department of the Interior concerning a pension claim, R. Nelson, Handwriting Examiner, Minneapolis city police department, identified these twelve similarities in his September 30, 1982, report. This was twice the generally accepted number for a "highly probable" identification.

Zora Davis, around 1920. (Courtesy of Esther Lebel)

Lillian Burton shortly before her death in 1922. (Courtesy of Esther Lebel)

A newspaper cartoonist mocks the candidacy of Morrie
Preston, the first person ever nominated by a political
party to run for the U.S. presidency while imprisoned.
(Nevada State Division of Archives and Records)

In this front-page cartoon by Buel, entitled "Nothing Doing" (*Reno Evening Gazette,* December 8, 1908), Justice sternly rejects the union's petition for the pardon of Preston and Smith.

A Buel cartoon from the *Reno Evening Gazette* (January 5, 1910) shows Justice pointing an implacable finger at Silva's grave while Preston and Smith, in convicts' stripes, vainly plead for clemency.

Morrie Preston's photo from the frontispiece of his pamphlet, "The Smith-Preston Case," originally published in 1915.

Carson City, far from the heat of battle. And Preston knew that these were not ignorant jurors whose emotions could be easily molded by a clever prosecutor but experienced jurists dedicated to impartial justice before the law. Justices George Talbot and Frank Norcross were men of some legal distinction and similar background, both sons of Nevada pioneers of Yankee stock. Talbot, then in his fifties, had served as district judge for eleven years before his election to the supreme court in 1902. Norcross, a supreme court justice for three years, was less experienced than Talbot but a veteran compared with their young colleague James Sweeney, who had just taken his place on the court in 1907. A Catholic of Irish descent like Langan, Sweeney was said to have been the youngest state attorney general in the nation's history at the time of his election to the post in 1902 at the age of twenty-four. He was also a man of no small political ambition. This had recently been revealed by his abortive attempt to wrest the Democratic gubernatorial nomination from incumbent Governor Sparks in 1906 and would presently be seen in his unsuccessful bid for the Democratic nomination for U.S. senator in 1910.[31] To these three men, Preston and Smith now turned for justice.

According to his own Socialist beliefs, as Preston had once enunciated them beneath the red banner, no justice was likely to come from a capitalist court. Moreover, Sweeney's attitude to radicals was already abundantly clear. In a 1907 Labor Day address, the judge had castigated "men of anarchistic tendencies" and "extremists or radicals who are not workers but shirkers" as the "real enemies" of labor when he declared: "The strike in the Southern district last winter and the early spring has proved most disastrous to mining industry, crippled thousands of men financially, driven capital from out the state and repelled capital which was fast flowing within our borders . . . and for a time it looked as though the prosperity which Nevada had so long needed was to be paralyzed in its infancy."[32] Preston had publicly and consistently plighted his troth to the Socialist dogma that a capitalist was no less a capitalist when he donned a black robe. Yet the man and the creed never entirely fused, and the man who had lived his life according to the rules was never able to eradicate the expectation of justice. Each time it was thwarted, Preston's indignant reaction betrayed the measure of his hope.

Then the blow fell. The Nevada supreme court refused to hear the case on a technicality, a decision widely interpreted in Goldfield as an attempt to sidestep the issue. Citing precedent, the justices centered their decision on a minor variation in phraseology that modern jurisprudence would reject as "a distinction without a difference." Hangs, his legal knowledge forged in the crucible of Cripple Creek, had bungled the form of the appeal—according to the justices. Instead of declaring "we do appeal," the defense attorneys had announced their *intention* to appeal.[33] It was over. There was no recourse, no redress, no hope. The appeal of Preston and Smith would never be heard. "We remember being told as a child in school that one could not be deprived of his right of appeal," Preston later wrote, "and that therefore this right was the citizen's safeguard against false conviction. Here we see another of our patriotic fancies of childhood shattered and laughed to scorn."[34]

IX

NOTHING DOING

The smoke signals rising from the Nevada supreme court continued to be highly inauspicious for those union men who clung to the diminishing hope that the court might somehow be persuaded to reconsider its decision. In the same month that they sidestepped the Preston-Smith appeal, the justices heard an appeal from Lindley Branson. The newspaperman had sued the IWW—Bowler once more represented the union, with the usual disastrous results—for boycotting the *Goldfield Sun* in 1906 and so injuring his business that he was compelled to sell the paper. His complaint had been dismissed by the trial judge, but the supreme court reversed this decision and remanded the case for trial. Several of the points decided in Branson's appeal enunciated the court's philosophy on union matters. Under the heading "CONSPIRACY—CRIMINAL RESPONSIBILITY—ENTICING SERVANTS," the court declared that a combination of workmen seeking "to injure another's business" constituted an "indictable conspiracy." The court's official definition of a boycott was "a confederation, generally secret, of many persons whose intent is to injure another by preventing any and all persons from doing business with him through fear of incurring the displeasure, persecution and vengeance of the conspirators."[1] In the face of this authoritive pronouncement, the reiterated claim by Preston and Smith that the boycott against Silva's restaurant had been both peaceful and legal swiftly evaporated. With the March injunction decision, the Preston-Smith decision, and the Branson decision, Nevada's highest courts had placed the imprimatur of legal approval on the persecution of the union. Preston called it the victimization of the "undesirables," and he had plenty of time in which to analyze its sources:

> Powerful property interests are invariably opposed to Union men charged with conspiracy when these charges grow out of labor troubles. But, over ninety per cent. of the law, both theoretical and practical, deals with property and property rights. Students of law have property rights in the class room, at meal times and for night cap. Their thought is riveted constantly on the preservation of property rights. They are trained to look upon property rights as the fundamental basis of all life. They are supposed to take cognizance of social rights, of course, but actually their studies of property rights in time absorbs their whole attention. Property becomes the essence of every brain cell; the personification of intelligence, and they come to think only in terms of contract, tenure and herditaments.
>
> Added to this training, Judges have every day court experiences which still further concentrate their attention on "property rights" and distract it from "social rights." Having developed this property psychology, in which property rights is the absolute and only foundation of intelligence, is it any wonder that Judges are prejudiced against Union men whose sole claim to consideration is their social rights? Judges are instinctively and inherently prejudiced in favor of property rights and the Union man charged with conspiracy has no terms in which to couch an appeal to the intelligence of the Court.[2]

The last, fragile legal lifeline which Preston and Smith might grasp, the last appeal to the intelligence of the court, was a petition for rehearing. This was duly filed in June by Hilton and Bowler; their brief argued that the supreme court had erred in dismissing the appeal without ordering it redocketed on a writ of error to be reviewed on its merits. While the prisoners awaited the results, no doubt with scant expectations, their union supporters continued to rely on publicity and agitation by the rank and file. Daniel DeLeon, who had visited Goldfield just before Preston's indictment, and the leaders of the Socialist Labor party attempted to focus national attention on Preston by nominating him as the party's presidential candidate at their New York convention in July 1908. Political candidacy was a publicity device that had earlier been used with great success when the Socialist party of Colorado nominated Big Bill Haywood for governor while he was in the Idaho penitentiary in 1906, and Haywood sailed into his role with all the enthusiasm of an old ham landing on the right platter.

Preston initially seemed pleased. Interviewed in his cell, he told a reporter that he was "a Socialist from the ground up" and felt proud of the honor bestowed on him but in no way surprised. However, the publicity device soon fizzled. Instead of investigating the circumstances of Preston's imprisonment and focusing public attention on his plight as Socialist Labor party leaders had hoped, the Eastern press reacted derisively to his nomination. One newspaper called it a "burlesque on Socialism" and termed him the "freak candidate of all history." The *New York Post* sarcastically wondered if the candidate would be able to pardon himself after his election. Although Preston probably learned little of this, he almost immediately reconsidered and decided to decline the nomination, explaining that he was compelled to compromise because his chances to win freedom might be jeopardized.[3] Let others flaunt their defiance, risk all, and win immortality. Preston preferred restraint by the radicals who would elevate him to martyrdom on the burning pyre of public opinion. In the summer of 1908, as always, he prudently drew back from the invitation to become a celebrity.

Beneath the headline "A CALL FOR ACTION, A COMMAND TO BE TRUE" on the front page of the September 5 issue of the *Industrial Union Bulletin,* the editors endeavored to drum up support for Preston and Smith, claiming, "It was the voice of millions that forced the prison doors open for Moyer, Haywood, and Pettibone." Readers were reminded that they had an even greater duty to support "those who are considered common soldiers only on the battlefield of labor," and were exhorted to mail coupons to the Nevada supreme court and to give contributions. Workingmen throughout America dutifully deluged the court with coupons clipped from the *Bulletin* urging a hearing for the Preston-Smith appeal on its merits because the technical errors made by the attorneys were no fault of the defendants.

It was not the sort of logic that animated the supreme court. On September 30 the petition for rehearing was denied, and the court delivered an opinion so cloudy and confused as to be nearly unintelligible. The only clear impulses to be discerned in the thickets of legalistic language were the justices' distaste for carpetbagging out-of-state attorneys uninitiated in the legal customs of their bailiwick and the relish with which the justices used Hilton and Bowler's own arguments to strangle them. Theirs is "a position entirely new," observed the justices disapprovingly in their comments on the defense brief, and "not a little startling in view of the practice that has prevailed in this state from its organization to the present time."[4]

After this final coup de grace, Hilton assumed full charge of the legal effort. As for "the lawyers(?)," as one WFM leader disparagingly referred to them, Bowler would make but one brief reappearance in the case, and Hangs's services had already been terminated after the appeal disaster. The next round would be an appeal for pardon to the Nevada Board of Pardons, a body whose membership offered little ground for optimism. It included the attorney general, Richard Stoddard, and the three supreme court justices who had just refused to hear the appeal and rejected the petition for rehearing. But its fifth and most essential member was a man of a different stripe. Governor Denver Dickerson, who had recently assumed the office after the death of Governor Sparks in May 1908, was a former union man with strong ties to labor. WFM leaders felt free to address him in their letters as "Dear Sir and Friend." Although under the Nevada constitution the governor had no power to issue pardons alone, his attitude was crucial because no pardon could be granted unless he voted with the majority in favor on the Board.

From Midas, Round Mountain, Rawhide, Manhattan, Virginia City, Fairview, Millers, Helena, Chafey, Silver City, Searchlight, Tenabo, Goldfield, Clifford, Klondyke, Vernon, Mazuma, Rhyolite, Ely, Kimberly, Hilltop, Battle Mountain—a roster of Nevada's mining camps— the petitions poured in to the Board of Pardons respectfully requesting a full and unconditional pardon for Preston and Smith because the supreme court's refusal to hear their appeal left them with no other means of redress. The WFM claimed to have collected three thousand signatures in all, a good showing, though twice that number had been collected in Idaho during the 1901 drive for Paul Corcoran. Those petitions, signed by eight of the twelve jurors who convicted him, had brought Corcoran a full pardon after serving two years of his seventeen-year sentence to hard labor.[5]

WFM president Charles Moyer, the Idaho charges against him now dismissed, spent much of December in Nevada investigating the Preston-Smith case and speaking to union locals, a dedicated effort which multiplied the number of petitions raining on the Board. His announcement that the WFM would petition the Board in January on behalf of the two prisoners was ridiculed in a cartoon entitled "NOTHING DOING" prominently displayed across the front page of the *Reno Evening Gazette:* as a sinister man, with a slouch hat pulled low over his brow and a clamoring crowd behind him, presents the "demand" signed by Haywood, Moyer, St. John, Orchard, Tregonning, the "Gum Shoe Kid," and other names certain to bring fire to the eye of a conservative, the white-robed figure of justice stands guarding the cell door and orders him away; in the lower right hand corner, the little donkey that voiced the comments of cartoonist Arthur V. Buel brays, "Now wouldn't it be a nice move to turn those two assassins loose in Nevada!"[6] The respectful tone of the union petitions notwithstanding, opponents accused the WFM of attempting to strong-arm the Board. That body's reaction to the petition effort remained an open question as Hilton completed his final preparations. In a letter written to Swallow shortly before the January hearing, the attorney indicated that his clients' application for pardon would primarily rest on the inapplicability of the manslaughter verdict and "the ill health of Preston and the petitions of his friends."[7]

Despite his youth and burly physique, Preston's health was showing signs of deterioration under the harsh and primitive conditions of the Nevada state penitentiary. At that time the prison contained slightly more than two hundred convicts, with two men frequently crowded in the small four-and-a-half by seven-foot cells and three in the larger ones. The cells were often cold in winter, when scattered wood fires provided the only source of heat. Some prisoners occupied themselves with the old cowboy craft of braiding rawhide, done for a while under the aegis of a convict who subcontracted the work to others and paid them in smuggled yen-shee (ashes of opium). This rawhide braiding brought welcome relief from the prisoners' customary work, breaking their daily quotas of rock with small hammers in the quarry. One progressive warden expressed doubts that rock breaking was "conducive to the best results" among the "better class of prisoners," but the practice was not soon discontinued.[8]

"He does not often complain, and upon being questioned as to how he feels almost always replies that he feels all right," wrote prison physician Anthony Huffaker, emphasizing his belief that Preston was no malingerer. Yet the rest of Huffaker's letter to the Board of Pardons showed that Preston had been unwell for several months. The lower drum of his left ear had perforated and opened, exposing the infected cavity of his middle ear. An area of abnormal sensitivity had developed behind his ear, and nearly every other night he suffered from severe headaches lasting three to four hours.[9]

In addition to Dr. Huffaker's statement on Preston's health and the several depositions entered in May 1907 in support of the motions for a new trial, Hilton also planned to present a series of glowing testimonials to Preston's character from his friends and neighbors in Los Angeles. The family doctor, William Harrison, remembered him as a "quiet industrious, honest, and hard working boy," whom he had often seen doing household chores and ministering to the sick during his professional calls at Lillian's home; another friend called him "an honest and industrious young man, being the only support of his mother before the trouble in Goldfield, always studious, devoting most of his time to science . . . and in no way anarchistic in his principles"; the Halls, friends of eight years' standing, urged the Board to give him "the most merciful consideration possible." Dr. George Pitzer wrote that Preston used to visit his house three or four times a week: "I became very well acquainted with his habits, disposition motives and ambitions. I regarded him as a modal [model] character for industry, truthfulness, honesty and charity. . . . I should certainly recommend the greatest leniency possible for he is not a bad man, nor a dangerous man, and his present unfortunate confinement is only the result of being misguided by an association which he thought to be representing a just cause. He simply made a mistake. He is a good man."[10]

Since even the worst of men may have a few friends who find some virtue in him, far greater persuasive power rested in the extraordinary pleas for clemency collected by Zora from several of the jurors. According to Preston: "Some of the jurors were located in almost inaccessible parts of Esmeralda County which necessitated travel by wagon through desert stretches and a-foot over rough mountain trails. When seen, several jurors demanded proof that Preston had never been in Colorado, and that he was not a 'dynamiter,' thus showing that their verdict had not been founded upon the evidence but upon the lies they had heard."[11] After obtaining Preston's school and employment records, Zora had revisited the jurors and secured the statements she sought.

Zora had by now arrived at the certainty that she was destined for an interesting future, perhaps as an artist, a seeress, a masseuse, a dancer, or an actress, but definitely not as a farmer's wife, birthing a batch of large, fair-haired children and tending Gottlieb's rows of beans. Her off-and-on marriage was over. During this period she was bursting through the social conventions of her time like a fledgling cracking out of the shell, setting out to live the life she wanted. In her own way she would do a great deal for those she loved, but no longer should anyone expect her to be a conventional wife, mother, or sister.

In the autumn of 1908 that was probably fortunate for Preston. Few conventional women would have dared what Zora set out to do. Her son Louis later remembered how she had sold all her possessions to finance her fight for Preston.[12] It took a woman with considerable mettle to plead for Preston before politicians conditioned to see him as a convicted assassin from an anarchist union. It took a woman of Zora's boldness to search out the former jurors with six-year-old Louis in tow, undeterred by the long miles of desert before her, the rough company in isolated ranches and mining camps, and her own vulnerability to the harassment and savagery of Preston's sworn enemies. It took a woman of rare persuasive powers to change the minds of men who but for Jarvis might well have sent Preston to the gallows. Against the varied backdrops of low, white ranch houses, weathered barns, and mining towns, her small, dark-haired, well-dressed figure, perhaps with a white handkerchief clasped in her beautiful hands, must have made a sight so touching as to soften the hardened heart.

It obviously softened the heart of W. E. Steineck, former juror, erstwhile drinking companion of the district attorney, mining man from the Salmon River country, and one of the founders of Boise's *Capitol News*. Little more than a year after the trial, the man who had virulently opposed Preston during jury deliberations became an ally and confidant willing to aid Zora's "unfortunate brother" in his bid for freedom and often to advise her from a distance as he pursued the life of an itinerant mining engineer in Nevada, San Francisco, and the Rockies. Perhaps, far from the heated atmosphere of Goldfield's labor war, Steineck had experienced second thoughts and the events of the trial had taken a different perspective; perhaps his own large role in Preston's conviction had left him with a guilty conscience. But assuredly his admiration for Zora, whose visit he awaited with "pleasant anticipation" in Carson City, did much to move him from doubt to open advocacy of her "heroic effort."

The conspiratorial tone of his letters to her revealed the pitfalls besetting an effort that sometimes turned into an undercover operation because Preston's opponents remained as active as ever. It was Steineck who told Zora how to reach the other jurors, exacting a promise to keep the information confidential, Steineck who warned her to waste no time on juror Ross Woodward because he was hopelessly prejudiced, and Steineck himself who offered to help with juror James Wichman, though his efforts did not succeed. "Once we get them on paper," he assured Zora, "their appeal could not be very well ignored."[13] Union labor in Goldfield was finished, but Steineck came to believe that the victors were not finished with Preston, and that spies had been placed near him, even in the penitentiary. Much of this appears in one of his letters to Zora: "I also wanted to especially caution you, to keep your own counsel, not confide in every one and to be very careful that nothing of your proposed plans will get to the people that are fighting against your present movement. I have some means of knowing that some of those whom you think confidential in your conversations with your brother are in an official capacity that does not permit them from keeping everything to themselfs. Lay your plans carefully and act only on the advice of *your attorney. . . .*"[14]

Aided by Steineck, Zora succeeded better than anyone could have anticipated. Jurors Bettles and Atcheson and the two Morgans petitioned the Board for a full pardon for Preston, while Steineck wired the same plea from Colorado, citing "facts presented and knowledge gained since trial." Jarvis made a statement that provided a vivid and graphic glimpse of the jury in action. "In the first place I had never been on a jury," Jarvis related, and so he had not objected when other jurors wanted to ballot separately on Smith after compromising on Preston. "Then they goes to work and cinches Smith simply through my ignorance." Jarvis had learned of the threatening letter to Judge Langan several days before the trial was over (surely grounds for a mistrial, as Bowler and Hangs had argued before the judge shortly after the verdict). At an earlier stage, Bettles had attempted to sound out other jurors to determine where they stood, violating the prohibition against discussing the case in advance of jury deliberations. Jarvis was satisfied that Preston had been wrongfully convicted because the "jobbers," Bettles and Steineck, had simply decreed that the jury would consider only the evidence of the prosecution. "I tried to argue the case with them," said Jarvis, "but got so rattled I could not argue." Steineck had told him that when "your brother" saw Silva take down the gun he could have avoided the shooting by running away. Jarvis's efforts to argue about Smith were equally unavailing. When he objected that Smith had not been present at the scene of the crime, Steineck told him that Smith was more guilty than Preston. Said Jarvis: "If it had not been for them two jurymen the thing would have been a whole lot different, or even if I had knowed as much as I know now, or half as much, it would have been different. It could not have been otherwise. But, I was never on a jury. We were jobbed from start to finish. And, another thing, we were on that jury for three or four weeks, locked up in the jury, and a man aint himself as he would be if he wasn't worn completely out. I know he was wrongfully imprisoned. I am satisfied of it, not according to the evidence, for all the evidence was thrown out."[15]

Although Hilton must have presented these petitions, he totally ignored them in his deferential address to "Your Honors of the Supreme Bench," "His Excellency, the Governor," and "General" Stoddard when the Board of Pardons convened in January 1909. Nor did he make more than brief reference to Preston's illness, observing that a "disease, in the ear, in the most intimate connection with the brain, is a constant menace," likely to result in death or insanity. Instead he laid out a full-scale appeal. The major thrust of his argument was that Judge Langan had committed prejudicial errors in slanting his instructions toward the prosecution and in allowing the Muller testimony, as well as at numerous other junctures throughout the trial; he should rather have ordered the prosecutors to "desist from such trifling with the life and liberty of the defendants." Hilton also labored long to prove that Inman's persistent leading questions had dictated the substance of Silva's dying declaration. This was probably true enough, but the case that Bowler had called a "comedy of errors" surely contained matters of greater significance.[16] Hilton's argument had the ring of a speech the busy attorney had prepared for the appeal the previous spring and felt disinclined to much revise in the light of the new affidavits. Even if he thought rumors of WFM coercion might have diluted the impact of the jurors' reversal, had he so misjudged the Board that he failed to gauge the weight they would consistently accord to the statements of those who had taken part in the trial? After a long and perhaps heated session, the Nevada Board of Pardons rejected the Preston and Smith application.

The next step was to secure another hearing as quickly as possible. In May, Hilton sent the Board a letter of Machiavellian sinuosity requesting permission to apply for pardon at the July session, despite the legislative requirement for the lapse of a year between hearings. Thanking the Board for their "very many courtesies," Hilton expressed his agreement with them on matters of expediency, "and we use the word expediency in its higher and broader sense, as meaning, safe-guarding of public as well as private interests, until such time as further investigation and maturer consideration, might lead to a different conclusion." How right the Board had been to "hold matters in status quo until public opinion can steady itself, and reflect." While conceding that Smith's imprisonment was illegal, Hilton declared it justified as a "salutary measure" until community opinion was ready to approve the union man's release. He assured the Board that the many workingmen in Nevada mining camps who urged him to take action "are very moderate and very earnest in their presentations." By this attempt to flatter the Board by condoning the denial of justice to his clients, Hilton hoped to provide justification for granting a favorable hearing after the issues he had raised had just been rejected in January, but he failed entirely in his purpose, and his request was denied.[17]

Another summer passed, as hammers rang in the prison rock quarry beneath the hot sun, another autumn also, with aspen turning gold in the canyons of the high Sierra that rimmed the valley west of the penitentiary, another winter came, blanketing the mountains in a whiteness marbleized by dark blue streaks and patches of shadow and pine, before Preston and Smith received a second hearing before the Board in January

1910. By then a sensational development had entirely altered the complexion of their case. Bliss had died a bloody death in a burst of gunfire, and his cover had wholly unraveled. Now the world knew what Mary McKune had clearly implied at the trial: Bliss was not simply the Utah mine owner he claimed to be but also a marauding member of the Wild Bunch who was known as "Gunplay Maxwell."

Indeed, despite the general silence surrounding Bliss's activities, the unraveling had begun even earlier when Bliss and his partner William Walters were arrested in June 1908 for robbing the Wells Fargo strongbox in the Rawhide stage of over a thousand dollars in diamonds— surely an event deserving more than passing mention in the newspapers. Jailed in Goldfield, Bliss wrote to one of his wives that he would be unable to post bail. But the next day he reported that "the unexpected" had happened: he was out on bail and would presently join her in San Francisco. He was as good as his word, for once, and was sometimes seen in the Bay area that autumn sporting a dazzling array of diamonds on his vest. Observed with Bliss soon after the stage robbery, jailed on charges of auto theft, and swift as his notorious companion to depart from Nevada without standing trial, was that young scion of the Southern aristocracy and leading legal light, William Claiborne. Preston found these events not really so unexpected:

> Claiborne declared in the presence of other jail inmates: "if they don't get me out of here pretty soon I'll tell what I know about sending up Preston and Smith." Needless to state, he was bailed out the next day.
> In the "Goldfield Daily Tribune" mention is made of the fact that Maxwell jumped his bond, but the "Tribune" fails to state that Maxwell was permitted to take his departure and that no attempt was made to ascertain his whereabouts or bring him back, simply because Maxwell held a club over the Mine Owners' Association and Citizens' Alliance, which made it dangerous for these combinations to interfere with his personal liberty.[18]

This time, as Hilton and his partner arrived from Colorado amid renewed flurries of activity among the mine owners' attorneys and press allegations that the WFM was trying to bully Board members, he had some very heavy ammunition in hand. The major thrust of Hilton's argument before the Board was an attack on the unscrupulous tactics of the mine owners and the character and credibility of the three witnesses on whom the prosecution's theory of conspiracy depended—Davis, Claiborne, and Bliss. His study of the record, said Hilton, had convinced him that the atmosphere of "avarice, restlessness, turmoil, and distress" in Goldfield during the labor disturbances had prevented Preston and Smith from receiving the impartial trial to which they were constitutionally entitled. At the moment when "two vituperative attorneys" were hired by the mining corporations and "forced upon the prosecution," the trial became a struggle between corporation interests and organized labor. "It frequently happens in every community, that some man has been successful in business or his political aspirations and he soon comes to regard every incident in his community as bearing either favorable to himself or as an affront to his interests," said Hilton, and there can be little doubt to whom he referred. "He grows to feel that the community exists and has its very being as a setting for his personal interests. . . . Now mark you well, that this was the dominating element of the trial." In effect such a man was saying, "Here's money; get into the ring; convict these men; I'm running this community." The aim of such a man was "not to punish crime but to punish the effrontery of an organization."

At this point, Hilton directed his beam upon Claiborne, Davis, and Bliss. He attacked Claiborne as a "predatory camp follower" who had fled a charge of forging an insurance policy in Arkansas, but he clearly had meager clues to Claiborne's true identity. His heaviest fire was directed at Claiborne's "miserable story." Why had Claiborne failed to warn Silva of his impending assassination, demanded Hilton? Why was he unable to identify the conspirators in court?

Hilton presently turned to Bliss, whom he identified as a member of Butch Cassidy's Wild Bunch at Robber's Roost. The attorney briefly sketched the outlaw's recent history: "Implicated in the Schurz stage robbery; arrested; brought to Goldfield and jumped his bond . . . in trouble all through Nevada, Wyoming, Colorado and parts of Utah; principal witness against Preston and Smith; visited the Sheriff's office with his customary bravado to demonstrate that he stood in with the authorities." Hilton then related his version of Bliss's death in Price on August 23, 1909. In fact, new evidence uncovered by Richard Johnston indicates that Bliss was not merely planning a bank robbery in Green River, as Hilton believed, but rather a series of robberies, some from the payrolls of Utah coal companies. Anticipating his plans, the coal companies placed Deputy Sheriff Edward Black Johnson under orders to kill Bliss as soon as opportunity arrived. A quarrel between Bliss and railroad detective Thomas Burge provided Johnson with the pretext he needed to shoot Bliss down in the street. As he lay dying, Bliss recognized Johnson. They had first met in Winter Quarters, Utah, in 1904 when Bliss bought a meal and a bed for the night at the Johnson home while working as a guard for the coal companies during a strike. They next encountered each other in the autumn of 1908 at Goldfield on the occasion of Bliss's testimony against several fellow prisoners who had attempted a jailbreak, and no one had much cared to listen when Johnson identified him to the judge as the notorious outlaw Gunplay Maxwell. They had to listen now. Hilton sonorously intoned, "His career was closed, but the evil he had done lives after him."

Davis's turn came next. Unlike Bliss, with his two wives and three identities, and the chameleon Claiborne, Davis remained the same tough gunslinger as always, but Hilton argued that the full implications of this had been insufficiently appreciated. After reviewing Davis's Idaho murder trial, the attorney demanded, "Where in all the history of ribald depravity can you match the low cunning, the absolute villainy of this man, who shot men to death in the back, and in his blasphemous insolence boasted that Jesus Christ could not track him?" Would the members of the Board accept the testimony of such men against their near and dear ones? "It was manufactured for a price and to feed the colossal egotism and vanity that is always part of such criminals. Is it not in keeping with this thought and this vile creature that for all his stay in Goldfield he proudly displayed the rope with which he was to have been hung in Idaho?" Hilton suggested that the appearance of these three witnesses on behalf of the prosecution had intimidated the jurors: "Bliss and Claiborne and Davis might at any future time, in the solitude of the desert, meet these men and like the cowardly jackals and hyenas of the plains that they are, taking acquittal as a personal affront to their testimony, just as certainly and with as much safety slay the jurors as the lonely sheepherders were slain in Idaho. . . . The fear of the hidden assassin made itself felt all through that trial and was voiced unmistakably in the verdict. The jurors knew the utter helplessness of the law to protect them. . . ."[19]

Hilton went on to praise the conduct of his clients in prison, where they had abstained from "joining themselves to the baser elements" and had demonstrated that they deserved parole. He concluded with a Darrowesque appeal to the impartiality of the Board in the name of "that great class who do the world's work" yet are denied the right to claim anything beyond the bare necessities.

When Justice Sweeney went in for politicking, he was known as "the man with the smile that won't wear off." At the pardon hearing, however, no smile stretched his plump cheeks, and the expression in his pale eyes was anything but affable. "Does not Preston's testimony alone convict him of murder?" demanded the justice. Hilton answered that Preston's testimony had been very unfortunate for his cause but the evidence of others showed that Silva had threatened his life.

The justice's attitude toward Smith and his radical views was even more antagonistic. Sweeney recalled hearing Smith speak at Union Hall in Goldfield. He had been noisy and turbulent, and Sweeney had recognized him for an anarchist. Sweeney had warned the IWW organizer that the people would take him out and hang him to a lamppost if he wasn't careful. Hilton's entire argument on Bliss, Claiborne, and Davis was then swept from the table in a single stroke when Justice Sweeney refused to consider any evidence outside the record. The young and politically ambitious Sweeney, in the words of one reporter, was "known as an avowed antagonist to the pardon of either Smith or Preston and has done more than any other member of the Board to hold the men behind bars." The Board went into an executive session lasting more than three hours, which again suggested heated disagreement among its members. Darkness had fallen by the time their decision was announced that evening: once more pardon was denied. The Board's calendar reveals that all five members had voted against pardoning Preston, but Governor Dickerson and Chief Justice Norcross had voted in Smith's favor. The front page of the *Reno Evening Gazette* featured a huge cartoon in which Preston and Smith, in convicts' stripes, pluck at the arm of the white-robed figure of justice as she points implacably to Silva's tombstone. The caption read, "THEY SHOWED NO MERCY—SHOW THEM NONE."[20]

As spring drew nearer, two items of relevance to the case appeared in *Daily Forum*, the short-lived Socialist newspaper published by attorney Ashley Grant Miller in Sparks. Although Miller had never met Preston or Smith, he was highly indignant at the "travesty on justice" they had suffered. On January 20 he published a front-page story charging that Douglas had assaulted and beaten two reluctant witnesses for the prosecution until they agreed to give the testimony he required (an interesting parallel to the Muller affair, of which Douglas had made so much). Miller believed that "but for certain influences" Preston and Smith would have been pardoned long ago. "The bitterness engendered by the Goldfield strike evidently persists in the minds of some editors of papers owned by the mine owners but that is no reason why these men should be unjustly imprisoned."[21]

Three weeks later Miller featured another story of considerable interest to those following developments in the Preston-Smith case. Claiborne was in the news once more, not in his capacity as an attorney educated at the finest colleges, or at home on the family plantation as befitted a Southern aristocrat, but as a detective entrapping an adulterous wife in a messy Los Angeles divorce suit. Since the time of the trial it had been common belief in Goldfield that Claiborne was in fact a detective (many said spy) working for the mine owners. What could be more natural than continuing to pursue his vocation in Los Angeles? But if final proof existed, it remained—and still remains—locked in the safe of Goldfield Con.[22]

These, and other stray bits of information on the witnesses for the prosecution, kept washing up on the beach. Even Dyer, the only man who claimed to have seen Preston and Smith together in the street before the shooting, was emerging as a rather different person from what had been supposed when he took the witness's chair at the trial. "I just found out that I could get affidavits in Tuolumne County, that he was never anything but a pimp and was finally ordered out of Summersville by the officers there and then came to Goldfield," Fred Clough, a former president of No. 220 and a member of the WFM national executive board, wrote to Governor Dickerson.[23] Hilton, however, was preparing to use a different but no less sensational tack in his next application to the Board in July 1910. His January oration was by now regarded as such a "classic" that the editor of the Carson City News, despite his ultra-conservative political views, had been offering it for sale in five-cent pamphlets for months. But, while it may have augmented Hilton's reputation and swelled the coffers of the Carson City News, it had done nothing to unlock the penitentiary doors for Preston and Smith. Hilton knew that if the powerful offensive he had mounted against the credibility of the unholy trio had failed to sway the Board in January, additional information impeaching the prosecution witnesses was unlikely to have much effect. He would continue to remind the Board of the witnesses' "utter unreliability and career as self-confessed criminals," but he thought it wiser to turn to something new, and he began to center his effort on Smith. With Sweeney and Stoddard dissenting (any assurances Stoddard had given Haywood cannot have been worth much), the Board voted to hear Smith's application for pardon or parole on new grounds at the July session.

In an effort to counteract the personal attack on Smith by Justice Sweeney at the January session, testimonials were belatedly collected to Smith's quiet, peaceful, thrifty, industrious, and law-abiding character.

R. E. Crosky, who knew him in Colorado in the 1890s, recalled Smith's "quiet and law abiding disposition" and his opposition to labor agitation. The O'Malleys, neighbors of Smith's in Goldfield, remembered him as "devoted to his wife and always at home outside of working hours," "a very neighborly man" who gave away any food he could spare during the hard times. Although Smith attended union meetings, "he was not in any way a violent man," nor was he given "to swearing nor to loud talk nor to rough conduct."[24]

All this was fairly standard, though heartfelt. Hilton's characteristically sensational touch appeared in his own deposition. Here the attorney charged that two weeks after the verdict Swallow had told him that Nixon had offered to assist in the conviction of Preston and Smith because they were WFM members "and as such obnoxious to him." Swallow had advised Nixon to engage Malone, which was done for the price of $5,000 "solely for the purpose of conviction and paid by the said Nixon out of his own moneys." Hilton went on to say that Malone had admitted to him shortly after the trial that he himself believed the "intemperate, passionate and prejudicial statements" the prosecutors had made in "the frenzy of the moment" were grounds for error. Malone had also allowed that he was "somewhat troubled because at that time he had failed to get his money, as said Nixon deemed said fee exorbitant," although he later told Hilton he had received payment in full.[25]

Some of the politically astute saw a more nefarious purpose in Hilton's maneuverings than a desire to jolt the Board into action with fresh evidence, and concluded that his concentration on Nixon to the exclusion of Wingfield or any other major figure behind the prosecution was far from accidental. Sweeney was then in the midst of his campaign for the Democratic senatorial nomination; if he won, Nixon would be his Republican opponent for the senatorial preference vote in the autumn. (Although direct election of U.S. senators was still three years in the future, the Nevada candidates would pledge to abide by the popular vote; the losing candidate would withdraw after the election, and the legislature would formally elect the winner of the popular vote as the next senator.) With the primary election campaign already in progress, Hilton may thus have calculated that he could neutralize the foremost enemy of Preston and Smith on the Board by exploiting his natural antagonism to Nixon and providing him with political ammunition to use against his rich and powerful rival. Charges first raised in late May 1907, during Hilton's court appearances for St. John, and not heard since, were suddenly resurrected. Once more the shrewd writer of the

expediency letter sidled to the fore, while the ringing voice of conscience that had resounded in January remained packed in Hilton's
suitcase. What effect these dizzying alterations in persona exerted on the
Board can well be imagined.

In the wake of the Independence Day celebrations, Smith's plea was
denied. Justice Sweeney had declined the bait, and though hot words
reportedly passed in the governor's private office, the Board was no
more moved by this fresh revelation than by those that had preceded it.
The character testimonials had only served to provoke a new and uglier
outburst of temper from Sweeney. He declared that he considered Smith
the worst of the two and went on to say that both men should have been
hanged. Now they were where they belonged, and if Sweeney had his
way, they would stay there. Governor Dickerson thought otherwise and
was roundly condemned by his editorial critics for his vote in favor of
letting Smith loose to "avenge his hatred." Both Swallow and Nixon
denied Hilton's charges, the former district attorney making clear that he
opposed pardon for the two union men and Nixon recalling the "splendid
effect" of the case on conditions in Goldfield.[26] The one positive,
though hardly splendid, effect for Preston and Smith from the hornet's
nest Hilton set buzzing was the airing that the flamboyant Colorado
attorney's charges received in the press, where some would read them
and draw their own conclusions on the role the mine owners had played
in the case.

A year would pass and a great deal would change before their
applications were again heard in the summer of 1911. Less than two
weeks after Smith's pardon was denied, and a little more than a month
before the primary election, a report was made public by the Nye County
grand jury on the 1907 crash of the Nye and Ormsby County Bank,
which had blotted out the life savings of many Nevada depositors.
Among the bank directors scathingly condemned by the jurors was
Justice Sweeney, who "at all times was allowed to borrow large sums of
money" from the bank and received a substantial fee for his legal
services in the bargain. The report noted, "He was one of the most active
directors . . . and undoubtedly knew of the insolvent condition of the
bank at all times." After particular reference to Sweeney and one of the
other sixteen directors, the grand jury report concluded, "No excuse can
in our opinion be offered by these men for their activity in the later days
of the life of the bank and their apparent utter disregard for the interest of
the depositors."[27] This disclosure may have played some part in
Sweeney's crushing defeat in the Democratic senatorial primary that
September, a defeat to which Goldfield, where there were more Demo-

cratic voters than in any other Nevada city, made a substantial contribution. "The man with the smile that won't wear off" was much less heard from after these chastening events. He who had burst into politics as a boy wonder eight years earlier, who had enlivened the otherwise lethargic election of 1906 with his burgeoning ambitions, who had so often pushed forward to voice his conservative opinions, had now virtually retired from public life at the age of thirty-two. He would never again run for state office in Nevada.

Although all three supreme court justices remained in office, Norcross having won reelection, the membership of the Board of Pardons altered after the 1910 election. Attorney General Stoddard, a participant in the appeal debacle under the aegis of Malone and Douglas and an unyielding opponent on the Board, had been replaced by young Cleve Baker of Tonopah, former Nye County district attorney. Baker, despite his Democratic affiliations, was linked to the Southern Pacific machine that dominated the Nevada Republican party; but, in keeping with the state Democratic party's drive to win the allegiance of organized labor, he apparently gave the WFM to understand that his attitude toward Preston and Smith was favorable. While Baker was too weak a figure to propel the Board in a new direction, the enfeebled Sweeney might find himself in an isolated and ultimately untenable position without Stoddard during the Board's 1911 sessions.

If the departure of Stoddard was a hopeful development for the two prisoners, the defeat of Governor Dickerson was not. There were several reasons for Dickerson's loss, predominant among which were the vast expenditures by Senator Nixon and the Southern Pacific machine for the election of docile Republican candidates and the disaffection of the Democratic faction which still identified with the late Governor Sparks. But other politicians would have noted that his popularity with organized labor had failed to bring him political victory. Dickerson's replacement, the first Republican governor Nevadans had elected in two decades, was Tasker L. Oddie, a popular and affable New Jersey lawyer who had made and lost a fortune in the Tonopah boom. To his detractors, the bald-headed, forty-year-old governor with the long, prim upper lip was known as "Easy" Oddie, a weak politician who, in the words of his campaign manager, "always did what he was told." Those likely to do the telling were the bosses of the Southern Pacific machine, who had worked assiduously for Oddie's election, and Nixon and Wingfield, to whom his ties were even closer.[28] But when Oddie took office in January 1911, his attitude toward Preston and Smith remained a cipher, and it is not known whether his mentors had as yet communicated their preferences to him.

Meanwhile public sentiment in favor of clemency for Preston and Smith was beginning to build. Local mining unions throughout the state had never ceased to agitate on behalf of the two prisoners, and now, four years after their conviction, the campaign was gathering new momentum. Petitions to the Board from union men continued to arrive. So did letters to the new governor. One correspondent from Battle Mountain wrote that Preston had no criminal intent and during his years in prison had already "amply atoned for any indiscretion." Others reminded the governor that the severe punishment inflicted on the two men deviated very far from the norm in Nevada jurisprudence; a letter attached to a petition from the Manhattan (Nevada) Socialist party pointedly noted, "Had the killing been the other way there would have been no conviction." To all these letters and petitions, Oddie noncommittally replied that he would give the cases "careful consideration and study."[29]

Some respected local jurists were also beginning to recognize the case as a miscarriage of justice. Peter J. Somers, a former congressman from Milwaukee and a district judge in Goldfield since 1909, wrote the Board urging a "thorough investigation" of the Preston-Smith application because the pair had been convicted in the midst of "great agitation" when a fair trial would have been difficult to secure. Samuel Belford, a highly regarded Colorado attorney who had moved to Nevada in 1908 and quickly climbed to an influential position in the state Democratic party, and Charles H. Tanner, the WFM organizer who was orchestrating the union effort on the prisoners' behalf, informed the governor that they had arranged a job for Preston in the hope that even if the Board "could not see your way clear to grant Preston a complete pardon . . . perhaps you might look with more favor upon a parole, providing it could be shown that when granted Preston would have a situation to go to."[30]

Even more encouraging than these individual straws in the wind were the actions taken by the Nevada legislature during the 1911 session. With only two dissenting votes, the assembly had passed a resolution noting that Preston and Smith had lost their "great and substantial" right to appeal through an error which was in no way their fault and respectfully requesting the Board to investigate the trial record, to permit the petitioners to be "fully heard," and to determine whether theirs was a case where "clemency should be exercised." The legislature had also appointed a joint committee of senators and assemblymen to review the Smith case. In their report to the Board, the committee recommended parole for Smith, stressing their conclusion that the verdict against him had been the result of inflamed public opinion. Smith's parole had for some time been viewed as probable in the unsympathetic eyes of the *Reno Evening Gazette*. The *Carson City News,* as well as other papers of more liberal bent, had been strongly advocating it for nearly a year.[31]

Perhaps believing new pyrotechnics unnecessary in view of this unmistakable shift in the tide, Hilton decided to rely on the by now standard but still powerful arguments on his clients' behalf in this his fourth appearance before the Board. He sounded optimistic when he wrote Preston in June, "I am very much grateful to learn of the good record you are making, because that is of the greatest help in presenting your cases to the Board." Preston did not share his optimism. "Am well, working hard," he wrote grimly to his foster mother in Los Angeles. "Don't enthuse over prospects. Don't come."[32]

His intuition was right, though he had no knowledge of the machinations occurring behind the scenes. In August Oddie received an extraordinary letter urging parole for Preston from Diamondfield Jack Davis in Kansas City, where he was attempting to finance a "good hog ranch" for a friend:

> Now I saw where Smith and Preston were up before you for a pardon. Of the two men I would parole Preston. Smith ought to had life. Preston was a boy and they made him think he was in a great cause. Smith cold bloddledly and deliberately planned the murder of that poor fellow Sylvia. They filled Preston with whiskey and all other stuff . . . Smith and Preston beat up old man McAllister a few nights before that and the Thursday night before that they beat up young Muller. Smith, Preston and other among them Jerry Sexton, Ben Donnelly those two James boys and others. If you people parole anyone, parole Preston he may have had a lesson and he has nerve but it was wrong directed. I heard he threatened to kill m[e] if he got out but I am still able to take care of myself and I doubt it of cours I know they said a lot against me in ther papers and Hitton used all kinds of abuse, but I overlook that. Smith should had been hung or had life. . . .[33]

This strange letter raises a number of possibilities. Perhaps Davis, though activated by personal animosity against Smith and too publicly committed to the prosecution to entirely reverse himself, had grown uneasy over the prospect of the innocent Preston's prolonged imprisonment. It is also possible that Davis really gave credence to the story of a conspiracy masterminded by Smith. If, as Preston thought, the whispering campaign had implanted in the minds of many the belief that the most damaging evidence had not been presented at the trial, Davis may have been unusually susceptible. Although not close enough to Wingfield to have known the entire strategy for conviction, he took pride in his position as an insider and would thus have been especially prone to credit the bogus bits of information divulged to him as confidences that appeared to confirm his superior status.

In fact, the issue was probably no longer in doubt by the time Davis's letter arrived. On July 2 George Wingfield wrote noncommittally to Oddie, "The Western Federation is making a very strong effort to get these men released, but I do not think that they are getting much support outside of their own ranks."[34] Days later Wingfield's wishes were conveyed in very plain terms to the governor through a third party, Oddie's brother-in-law and close friend, mining engineer Frederick J. Siebert: "I have been talking with G. W. about the Preston and Smith case which we understand is coming up shortly before the Board of Pardons. We both agree that it would be best to let Smith go on parole, as he has been sufficiently punished and was only a poor boob in the thing in the start. So far as Preston is concerned, however, we sincerely hope that he will stay there until he rots."[35]

Subsequent events conformed to this scenario. The Board postponed a decision until November, announcing that Oddie and Baker needed more time to study the case. Smith was willing to accept parole in place of the unconditional pardon for which he had originally applied, and his parole could conveniently be ascribed to the legal monstrosity of the inapplicable verdict without raising the issue of the perjured witnesses and the men behind them which was inextricably linked to Preston. Because his sentence was the shorter, parole could be more than amply justified by the time served relative to his sentence. The public demand for justice had now centered on him and might be expected to defuse if he were paroled. Should further legal justification be needed, attorney Belford provided it during the interim in a lengthy and closely argued letter to Justice Norcross urging "favorable action" on Smith's application because the verdict of manslaughter against a man absent from the crime was "the veriest travesty upon justice" and ought to have been set aside by Judge Langan. Whether Belford's opinion had been solicited by the Board or volunteered at the behest of the WFM is not known. The Board's penchant for buttressing controversial decisions with the pronouncements of leading local attorneys, and the likelihood that some discussion preceded the sending of the case file to Belford, suggest that it may have been requested, and that the Board was moving toward a decision on Smith in compliance with Governor Oddie's wishes.[36]

Smith's surprisingly stylish slanted signature appeared on his application to the Board:

While I am a working man I have always conducted myself as a citizen should and I have never been in trouble of any kind and have never been the cause of any trouble. During my imprisonment, my wife and child are dependent wholly on charity. . . . My conduct at the prison will show that I possess the character that I claim. Honesty, as my business record shows, peaceable as my friends know me to be, and a willingness and a desire to do right.[37]

On November 14, 1911, Smith received his parole with only the implacable Sweeney voting against him, while Preston's application was once again unanimously denied. A week later Siebert assured Oddie that Wingfield's permission had not been rescinded: "George asked me to tell you that he had no particular kick about the pardoning of Smith but that the pardon was decidedly unpopular in Goldfield."[38]

When Smith arrived in Reno on his way to rejoin his family on the coast, he warmly praised state prison warden Ray Baker, thanked all who had worked on his behalf, and added, "I am not of a vindictive spirit and hold no ill will against those who conspired against me." He spoke of entering "some business where I can make a living" but made no mention of the union.[39] The affable, conciliatory figure waiting on the station platform bore no visible relation to the radical union enforcer or the man reporters had once watched receive the jury's verdict with cold, hard defiance. Freedom was all that mattered, and he embraced it gratefully. In December, and again in January 1913, he wrote to *Miners' Magazine* from San Francisco urging union members to raise money for Preston's family by holding a benefit dance or raffling off an item of Preston's handiwork: "If it is only a two bit piece it will help. . . . I believe that everything is being done by the W. F. of M. to get justice and freedom for him; but in the meantime his family has got to eat."[40] (It may be noted that the friendship of Preston and Smith had better withstood the strains of imprisonment than that of Haywood and Moyer.)

Smith can be traced in the San Francisco city directories until 1914–15, when he is listed as a waiter living with his family on Baker Street. After that he sinks back into the masses that had long been the stuff of his ideology. He sent no reports to the Nevada parole officer. No further traces of him appear in the public records or the press. He disappears with the suddenness of a stone dropped in a dark pool.

X

A MORAL VICTORY

"I have tried to show my intentions by my conduct," wrote Preston. "I have tried to bear my punishment meekly, fully believing that time would discover the facts and I would be pardoned."[1] Over the years that belief had been severely tested, and during 1912 he made no new bid for pardon, probably because strict interpretation of the statutory requirement for a year's lapse of time between applications could prevent him from reapplying in April 1913, when a new legislative resolution could be expected to maximize his chances.

In the year since Smith's release, Preston had watched seventy men go forth on parole, including eight second degree murderers. Some of them no doubt confirmed his worst suspicions about Nevada's system of justice. The favorable action taken on Goldfield gunslinger George Gibson's parole, despite his poor record in prison, suggests that Wingfield's wishes on such matters were not taken lightly. Hung juries, technicalities, and Diamondfield Jack's threats to stamp a key witness's head into the ground had enabled Gibson to wriggle out of a murder charge for shooting a young mining engineer during a brawl in the tenderloin, but he was finally dispatched to the penitentiary for attempting to shoot the deputy sheriff who arrested him for beating his common-law wife. "In case George Gibson comes up for pardon at the next meeting," wrote Wingfield to Oddie, "I shall appreciate anything you may do for him upon his promise to leave the state."[2] Gibson quickly received his freedom but landed in trouble in at least three Nevada cities almost at once, and later came gunning for the prosecutor who had convicted him. The notorious J. C. Schwick, convicted of second degree murder in Goldfield several months after Preston and considered so dangerous that he was transported to Carson in an "Oregon boot," was another distinguished parolee. Preston, as a first offender without a life term, had become eligible for parole after serving only a single year of his sentence.

In 1913 the composition of the Board of Pardons had shifted once more. Sweeney left the supreme court, and former Nye County (Tonopah) district attorney and future U.S. senator Patrick A. McCarran took his place. Although McCarran's liberalism was fitful and inconsistent, he at least lacked Sweeney's long-standing opposition to Preston. The other change in the Board's membership occurred in December 1912, when young Cleve Baker suddenly died. While Governor Oddie was away at a conference, Democratic Lieutenant Governor Gilbert Ross hastily appointed Democrat George Thatcher, another Tonopah attorney, to the post. Thatcher would later become right-hand man to George Wingfield—perhaps strong links had already been forged between the two—but he was also a brilliant lawyer who showed some signs of sympathy for labor.[3]

In early 1913 the Nevada legislature convened again, and the assembly unanimously enacted a resolution introduced by George Cole, a powerful, cigar-chewing, Democratic legislator from the mining camp of Manhattan who had for some time been endeavoring to build a political base through the WFM. There is a strong likelihood that support for the resolution was orchestrated by Socialist "kingpin" Grant Miller, who was active behind the scenes during this session. The legislators reminded the Board that "punishment should be corrective and deterrent, never arbitrary" and cited Preston's conviction "at a time when the better judgment and reason of the community was suspended," his unheard appeal, and his exemplary conduct and "wide influence on his fellow prisoners for good" during six years of imprisonment. The sharp tone of the final section of the resolution clearly suggested that public awareness of the wrong done to Preston had taken a quantum leap during the past two years: the 1911 resolution had "respectfully" requested an investigation to determine whether clemency should be exercised, with no specific mention of pardon; the 1913 resolution, with only the slightest obeisance to the judgment of the Board, and without respect, demanded a "careful, thorough and exhaustive investigation" into Preston's case and urged the Board to allow him "to be paroled or to be fully pardoned."[4]

Preston had his enemies still. The *Carson City News,* for one, greeted the resolution with a false accusation (authoritively contradicted by prison records) that Preston had been consigned to the dungeon for his recurrent infractions of the rules. But local support for him was snowballing all the same, and to be on his side was no longer regarded as a form of political hara-kiri.

In his April 1913 pardon application, as in his earlier ones, Preston tried to distance himself from the WFM-IWW by mentioning that at the time of the shooting the union had already elected a new business agent in his place and he had made plans to return to Los Angeles. He went on to reiterate the circumstances of the crime and to urge the Board to consider that he had served so many years of his sentence that even if he were guilty his release was due. He closed with an act of contrition: "I can never get over the sorrow of the wrong, but from the very first day I was in prison I have resolved to show repentance. . . ."[5]

Issuing a statement that more time was needed to review the testimony, the Board took the application under advisement, where it remained for eight months until the Christmas holidays approached. It was a season draped in black for those mourning the latest and most grievous WFM tragedy: seventy-two children and parents of striking miners at Calumet, Michigan, had been smothered to death in a stairwell after someone falsely cried "Fire!" from the door at a Christmas party. When WFM President Moyer refused relief money from the mine owners, he was shot in the back, dragged through the streets, and shoved on a train. A heavy snowfall blanketed the Sierra with an illusion of purity and peace, so isolating northern Nevada from events in the outside world that some communities received only belated bits of news brought by a courier on snowshoes. When the Board of Pardons finally cast their ballots on Christmas Eve, four voted in Preston's favor and one opposed—Governor Oddie. Because the state constitution required that the governor must vote with the favorable majority, pardon was once more denied.[6]

Although Preston could not have imagined it, Oddie, alone among the Board members, had particular reason to know that Preston had been framed. In the course of the preceding year the governor had received another letter from an old friend now fallen on hard times—Diamondfield Jack Davis. Wingfield's former bodyguard had pursued various mining ventures with indifferent success after leaving Goldfield. By 1913 he had turned against Wingfield, partly because he blamed his recent losses in mining investments on Wingfield's machinations, and he wrote the governor a disgruntled letter from Salt Lake City in the hope that Oddie would use his influence to secure payment of Wingfield's debts to him:

I am dropping you a few lines about the latest attack the I.W.W.'s made on me in Butte. . . . They did not get me. That is enough. There were three of them and they all had guns, but they did not dare use them for fear of shooting each other. Only one of them used his gun. He had it pointed at my left eye, and said you are dead, you son of a so and so, we have you now. Wingfield is the next. I guess he can look out for himself. Certainly what they do to him is no concern of mine.

I stayed with Wingfield through thick and thin. Did he stay with me? He sold me out. . . . I owe Wingfield nothing, not even good will. I have this shot through the jaw as a reminder of his loyalty to his friends, and I have the loss of nine teeth also by that bullet, and I made enemies over him. I would do the same to-morrow, thinking as I did then, and I am not making any apologies to those I.W.W.'s, but I would not trust George Wingfield as far as I could throw a bull by the tail. His motto is to use any one that he can and then throw them aside like a broken branch. He cannot do that with me. Had he tried to take his seat in the Senate I would have fought him off the cross. He showed good judgment in laying down. The reason I have not filed suit before is not on his account but because I did not want to have your name mixed up. . . .

(In 1912 Wingfield had declined the seat in the U.S. Senate offered to him by Governor Oddie after the sudden death of Senator Nixon.) Davis went on to say that he would refrain from suing if Wingfield made an "honorable settlement" on two points, the first of which was Wingfield's agreement to sponsor a shotgun wedding for the wronged daughter of a former mistress:

That is one of the conditions. The other is that he pay me $6,000 of the $9,500 he owes me. I put up money at his request to hold witnesses together and other things in the trial of Smith and Preston. I must get it back, that is all. I know you are my friend. Don't mix up between us. If you will hand him this letter, you will do him a favor. . . .[7]

Oddie now knew that Diamondfield Jack had paid other witnesses to give false evidence on Wingfield's orders. He nonetheless continued to reject Preston's pardon application in the face of the united opposition of the rest of the Board.

Preston appears to have emerged from this latest, and perhaps cruelest, of setbacks more encouraged than not. After all, the months that his application remained under advisement had clearly signaled trouble, and he may have feared the emergence of even broader opposition within the Board. Instead, some good omens could be read in the result. Although the governor remained irrevocably opposed to Preston, the Board's two new members had voted in his favor, and Justices Norcross and Talbot—masters of his fate, if not captains of his soul, since 1908—had abandoned their old antagonism to him.

Heartened by these developments, Preston began a major drive to forge past the final obstacle to his freedom. He recognized that there was "little chance of getting justice through pardon" as long as Oddie remained on the Board. If Oddie won reelection to a second term in the fall of 1914, as appeared likely, Preston's chance of pardon would remain foreclosed for the next five years until 1919. But since 1909 the Board of Pardons had also served as the Board of Parole Commissioners, with the important difference that the statute permitted paroles to be granted even when the governor did not vote with the majority in favor. Preston wrote to WFM headquarters requesting sanction for a parole effort and expressing his wish to "personally" take charge of his own case.[8] The suggestion that his release had been so long delayed because he would not accept parole until pardon appeared entirely out of the question cannot be confirmed, nor can the even fainter suggestion that he had pursued pardon, and nothing less than pardon, for all these years on the advice of the WFM. His own visceral belief in the American legal system, bolstered by such hopeful signs as the legislative resolutions, must have led him to think that pardon was within reach during the two years that followed Smith's parole, and the Board's lopsided vote in his favor had shown him almost right.

Preston was no man for ingratitude, and the explanation he offered for disassociating himself from the WFM after seven years was a tactful one: because the strike in Michigan was straining WFM resources, and because the union's effort for him had "always been opposed by powerful secret influences," it was decided that "these forces might prove less active" if Preston sought parole on his own.[9] Time and again, at the hour of Preston's pardon application, Hilton had thundered across the Rockies as his aristocratic British ancestors had pounded forth for centuries upon medieval battlefields from Faversham to Agincourt—generally to be slain there. Neither Hilton's sensational disclosures, nor his attempts to flatter, nor his political maneuvers, nor the compelling documents that fate and Zora had laid within his hands had proven of any avail to

Preston. At the outset, it is true, Hilton had contended against heavy odds, but the 1911 and 1913 legislative resolutions had reflected a significant shift in public opinion, a shift from which another attorney less prone to arouse antagonism in his own right might be able to draw greater advantage. Hilton apparently shared with his notorious client St. John an unfortunate talent for setting a conservative's teeth on edge. By now the suspicion had surely arisen that despite his eloquence and his prestige as a union troubleshooter, Hilton's stewardship of the case had proved scarcely more successful than the inept efforts of Bowler and Hangs. A local attorney would be better attuned to the personalities on the Board and the political currents affecting it. He would be able to give the application his attention whenever the need arose, in a way that Hilton, on one of his whirlwind visits from some distant union crisis, had never been able to do.

Hilton, for his part, may have been more than willing to abandon his increasingly perfunctory effort on Preston's behalf. During 1912 he had been much occupied with the legal affairs of striking WFM copper miners in Bingham, Utah; the following year he was busy with the WFM strike in Calumet, for which he would testify before Congress for the WFM in February 1914. On January 10, 1914, Joe Hill was convicted of murder in Utah, and Hilton began to devote himself to the sacred cause that was capturing the imagination of the labor movement. It is for losing his appeal to save the life of the famed IWW poet that Hilton is best remembered today.

As Hilton's replacement, Preston chose Reno attorney Grant Miller, a sympathetic partisan of his cause since Miller had edited the short-lived Socialist newspaper *Daily Forum* in 1910. Miller saw the case as "one which brings great shame to the State of Nevada and shows the extent to which capital will go in order to work injustice to the men who toil."[10] Michigan born, the son of a Baptist minister and early organizer of the Republican party, from whom he may have acquired his forceful style of speaking and his understanding of politics, Miller originally came west in search of a healthier climate—obviously the right prescription, for he would live to the venerable age of ninety-three. His education was sketchy, and his career had been erratically pursued between interludes of homesteading and poking hopefully around in mining camps, but he may have gained an intellectual dimension lacking in many of his provincial colleagues through travel to England and a stint at the University of Chicago. After his arrival in Nevada in 1907 at age forty, Miller quickly made a place for himself as the state's leading Socialist politician. For reasons that must have lain in his personality rather than his ideology, he almost made Socialism respectable and became the most popular Socialist ever to contend on the Nevada ballot. Still more important, from the viewpoint of Morrie Preston, Miller had gained the respect of other lawyers of all political persuasions, and he knew his way around.

This time Zora was not on hand to aid Morrie's drive for freedom, because she was enmeshed in a new romance and a new career. The man was mining engineer Ernest H. Liebel, remembered by her family as a "real toff," with whom she spent an interlude in Arizona. In 1911 she accompanied Liebel to the East, where she subsequently became a New York chorus girl. But the devoted Lillian could still be relied on. She sacrificed her meager possessions to move from Los Angeles to Carson City so she could plead for Morrie, and Lillian was a lady not easily turned aside.[11] Who among the members of the Board could refuse to see the woman with the broad, motherly face who waited so patiently at the door? How many could remain entirely unmoved under the gaze of her dark eyes? It might not have been easy to maintain the stereotyped image of Preston as a criminal labor agitator in the presence of this articulate schoolmistress.

Of still greater significance to the prisoner was the quiet investigation into the case begun by Justice Norcross early in 1914. As vice president of the American Institute of Criminal Law and Criminology, Norcross was especially well equipped to note the discrepancies in the trial, and as a judge so popular that no rival had found it worth the trouble to oppose him in his last election in 1910, he was politically secure enough to act as he saw fit. If he had already decided not to seek reelection to the court in 1916, this only enlarged his freedom of action. Norcross probably wrote to several of those involved in the case, but the only reply that survives is one from Douglas, written from the St. Francis Hotel in San Francisco. The former special prosecutor had returned to California when it became evident, following his defeat in the Nevada Republican congressional primary in 1910, that he would be unable to parlay his connections with the Goldfield elite into a successful political career. In his letter of February 18, Douglas put himself on record in favor of Preston's parole on the ground that the convicted man could be rehabilitated:

Prior to his trial I have never come in touch with Preston, but from his demeanor during the trial, and from quite a long talk I had with him at the prison after his conviction, I came to the conclusion that there was nothing of a vicious character in his makeup. There is little of an extenuating nature that can be said in his defense as far as the shooting of Silva is concerned, but I have often thought that he was carried away with an unholy zeal that seems to characterize a good many of our latter day labor agitators, rather than believe that he belongs to the criminal type. His sister has told me in many conversations that he was exceptionally thoughtful and good to his mother and to her, and we could find no record of his ever having been in any kind of trouble before. If my opinion will have any weight in his behalf, I believe that the ends of justice will have been served and the prospect of making a good citizen out of him enhanced if he is given his release.[12]

Norcross, however, was less interested in Preston's prospects for rehabilitation than in the prosecutor's opinion of the testimony of Claiborne and Bliss. At last, four years after Hilton's eloquent diatribe against these witnesses, their credibility was belatedly being recognized as a legitimate issue. In response to another letter from the Board, Douglas made a startling admission which, despite its qualifications, probably did more to set Preston free than all the boxes of petitions carted in to the Board during seven years of union agitation:

I have no hesitancy in stating that I became convinced at the time of the trial and from information which came to me subsequently thereto, that both the above named witnesses [Claiborne and Bliss] perjured themselves at that trial. Certainly enough of their testimony was perjured to create grave doubt as to the truth of it.

However, I am thoroughly convinced that the testimony of neither of them had any material weight with the jury in that case. The record will disclose that their testimony was directed largely to the question of conspiracy on the part of other members of the Goldfield Miners' Union, who were then under indictment.[13]

Douglas must be given a large measure of credit for coming forward, however tardily, and making a statement that cast considerable doubt on his own role in the case rather than allow Preston to remain in prison—at least after his departure from Nevada and the collapse of his political ambitions severed his dependence on Wingfield. Douglas was probably the prosecutor who bore the main responsibility for Preston's conviction; he had questioned numerous witnesses, made the opening statement, and delivered the first closing argument, an argument that even shocked opponents of the union. If there were any uneasy consciences after the trial, few were more likely to be troubled than his.

Whatever it was that impelled Douglas to break silence after seven years, his statements remain extraordinary in their implications. The suggestion that the Claiborne and Bliss testimony carried no weight with the jury may be set aside as a face-saving device; the Board well knew that on it hinged the critical difference between Preston as union assassin or as participant in an unforeseen fracas. As Preston himself pointed out, the conviction of Smith had shown that the perjured testimony weighed heavily with the jury, unless the verdict bore no relation to the evidence at all.

"While realizing that Mr. Douglas has bravely acknowledged the truth as to the perjury, and while appreciating the value of that acknowledgement," wrote Preston mildly, "we are yet compelled to criticize his logic."[14] Not only his logic but also his professional conduct demanded criticism. If, as Douglas admitted, he became convinced *at the time of the trial* that Claiborne and Bliss had perjured themselves, thus vitiating the prosecution's conspiracy theory, why had he called Preston "an assassin of the lowest type" and a "cold blooded killer of men to gain his own ends" in closing argument? Had he informed the other prosecutors of his knowledge? Why hadn't he immediately drawn the perjury to the attention of the court? Why had he instead participated in an obvious effort to convict Preston in spite of the discrepancies in the perjured testimony? Why, when the supreme court refused to hear the appeal on a technicality and it was clear that Preston and Smith were to be imprisoned without hope of redress, had he not written to the Nevada attorney general confessing error and requesting a new trial?[15] It did not lie within his discretion to deprive them of their rights because he thought the jury had given more weight to other testimony. And why had the prosecutors waited five months before moving for dismissal of the charges against the union leaders, whose indictment rested solely on Claiborne's testimony?

In addition to Douglas's letters, the Board received another letter from Esmeralda County District Judge Peter Somers. While undoubtedly less significant to Board members than Douglas's letter, it lent a broader dimension of legal authority to Preston's cause. Somers vividly recalled the atmosphere in which the trial was conducted:

> It is generally conceded, and I believe the fact to be, that those witnesses [Davis, Claiborne, and Bliss] were entirely partisan. Public excitement ran very high at the time of the trial. Meetings were held during its progress, giving vent to public sentiment which was distinctly hostile to the defendants. The proceedings of those meetings were published, undoubtedly reaching the jury. It was claimed a threatening letter was received by the presiding judge, which letter was also published, tending to inflame the

passions of the people and prejudice them against the defendants. The jurors, and even the judge, were guarded by deputy sheriffs in a dramatic way, which would necessarily have a tendance to cause the jurors to believe that the defendants and their associates were desperate and dangerous men. The witness Davis took part in demonstrations hostile to the defendants. . . . I do not think a conviction could be secured at the present time in Goldfield of anyone upon the uncorroborated testimony of such witnesses.

An industrial war existed in Goldfield at that time. . . . Much vehement language was used upon the streets, for and against either side. Crimination and recrimination were hurled from side to side in angry denunciation. There were few people in the camp who did not take sides in this industrial warfare, and I think that all these circumstances should be taken into consideration. . . . Is it asking too much to consider for a moment the turmoil and confusion in Goldfield during the time of the trial?[16]

Judge Somers wrote of giving Preston the benefit of the doubt and taking a "merciful view"; significantly, the redress he urged was not parole but pardon.

No small part of the Board's growing inclination to take that merciful view undoubtedly hinged on the attitude of Preston himself, who appeared to meet every standard as a likely candidate for rehabilitation. He declared that he had been studying ethics, psychology, and philosophy, among other subjects, to prepare for a "useful and profitable life" after his release.[17] Preston was no Tom Mooney rejecting parole as an unacceptable substitute for pardon, no Joe Hill cursing the capitalist system of justice to its very face in proud, wild defiance, but a man who wished to reclaim his place in society. From the outset he had operated within the rules of the system, turning himself in voluntarily and testifying in his own defense. His writing on the case has a tone of injured indignation, as though he had expected the law to deal justly with him. All this is consistent with the possibility that Preston's adherence to revolution was nothing more than a young man's fling with radicalism. On the subconscious level where the reflexes are triggered, Preston probably had never fully accepted the implications of being a revolutionary.

Seven years later the Morrie Preston who once spoke with St. John before a stamping, cheering crowd after the Bloody Sunday parade had been replaced by a good candidate for parole who had consistently resisted transformation into a union martyr. Although *Industrial Union Bulletin* promised its readers that their letters and agitation could win his freedom, such demonstrations proved counterproductive more often than not. Preston was probably fortunate that no thousands marched for him in national demonstrations as they would march for Mooney, and no worldwide storm of indignation flooded the mails for him as for Hill. Mooney was to spend twenty-two years in prison before he was pardoned, and Hill died before a firing squad. Intense agitation and the transformation of a prisoner into a symbol, as Preston seems to have recognized when he declined the 1908 presidential nomination, make it difficult for politicians to exercise clemency without appearing to capitulate under pressure. The most significant effect, however, is the transformation within the prisoner himself, the process Stegner has described as "the way circumstance has of taking a man out of his own proper and recognizable character and subtly transforming him, coating him with a new personality as a lead tray is glazed with silver in an electroplating tank."[18] He acquires a role in his own eyes—as Mooney did when he began to see himself as a symbol of the labor movement and rejected parole—that makes it impossible for him to accept anything less than total exoneration. No one would sing of Morrie Preston as the man who never died; instead he wanted to go free.

The Board decided to scrutinize the record as Judge Somers had urged them to do, and the consequences proved startlingly different from previous sessions. Suddenly, almost astonishingly, the arguments that had been ignored since 1907 became the Board's justifications for parole, announced in a public statement that virtually exonerated Preston. The Board noted that the verdicts of manslaughter and second degree murder, instead of first degree murder in both cases, "showed that the theory of conspiracy was not established to the satisfaction of the jury." They also found "much testimony" in the record impeaching Claiborne and Bliss (the delicate subject of Diamondfield Jack still passed without mention). Claiborne's inability to identify "men whose names he had freely used in testimony," combined with the admission in Douglas's letter, led the Board to state unequivocally that they were convinced the testimony of Claiborne and Bliss was perjury: "We are entirely satisfied that there was no element of conspiracy to the homicide." At the same time they recognized that "it is impossible to tell to what extent the perjured testimony, or any of the evidence offered to establish a conspiracy, influenced the jury."

Board members dismissed the evidence on what occurred while Silva stood in the doorway as conflicting. However, relying only on witnesses for the state and omitting the defense witnesses entirely, they placed great weight on the fact that Silva had armed himself, threatened to use the gun against Preston, and advanced to the doorway with it. Belatedly embracing the reasoning that had been advanced not only by Preston's procession of attorneys but also by Somers and Belford as early as 1911, by the Nevadans who wrote to Oddie on Preston's behalf, and by hundreds of union petitioners, the Board acknowledged that the trial had been held at a time of "bitter public feeling" and that "without fault upon his part" Preston had been denied a hearing for an appeal that raised "a number of grave questions of law." More than five years after Hilton presented the affidavits Zora had collected in her desert journeyings, and three years after Somers first wrote, the Board at last admitted their importance: "The judge and District Attorney of the county in which he was convicted, the leading attorney for the prosecution, the foreman and a member or members of the jury which tried the case, have recommended favorable action." (The only new element, of course, was Douglas's letter.) Citing Preston's "previous good character," his youth, and his exemplary conduct in prison, the Board concluded, "A good case, in our opinion, is made out justifying his parole, independent of other considerations, which appeal strongly in his behalf."[19] Preston saw the statement as a "pronounced moral victory for Justice," and he believed the Board felt compelled to issue it because the same "evil influences" that secured his conviction had "prejudiced a large portion of the public."[20] Well he knew that the old fears of Socialism and radical unions still lay just beneath the surface, and the lingering effects of the pretrial campaign of rumor and innuendo had not yet run their course.

An additional reason behind the Board's unusual public explanation may have been Governor Oddie's dogged adherence to the position he had assumed in 1911. The governor adamantly refused to sign the statement. He furthermore blocked Preston's release, demanding an opinion from the Nevada attorney general on the constitutionality of granting parole without his consent. The mortal illness of the governor's mother compelled the Board to postpone the meetings regularly scheduled in early April. Now further delay intervened, while Preston waited to learn whether Oddie would succeed in wresting away the freedom that dangled so nearly within his grasp. A negative answer at last arrived on April 25, to his immense relief. In an opinion reprinted by the local press in tacit recognition of its highly sensitive nature, Attorney General Thatcher held that despite the governor's dissenting vote a majority of the Board had the legal power to grant parole, although the granting of a pardon without the consent of the chief executive would clearly be unconstitutional.[21]

On April 28, 1914, nearly seven years after his conviction, Morrie Preston walked out of the state penitentiary. He was now thirty-one years old. Almost a fourth of his life had been spent behind bars. He would later compress all he cared to remember of that time into a few sarcastic lines:

> During Preston's seven years incarceration there was only one violent prison break, though there were several escapes, accomplished by stealth and a number by "breach of trust."
>
> Numerous fights occurred, some serious though not deadly, and much could be told of both the good and bad sides of men's nature when confined. In seven years Preston was under six different Wardens, each of whom had a different system of control, and he learned much about the management of prisons and the political intrigue connected therewith.
>
> Withal, Smith and Preston fared as well as could be expected in prison, but after all the greatest privation suffered by the prisoner is the loss of liberty and that is the feature that makes the best of prisons a hell.[22]

He entered a world stunned by the "Ludlow massacre" a week earlier. Miners in the Colorado coal fields largely controlled by the Rockefeller interests had been on strike since September. On April 20, company guards attacked and burned the Ludlow tent colony where the striking miners and their families lived. Fatalities included thirteen women and children who suffocated as they hid in a cellar. On the day of Preston's release, Colorado's mine war continued to dominate the headlines as events moved toward a familiar conclusion, the smashing of the strike by state troops.[23] If the world had altered a jot during Preston's seven-year absence, it was not apparent. Still, spring surrounded him, and home was no longer a barred cell but the yellow frame house on West Second Street where he lived while doing occasional carpentry work for Edgar H. Sweetland. As he walked the dusty, unpaved streets of Carson City, tasting his freedom, lilacs bloomed beside the little Victorian houses. Around the state capitol, its massive blocks of dark, gray stone quarried in a spot he knew all too well, the Dutch elm trees shimmered with the faint, diaphanous greening of early spring.

XI

DISCOVERIES OF TIME

Preston went forth a free man—yet not free, because he was still "held by the shackles of . . . unjust conviction and the burden is weighty." Although he found the board's statement a "complete vindication" for Smith and himself, he never ceased to glance nervously over his shoulder in fear that the state prison might reach out to reclaim him at any moment. He punctiliously reported to his parole officer at the beginning of every month; when the date once slipped past him, more than a year after his release, his hurried telegrams, explanations, and apologies reveal his anxiety. "He is still deprived of citizenship," he wrote of himself, "and the threat of further unjust punishment is still held over him, inasmuch as he is on parole, which limits his actions and *lays him liable to reimprisonment at any time.*"[1]

Freedom had not sufficed to cure him of the recurrent ill health that was to plague him the rest of his life, his years of imprisonment having transformed him from the "boy dupe" to a man of ruined health, prematurely aged. This emerges clearly in the report of an undercover detective who encountered the "old timer and rebel" during one of his trips to the mining camps. "He entertained Billy and operative with the wildest stories about the labor trouble in Goldfield . . .," noted Operative 18's report. "Operative got a good deal of good and valuable information from him . . ., he is broken down." Preston had talked about some Socialist miners recently fired in Goldfield, but he was fortunately spared the knowledge that he was being milked of information about his old comrades for the mine owners' benefit. A severe bout of "internal

neuralgia" incapacitated him for more than two weeks following his first
trip to Reno, Tonopah, and Goldfield. Once recovered, he worked a
while on the construction of a ferry at the Carson River before returning
to "literary work which, I have some reason to believe, will redound to
my financial benefit in the near future."[2]

The journey and the references to literary endeavor denoted that
Preston had begun investigating some leads and had started to write a
pamphlet on his case. He was still seeking a pardon, and would never
cease to seek it as long as he lived. His righteous indignation over the
legal frame-up had only been inflated by his unjustly prolonged years of
imprisonment. He had drawn back from the presidential nomination,
declined the martyr's role, seized freedom on any terms, but in his own
words and in his own way, among the moderate union men he regarded
as his own kind, he wanted to speak out.

Two pamphlets he wrote, the first in 1914–15 and the second probably two years later, reveal his own analysis of the case. Typically,
although his own role in the case was by any measure the predominant
one, he placed his codefendant right beside him in the limelight by
entitling both pamphlets "The Smith-Preston Case." This obviously
contrasts with Mooney, who repeatedly ignored Billings in his publicity
efforts. The first pamphlet incorporated a sizable portion of a 1911
report by Charles Tanner to the WFM on the case, and reprinted the
Douglas letters, the Board of Paroles statement, and other documents he
considered particularly important, including a portion of the trial testimony beneath the heading "FRAMED UP LIES." The circumstances of
the shooting were tersely summarized on a single page culminating in a
series of angry, staccato questions:

> What should Preston do?
>
> Run and be shot in the back?
>
> Stand and be shot down like a dog?
>
> Or, in self defense, shoot and shoot first? . . .
>
> Nine out of ten men in Goldfield at that time, except they were union men,
> would have been exonerated from all blame.
>
> But Preston was a union man—worse still—he believed in the industrial
> form of unionism—and worst of all, he was a Socialist.

As the brevity of these remarks suggests, Preston was unconcerned
with proving his own innocence; this he considered so obvious that no

proof was required. The main thrust of his pamphlet was to expose the conspiracy that had imprisoned him for seven years. He cast in capital letters the section of his 1914 statement to the Board in which he told them:

PERSECUTION IN THE GUISE OF LAW IS NONE THE LESS PERNI-
CIOUS AND AS IT IS MY DUTY TO CALL YOUR ATTENTION TO
THE ILL USE TO WHICH THE LAW HAS BEEN PUT IN MY CASE,
IT IS YOUR DUTY TO CLEAR THE FAIR NAME OF NEVADA OF
THE FOUL STIGMA ATTACHED TO IT BY THE IGNOBLE CON-
SPIRACY CONCOCTED AND DEPENDED UPON TO CONVICT ME.

Another section of the pamphlet attacked the "flagrant duplicity" of the unholy trio of witnesses. His discussion of Davis and Bliss merely recapitulated points Hilton had already pounded home in 1910, but Preston had obviously been pursuing some leads on the elusive William Lovett Claiborne, whom he accused of various petty crimes in Califor-nia. "It seems to me that he was not above taking the money of the money kings of Goldfield," observed Preston, "and that he got a nice little piece of money for his perjured testimony in this case, I, for one, am satis-fied." He reprinted letters from university registrars showing that Claiborne's claim to have attended the University of Virginia and Stanford was false, and he presented evidence that "the thug" had been convicted of perjury in San Francisco in 1915.[3]

In truth, this was but the tip of the iceberg. Tracing Claiborne's convoluted trail might well have posed an impossible challenge to the talents of Allan Pinkerton himself, and Preston was only to uncover the tiniest fraction of it. Rising phoenixlike from the ashes of disgrace, as he was to do time and again, Claiborne had soared away from his mysterious involvement with Bliss and alit in Los Angeles. No one there was likely to inquire about Bliss's sojourn at a Rawhide establishment known as "Claiborne's Cabins" just before the Schurz stage robbery; no one knew about the journey in which Claiborne chauffeured Bliss from Dead Horse Wells to Rawhide the day afterward; nor were any embarrassing questions likely to be asked about Claiborne's alleged theft of the car following Bliss's arrest. From his new perch, Claiborne added some novel embellishments and curlicues to the long-cultivated legend of himself as aristocrat and war hero and, with the effrontery of the born con artist, related it once again to the ever-sympathetic report-ers. Painstaking research by Richard Johnston has recently confirmed the preposterous dimensions of this evolving fairy tale. The *Los Angeles Times* informed its readers that Claiborne's direct ancestor had been the first colonial secretary of Virginia, where the family had received large grants of land from the English crown, and that his father and his three uncles, Patrick, Walter, and Thomas, had served as generals in the Confederate army, leaving Claiborne the "descendant of a long line of warriors." In fact, only one Cleburne (Patrick) appears in Confederate records, and he was an unmarried man with no brothers, only very remotely related to the aristocratic Virginia Claibornes; Claiborne's father was a hotelkeeper in Hot Springs, Arkansas. The *Times* went on to state that Claiborne had played varsity football at Vanderbilt University in 1893 and was chosen for the All Southern team. It seems, however, that Claiborne must have been a little small for varsity football in 1893, being no more than thirteen at the time.

Following his graduation from Vanderbilt, according to the *Times,* the football star was appointed to West Point, where he and his Southern friends objected to being hazed. Pitched battles with the upperclassmen ensued; "sometimes fists were used, more often clubs and finally guns." The lobe of Claiborne's left ear was nicked in one of these West Point gun battles, and one man was killed, which compelled Claiborne to depart without graduating. The United States Military Academy reports no record of his attendance.

Beneath the billowing smoke of legend, which he so assiduously fanned, burned one tiny spark: Claiborne may actually have attended Vanderbilt law school in 1903–4 under the name of Daniel Claiborne, the same name by which he served in the army. He later explained to army authorities suspicious about the several variations of his name in their records that he had enlisted using his father's name (Daniel W.) and lied about his age because he was too young. But evidence from other documents indicates that his enlistment may have been one of Claiborne's truthful lapses. The change of name raises the possibility that Claiborne was exceedingly anxious to shed the identity of Daniel W. for all purposes save pension claims.

Even in his earlier Goldfield phase, Claiborne had posed as a former officer in the Spanish American War. Indeed, "Colonel" Claiborne may really have enlisted in 1898 and served in the Philippines, though he could scarcely boast the status of an officer, having been busted from corporal to private and having served part of his enlistment as a cook and a wagon driver. To the receptive *Times* reporter, Claiborne now revealed some new facets of his war experience: during the Boer War he had made two trips to South Africa to supply the British army with mules and had sustained wounds in the right wrist and left leg and hip; after being wounded in the right shoulder and left thigh during the Spanish-

American War, he had fought with the relief expedition in China when the Boxer rebellion erupted, and at the siege of Tientsin was once more gloriously wounded, this time in the right knee. The army, however, listed his health as excellent when he was mustered out in 1901. In a physical examination of Claiborne for a railroad pension claim many years later, the doctor failed to notice any scarred and bullet-riddled limbs, except for the gunshot wound in the right knee. The only genuinely troublesome disability Claiborne had sustained, and the one on which he based his army pension claims, was a rectal fistula.

The following years were busy ones for Claiborne, according to the *Times*. He took charge of the American Hotel in Manila in 1900 (a particularly notable feat, since his war record shows that he did not leave the army until the spring of 1901), making a fortune of $100,000. Part of this he invested in a pool hall business in Hot Springs. He then graduated from law school, made and lost a $50,000 fortune in Goldfield mining claims, and was bereft by the San Francisco earthquake of the valuable 15,000-volume law library inherited from his father, the famed jurist. Returning to Nevada, he "acted as bodyguard for Governor Sparks," helped organize the state police, played a large role in settling the union troubles, and "gathered most of the evidence" that sent Preston and Smith to the penitentiary.[4] In a sense, Claiborne could lay some legitimate claim to the last of these accomplishments.

As usual, Claiborne emerged unscathed from his 1915 perjury conviction and the crimes with which he had been linked in southern California and went on to become a prominent Oakland attorney specializing in personal injury cases. He appears among the notables in *California and the Californians*, published in 1932. The saga of the scion of the Southern aristocracy remained unchanged in its essentials from earlier versions, and its tentacles of genealogy and partnership were creeping forth to embrace great families and business enterprises throughout the South. The list of his father's law partners had turned into a roster of eminent Southern jurists. "By intermarriage the Claibornes have been connected with nearly every prominent name in the South," the article noted. Claiborne now divulged that his mother was a Maxwell of the family that owned the famous antebellum Nashville hostelry, Maxwell House (the Maxwell Family Association has no record of her). This was but the latest of his efforts to upgrade his female relations. After the death in 1909 of his first wife, Ethel Gallie Conway of Arkansas, he had told the Goldfield press that she was the daughter of the prominent Frederick Bonfils, publisher of the *Denver Post*.

In the 1932 biographical sketch, Claiborne omitted mention of the All Southern varsity football team, West Point, Stanford, and the University of Virginia, but he did enlarge his education to include university courses in Manila, engineering studies in Boulder, Colorado, and "special work in analytical chemistry" abroad at Heidelberg. He also added a few wars. His experience in the Boer War expanded to include combat at Ladysmith and Spion Kopp and a commission as colonel in the South African army. (He does not, however, appear on the roster of Boer War veterans.) This was capped by six months' service as an officer during the war between Turkey and Greece. During World War I, he served for twenty-one months on the battlefields of France. A job as a railroad engineer was euphemistically referred to as joining the "transportation department of the Southern Pacific"; a period evidently spent as a laborer in San Antonio was passed over in silence. The fortunes made and lost after the Spanish-American War had now shrunk a bit to a stint as a clerk in a San Francisco furniture store, but Claiborne's activities in Goldfield had magnified amazingly: he disclosed that he had headed the state police during Goldfield's labor troubles and had prosecuted the "notable" Preston-Smith case.[5]

All these interesting revelations would have made Preston's wild, gray eyes blaze with anger if he had lived long enough to read them. As it was, Preston had long since lost track of the slippery Claiborne and abandoned the attempt to prove his perfidy. Shortly after the publication of the laudatory biographical sketch, the law once more caught up with Claiborne. He was sentenced to a term in the federal penitentiary in 1933. He would nonetheless emerge several years later to grow fat and gray-haired, to marry the last of his many wives, and finally to die at home of natural causes in his seventies.[6] It was Preston's ill luck to have as his adversary this supremely gifted and convincing liar, this fabricator of the legend of family breeding and heroism in war that newspaper reporters and word of mouth had so conveniently draped behind the witness for the prosecution as backdrop in the Hawthorne courtroom in 1907.

Preston never learned the last, and perhaps most interesting, addendum to the Claiborne story. Just after the trial, Hilton had suggested in court that the threatening letter to Judge Langan from the IWW had actually been written by a prosecution witness to influence the jury, and he demanded an investigation. It was a critical issue: the IWW had been severely condemned in the press; the letter had been interpreted as proof of the union's violent methods and had made the accusation that Silva's death was a union assassination appear plausible; the jury had undoubtedly been affected by it, and perhaps Judge Langan as well. At the time, Claiborne announced that he too had received threatening letters. The defense had dropped their charge, apparently for lack of proof. Preston thought that since the mine owners were "the only ones to profit by such an action it can be quite logically inferred that they who would pay $5,000 for special counsel to prosecute would also stoop to other methods to bolster up their case and prejudice if possible the trial judge against the accused,"[7] but it remained a logical inference and nothing more. Preston and his attorneys were never to learn the secret locked inside the threatening letter. The words menacing Judge Langan, "If you hang them, or send them up for life you will die for it you will be *killed like a dog,"* had not been written by those Branson customarily termed the Black Hand of the IWW. "Traitor . . . Claborne we will get him soon," the letter had warned, and Goldfielders had admired the heroic sangfroid with which Claiborne stood his ground. But we now know that he could not have been much worried, for our examination of an army pension application written in an identical and highly distinctive hand has revealed that the threatening letter to Judge Langan was written by star prosecution witness William Claiborne himself.*

Although the full extent of Claiborne's perfidy remained unknown to Preston, he ended his pamphlet with an indignant but clear analysis of how the conviction was accomplished. He believed that the public still lacked an "intelligent understanding" of the case because the Nevada press had prejudiced them:

> The policy of the press of the State generally has been one of misrepresentation and falsehood, influenced no doubt by the powers who control the industrial life of the state, and who, at considerable cost to themselves, were able to obtain a verdict against the men. It has been represented that they were two dangerous Socialists and agitators, men with anarchist tendencies, who wanted to destroy society, and that they were responsible for the strikes and industrial turmoil that marked the early history of Goldfield. If this were true, if every charge they make were true, as to their being undesirable citizens, still it would not justify the state in imprisoning men for a crime of which they were not guilty.

Preston thought such "raw deals" instead served to increase Socialist party membership.

*After an examination in which he identified individuality in the formation of twelve different letters in these documents, Robert M. Nelson, Document Examiner, Minneapolis Police Department, concurred with our conclusion.

At the time of the "unfortunate shooting," Preston continued, "a great labor war is raging in Goldfield and it is essential that the unions be put in bad with the general public, in order that the position of the mine owners and stock gamblers be strengthened." Darrow, Hilton, and other attorneys who usually defended WFM members were busy with the Haywood and Adams cases, so Bowler and Hangs were engaged (this muted suggestion was the only criticism Preston offered of his attorneys). "The allied corporate interests in Goldfield import one Malone, a crafty, skilled criminal lawyer from Denver, Colorado, at a cost of $5,000, to aid in the prosecution. . . . With the appearance of special counsel in the case it ceases to be the State against Smith and Preston and becomes instead Capital against Labor. Mine Owners against Mine Workers." Aided by Malone, the prosecution then advanced, through Claiborne, the preposterous theory of conspiracy. Only in enumerating the final element in his conviction did Preston slip into exaggeration. He declared that the mine owners had succeeded in prejudicing Judge Langan by arranging matters so that he was "constantly in receipt" of threatening letters purporting to come from friends of the accused.[8]

In this first pamphlet, Preston had recognized nearly all the ingredients in his conviction—public hysteria, second-rate attorneys, the mine owners' conspiracy, and judicial prejudice—yet the latter two were stressed most. As he continually reevaluated his ordeal in later years and as his perspective lengthened, the torch of memory would spotlight different aspects.

Even as he prepared to bring his case before the union world, Preston made ready to present it yet again to the Board of Pardons in the spring of 1915. Justice Norcross was now the only member still in office from the original Board Preston had faced in 1909. Governor Oddie had been defeated by Democrat Emmet Boyle in the 1914 election, and Justice Ben W. Coleman had replaced Justice Talbot on the supreme court. Oddie's departure, combined with the Board's declaration of the previous year that Preston had been convicted on perjured testimony, provided good reason to hope that the Board might go a step farther than 1914 and grant pardon. Aiming to secure an even stronger legislative resolution than before, Miller apparently planned a publicity blitz and wrote to Governor Boyle requesting special permission to hold the hearing in March while the 1915 legislature was still in session.[9] Then, inexplicably but entirely characteristically, Preston backed away from the plan to publicize his case before the legislature and told the governor that he had decided not to make his application until the Board's regular

April session. Most legislators seemed to feel that parole was an adequate response to Preston's demand for justice, and no further resolutions on Preston were passed.[10]

Although there was no small danger that the Board would take refuge in the same view, Miller had two new levers to apply. The first was Preston's excellent record during his year on parole, often considered ample cause for granting pardon. The second was the brief but highly significant letter that Miller had secured from Judge Langan himself recommending a full pardon for Preston. With no mention of the trial or of the perjured witnesses, Langan wrote that he believed Preston had "shown himself worthy of pardon" during his year on parole.[11]

Some judges would not have gone even this far, it is true, but the best of them would have gone much farther, and done it a good deal sooner. When Franklin Griffin, the presiding judge at the Tom Mooney trial in San Francisco in 1917, learned of new evidence suggesting that the principal witness against Mooney had committed perjury, the judge not only wrote immediately to the attorney general asking him to confess error and request a new trial but also urged two California governors to pardon Mooney.[12] In view of the importance the Board had attached to Douglas's letter, any acknowledgment from Langan on the perjured witnesses, the climate of public hysteria, or any other aspect of the trial might well have been sufficient to bring Preston's pardon. Instead Langan carefully confined himself to Preston's good behavior, a safe subject that could rub no tarnish on his judicial career by reopening the issue of his own impartiality.

By a rough kind of poetic justice, the seeds of Langan's undoing, like Preston's, had been sown in the mining camps years earlier, and also in an affair that mushroomed to consume his life—from a spore as tiny as Preston's casual impulse to picket the Nevada Restaurant. When the State Bank and Trust Company foundered amid a welter of questionable loans, fictitious dividends, inflated construction costs, and worthless stocks from the trust company operated by speculator George Graham Rice, Judge Langan appointed a receiver at the request of the Nevada attorney general. Little did he realize that the State Bank and Trust affair would drag on for over a decade, while the bank's directors sued the receiver, the angry depositors failed to recoup their losses, the legislature authorized an investigation, and Langan became the scapegoat for the entire financial disaster because many began to question his authority to appoint a receiver. In 1921 the receivership case remained deadlocked, and an effort to impeach Judge Langan fell short of a two-thirds majority in the state senate after a three-day trial. He was defeated in his

1922 bid for reelection in the district over which he had presided for fifteen years. Although he secured an appointment as district attorney in tiny Lyon County in 1924, even this minor office slipped from his grasp in the election of 1926. After this last defeat, in failing health, he moved to California, where he died in 1929.[13]

No decision on Preston's new pardon application was immediately forthcoming at the Board's April session. Indeed it is significant that no other applicant suffered such repeated delays and postponements. In late May, Board members found themselves still unable to make up their minds. A hearing was set for June 4 and a letter dispatched to the Nevada Bar Association inviting the attendance of the president and the executive committee or of other representatives and requesting comments on the case, an unmistakable sign that controversial action was contemplated. The cautious executive committee of the Bar Association tossed this political hot potato back in a hurry. By curious coincidence, every executive committee member claimed pressing business on June 4. Furthermore, President Robert G. Withers noted stiffly, "this hearing is not within the purview, scope or objects of our Association."[14]

In all probability the Board was seeking the extra thrust of legal authority that the Belford opinion had lent to Smith's parole and the Somers letter to Preston's, but none was forthcoming. Miller gave what the press termed "a strong talk," arguing that Preston had acted in self-defense but public prejudice had convicted him. The Board again postponed its verdict, this time until later in the month on the pretext that the new members needed more time to review the testimony. Further postponements ensued—to September, when Bowler appeared on Preston's behalf, then to December, as the scales wavered uneasily in balance.[15]

By then Preston was already on the road. In February he had been granted permission to leave the state. When the Board postponed a decision on his April pardon application, he saw no reason to linger. He had learned in 1913 how long these postponements could last and how little hope should be squandered on the result. During March and April he had devoted all his time to preparing his pardon application; he now left Miller to inform him in absentia of the anticipated negative outcome. He would spend the next five years moving from city to city in the Midwest and the East, speaking at union meetings about his ordeal, and supporting himself by the sale of his pamphlets and an occasional job.

He began by going back to the scenes of his childhood in Memphis and Little Rock to visit relatives and old friends and to sell pamphlets.

He had scarcely commenced his life as an itinerant union speaker, however, when his unlucky genius for being in the wrong place at the wrong time once more landed him in trouble. Arriving at the St. Louis post office on June 29, he was promptly arrested for a confidence swindle in Little Rock involving a gullible Italian and a woman named Lucy Preston. The coincidence of name and her departure for St. Louis at the same time as Preston had aroused law officers' suspicions. They locked him up overnight before realizing their mistake.[16]

He moved on to Chicago, speaking, selling pamphlets, and presenting his letters of introduction in union halls. In the process, however, he stirred up suspicion and trouble. The warden at the Nevada penitentiary received a letter from Chicago requesting a photograph and description of Preston to determine whether the pamphleteer was really the man he claimed to be; the Nevada press reported that Preston was lecturing for the IWW. None knew better than Preston the disastrous results of association with the still potent symbol of the red flag. Learning of this report, he dispatched an immediate and emphatic denial to his parole officer:

> I beg to add—I have *not* been speaking for the I.W.W, nor do I intend to speak for them for I do not espouse many of the principles to which they adhere and have no intention of adopting the tactics they advocate, whether I am granted my freedom or not.
>
> I have had no connection with the I.W.W. further than that I have met a number of members and have impressed upon them the fact that I shall not join their movement no matter what my position.[17]

By that time Preston had temporarily abandoned speechmaking and pamphleteering for a job as a molder's helper at a Chicago foundry. An unusually revealing report to his parole officer, in his characteristically sprawling, childish script, showed him deeply discouraged by the perils and disappointments of the preceding months:

> Have found that the conditions I am under together with an untamed scrupulousness as to honesty hamper me no little. I could have had steady employment at good pay long ago if conditions had permitted me to join a union but as that is forbidden I am shut out of a large field wherein the pay would be commensurate with my needs. There are too a number of soliciting propositions I could take up and succeed in but in all of them I find that the prime requisite is capacity for deception, and not being inclined to lie, however much the "American people want to be hum-bugged" I find myself shut out there.

Summing up—about the only work left to me is manual labor of the
harder and less remunerative kind. As the prospects now are good for me to
secure such a job, I shall be content with it.[18]

Three weeks later Preston's persistent bad luck struck again and he
was severely burned when the foreman spilled some molten aluminum
on his right foot while preparing to cast a mold. The burn did not heal
well enough to allow him to resume work for some time. The New Year
of 1916 found him again unemployed and in the midst of a winter of
discontent. During the first six months of his odyssey, he had been
arrested, tarred anew with radicalism, and injured in an industrial
accident, and he remained heavily in debt with no prospect of employment. In his own bleak assessment, he had "met with poor success."[19]

In February, when he moved on to Milwaukee and resumed selling
pamphlets, his life took an abrupt turn for the better. "I have transacted a
goodly amount of business," he observed with unusual optimism. "I
have no doubt whatever of my ability to provide for myself and those
dependent upon me from now on." That spring in Cleveland he was able
to make some payments on his Nevada debts and send a little money
home to Lillian. Disgust with the Board's perpetual postponements
probably lay behind his decision to withdraw his pardon application for
the time being.[20]

While Preston headed East and strove to "continue forging ahead
financially from now on,"[21] one of the lives that had briefly interlocked
with his at a Western boomtown in the spring of 1907 was suddenly cut
short. The *Tonopah Daily Bonanza* reported Patrick Bowler's death
beneath the headline "Intense Nervous Strain of Three Years Protracted
Litigation Snaps the Heart Strings of Attorney." After taking an early
morning walk around Tonopah and speaking briefly with his brother-in-
law, Edward E. Seylor, before going into court once more in the
intricate water rights suit in which he represented Seylor, the sixty-
eight-year-old attorney had lain down on a couch and died. The *Bonanza*
ascribed his sudden death to "his high sense of honor, which spurred him
in a law suit to overtax the strength of mind and body. . . . His advancing
years and failing health left his still brilliant mind overriding his enfeebled body till the snap came." A different story, swiftly denied, surfaced
in the *Goldfield Daily Tribune*. According to the *Tribune*, "A report sent
out shortly after the discovery of his death stated that the attorney had
taken poison rather than face a client whose case he had lost through

an inadvertent error, and that the dead man had left a note indicating his intention to take his life."[22] Whatever the truth, it is the inadvertent error—not his first—that lingers in the mind.

Bowler's demise was not to be chronicled by Lindley Branson, for the *Sun*'s editor had departed from Tonopah several years earlier. The large profits of the boom days had dwindled in calmer times, the failure of the Nye and Ormsby County Bank had brought heavy losses, and Branson had been forced to sell his large and expensive newspaper plant "at a sacrifice" in 1910. He launched unsuccessful ventures in several western towns during the ensuing years, finally arriving at Jerome, Arizona, to open yet another *Sun* in the winter of 1916. The chronicler of Branson's Jerome venture calls his editorials "windy" and "specious" and notes that over time his early "stridence" degenerated into a "banal whimper." The subject of Branson's banal whimpering was a new form of his old IWW paranoia: he perceived the United Verde Copper Company, which loomed large in Jerome, in collusion with his venerable union enemy in a plot to destroy the local AFL-affiliated miners' union. He quickly learned that a mining company was a far more dangerous adversary than the IWW. Circulation dropped, advertisers canceled, Branson lost his printing press, and the courts rejected his attempt to recoup his losses by a damage suit against the copper company's agent, a very different result from the affirmation he had received from the Nevada supreme court in his suit against the IWW.

It didn't take United Verde long to chew up the Jerome *Sun* and spit out the pits. Seventeen months after his arrival, Branson was forced to close the newspaper and leave town. He returned to Nevada, where he edited two newspapers in Ely, served in the state legislature, and made an unsuccessful campaign for governor as an Independent in 1934. He spent his last days in Seattle, reminiscing about the great rush to the Klondike in 1897, long before he ever drew blood from the IWW—or ran afoul of United Verde.[23]

"I have a large territory before me, and, barring sickness, feel that I shall be able to keep well ahead of financial distress," Preston wrote cheerfully to his parole officer in September 1916.[24] For the next three years he remained in the East, reporting from New York, Boston, Philadelphia, Trenton, Newark, Brockton, Albany, Troy, Rochester, Buffalo, Wilkes-Barre, Pittsburgh, never lingering very long in one place. Sometime in the course of these peregrinations he arrived at the destination that may have been uppermost in his mind as he gravitated slowly eastward—the New York tenement where Zora, now a dancer in the Anna Held chorus line, was living with young Louis and Ernest Liebel. The former mining engineer was now working sporadically as a salesman of industrial belts. Morrie and Louis passed several evenings in the tenement together swapping stories, but when Morrie told the boy what had happened to him in Goldfield, he did so with a serious purpose. During the brief time he spent with Louis, he quickly realized what Zora was too blind or too caught up in the gay nightlife of New York's cabarets and her tempestuous battles and reconciliations with Ernest to see. Louis was teetering on the verge of serious trouble. He had acquired a handgun. With that gun, the childish raids on fruit stands and ice cream trucks where he led the neighborhood boys in pranks could soon develop into something far more alarming. Morrie persuaded Louis to give him the gun, saying he would dispose of it in New Jersey, where he was then working. It was a moment Louis later remembered as a turning point in his life, brought about by a kind and caring man who took the time to know him instead of attempting to beat him into submission as Ernest did. Although Louis had been given the Liebel surname (which he would later anglicize to Lebel), this signified no fond relationship with his stepfather. Ernest's resentment was in ugly contrast to the special affection he received from Morrie because he was Zora's child.

It appears that Morrie took Ernest to task for his harsh treatment of Louis. Yet the shouting match between the two men which echoed through the walls of the apartment may well have had another cause, known to Louis ever since he was old enough to sense such things. Louis realized that Morrie was still hopelessly in love with his mother and that she harbored a feeling for her adopted brother that Ernest recognized as considerably more than sisterly. Her preference for Ernest was less easily understood. Morrie's reunion with Zora, nearly a decade in the making, had ended almost as soon as it began.[25]

Sometime after his arrival in the East, Preston wrote the tract we have labeled Pamphlet 2. An earlier version has been located, but it is virtually a duplicate with a different frontispiece and title page, and Pamphlet 2 stands as the final judgment we have from Preston on his own case. The most obvious difference between the two pamphlets is the latter tract's tone of biting fury. The longer Preston had to look back in anger, the angrier he grew. Perhaps he at last felt free to express emotions he had not dared to reveal earlier for fear that his parole might be revoked. There are also signs that he was beginning to shape, dramatize, and exaggerate his story as he told it in union halls, possibly spurred by the fervid emotions and expectations of his audiences. Ten years after the trial his memory began to falter on some details.

In part, Pamphlet 2 reprinted material that had already appeared in Pamphlet 1, but it also contained a good deal that was new. Here Preston spoke for the first time about the pretrial whispering campaign and Zora's desert journeys to secure affidavits and set forth his theory that Claiborne had transposed an executive session held in Union Hall on Wednesday to Saturday in order to lend verisimilitude to his story. The "coterie of snakes" (Davis, Bliss, and Claiborne) is covered in the chapter entitled "RECORDS OF GUN-MEN." In the final section of Pamphlet 2, Preston expounded the lessons he had learned behind prison walls on the conspiracy charge in union cases:

> *Experience leads us to say that the conspiracy charge is held in reserve almost exclusively for members of Organized Labor.* . . . Those who doubt may test the matter by calling to mind the cases in recent years wherein conspiracy has been charged. The first one coming to mind is invariably a "Labor Case," so also the second and probably the third, and after a while one possibly calls to mind a case involving other than Union men . . . [the union man] must face all the allied forces of the State as represented by the State's attorney, his help and Court attaches, if not, indeed, the Court itself; money is represented by hired prosecutors, crooked deputies and purchased liars, and thugdom is represented by gunmen, strikebreakers, and private detectives. The Union man must contend with malfeasance in office on the part of the prosecutor and his henchmen; malpractice on the part of hired prosecutors, garbled reports in the press, and other tricks on the part of money; and finally perjury, lies, jury-tampering, and a thousand and one other despicable devices on the part of deputies, thugs, and detectives . . . [the prosecution of the union man] is *persecution* stark and naked. It is a "rough-house" affair in which the presiding elder [the prosecutor] quite often is rougher and tougher than the other vicious factors, and in which there is only one possible victim,—the defendant.[26]

The prosecution, Preston warned, was allowed to submit evidence on unrelated crimes, to use the actions of one defendant as evidence against another, to present the inferences of their witnesses as statements of fact. The law as he saw it was primarily concerned with property rights rather than social rights. Prosecutors not only shared this concern but also received "special inducements to resort to every cunning device to abort justice":

Now comes an element always an active factor in conspiracy trials. If a
little perjury be added to the vicious combination just described, you have a
phalanx of chicanery and duplicity well calculated to convict the most
innocent among the propertyless. Be it understood, too, that the very
nature of the conspiracy procedure, and of the interests at stake when
Union men are on trial, makes perjury a welcome ally to the prosecution,
and the perjurer must be protected at all hazards. Knowing this, the
prosecution's perjurers unhesitatingly swear to the most atrocious lies.[27]

Preston strongly urged "Unions and other working class partisans" to
abolish the common-law conspiracy doctrine "by legislation, if possible, otherwise if necessary." He offered a final "word of advice" to
union men facing conspiracy charges: they should demand a preliminary
hearing "in order that the defense may gain some knowledge of the
prosecution's case and the perjury upon which the prosecution de-
pends"; they should insist on separate trials, so the jury could not
hold each defendant responsible for the acts of the other; their attorneys should adopt the aggressive strategy used by Darrow in the
Haywood case and accuse the prosecution of conspiracy. "This is
invariably justified by the facts," noted Preston, "for the prosecution does conspire, and such conspiracies always have for their
object the conviction of labor men whether guilty or innocent." The
pamphlet ended on a Socialist note: "As monstrous as is the injustice
inflicted upon workers by this judge-made device, it is only one of the
many schemes to defraud common men of their inalienable rights,
and the toilers are again urged to unite for the abolition of all forms
of tyranny and exploitation and for the ultimate emancipation of hu-
manity."[28]

It would be difficult to deny the fundamental accuracy of Preston's
analysis. The central point—and even after the passage of many years, it
never ceased to enrage him—was the "criminal injustice" of convicting
him on the basis of the preposterous conspiracy story concocted by
Claiborne. Preston knew Claiborne for a liar and could not fathom how
anyone could believe that union leaders would admit a stranger to their
council as they plotted assassination or that Claiborne would fail to warn
the victim. Indeed the story contained even more flaws than Preston had
named. As Stone has observed of Orchard's testimony against Haywood, it would be absurd to credit the supposition that the embattled
union leaders could sanction an act that they well knew would be
suicidal in its effects on public opinion.[29] Some evidence has indicated
that the union used to beat up its opponents and run them out of town.

Why should this method have been abandoned in Silva's case? If intimidating opponents was the union's objective, it would have made a great deal more sense to kill one of the AFL organizers, mine owners, or gunfighters with whom the union was so deeply and fundamentally embroiled, not a minor figure with whom the union had an isolated dispute. The suggestion that the union sought to intimidate all its opponents by killing one seems too haphazard to be taken seriously. Indeed the vast implausibility of selecting Silva as the union's victim was implicitly recognized when Claiborne appended his story on the list of citizens to be killed, including the logical victims Wingfield and Davis.

One of the factors that Preston, in his polite gratitude to anyone who had tried to help him, passed over lightly yet clearly implied in his advice to union defendants was the incompetence of the defense attorneys. It is true that they faced a formidable obstacle in public prejudice against the union, and that they were hampered by separation from their clients and lack of funds. They also struck some bad luck, when a juror's illness brought the trial to a temporary halt before they had completed their case, and in the coincidence of timing with the Haywood case—though the rift with the Goldfield radicals might well have disposed the union's national leadership to ignore Preston and Smith even if their attention had not been diverted. Granting all this, it is still difficult not to conclude that the defense attorneys failed at every turn. They failed in their basic strategy, as Preston implied in his warning to union defendants to insist on preliminary hearings and seek separate trials. They failed, despite the hints contained in the indictment of Smith and the rumors of secret indictments, to prepare for the conspiracy case that a brief glance at other union cases would have suggested as a strong likelihood. They failed in the day-to-day conduct of the case, bringing poorly prepared witnesses to the stand time and again and allowing vital points of evidence to slip through their fingers. Perhaps their most critical failure occurred in the initial business of jury selection, and it must be emphasized that this *was* a failure on the part of the defense attorneys. Although Preston and his supporters believed that public hysteria at the time of the trial had affected the jury, Darrow succeeded in finding an unbiased jury in the face of even more intense popular prejudice. So too did the attorneys for Tom Mooney's wife, Rena, although it took them hundreds of veniremen. Securing an unprejudiced jury meant the examination of prospective jurors would continue for weeks, not the span of three and a half days that Bowler and Hangs had devoted to it, but it could be done.[30]

In retrospect, the prosecutors' conduct of the trial certainly suggested an awareness that they faced a jury prejudiced in their favor. They dealt with radicalism in a highly allusive way, simply by mentioning symbols—the red flag, Burke, the IWW—and deviated from this approach only briefly when questioning Smith on the doctrine of class warfare. In Rena Mooney's trial, by contrast, the prosecutors read extensively from radical magazines and the works of Emma Goldman, Eugene Debs, and others in an effort to convince the jury that radicals were dangerous.[31] In the Preston-Smith trial, the prosecutors clearly thought these proofs unnecessary and instead relied almost exclusively on flashing the code words that would activate the jurors' preexisting prejudices.

Miller, and many others, believed that trying Preston and Smith "on a rush order" was among the foremost of the prosecution's dirty tricks.[32] It is true that the trial had followed the shooting with unusual speed, but less clear that this hindered the defense. Neither observation, nor experience, nor the indictment had given the defense attorneys a clue to the general thrust of the prosecution's case, so additional investigation time would scarcely have served them well. Indeed it would probably have been a disadvantage: given the high mobility of mining camp populations, many witnesses would have drifted away by the time the prosecution's theory was at last disclosed and the defense's requirements known. The witnesses produced—McKune, Luxinger, Sexton, and Whitkop, among others—were strong ones. Although more time might have meant more witnesses to Davis's whereabouts when he claimed to have seen the corral of men, this would only have provided additional confirmation for the two they presented. The defense needed not a larger number of witnesses but the capacity to build credibility with the jury for those they had, to demonstrate convincingly the importance of their evidence, and to select a jury willing to believe them. The fact that half the jurors had changed their minds within two years suggests that this should not have been beyond their powers.

While those witnesses present and accounted for were more than adequate for the defense, the issue of missing witnesses remains one of the lesser mysteries of the Preston-Smith case. These included Silva's cook, an eyewitness to the Muller assault; the union picket who preceded Preston at the restaurant and was needed to corroborate St. John's statement on the gloves; the two men Preston accosted after Dixon and Luxinger at Silva's door, both eyewitnesses to the shooting; Smith's companion Hoey; and Bliss's partner Frank Branch. If some of these witnesses had not been actively suppressed by the prosecution—and, in view of the long withholding of Schultz and the evidence on Silva's gun, this possibility cannot be discounted—fear of involvement must have driven them underground or the hope of finding better prospects elsewhere must have prodded them to move on. The only one of these mystery witnesses on whom a few scraps of information have been unearthed is Frank Branch, a blond, Kewpie-doll-faced young man of twenty-three from Price, home base for the Wild Bunch, the members of which were undoubtedly no strangers to Branch. He sometimes tended bar in Price at the Oasis, owned by his brother-in-law, Herbert Millburn, an investor in several of Bliss's mining enterprises. In 1907 Branch set off with Bliss to Nevada on what he supposed was one of these mining projects. He was probably unaware that Bliss, along with others who had worked as guards during the Utah coal miners' strikes of 1903–04, had been contacted by the mine owners to come to Goldfield. After the pair arrived in Goldfield in late February, young Branch's great adventure quickly soured. He went to Hawthorne with Bliss to testify in the Preston-Smith trial but apparently found perjury something more than he had bargained for. Harboring, and perhaps secretly idolizing, the romantic bandits around Cassidy was one thing and lying for pay to hang innocent men another, especially to a young man from a deeply religious Mormon family. Branch fled without testifying and returned to Utah before the trial ended. In late August he suddenly died from injuries the press reported had been incurred in a fall from a warehouse platform. There is a rumor, though, still repeated in Price, that Branch had not really tumbled from a platform at all but had suffered a fatal beating.[33]

In Pamphlet 2, Preston's specific recognition of the critical part Judge Langan's prejudice had played in the trial is more muted by his generalizations on law as the servant of capital than in the earlier pamphlet. His remarks on Judge Langan are not wholly reliable, because he was convinced that the judge's prejudice against him had been aroused by several threatening letters, a belief that also surfaced in the St. John affidavit and may have gained general acceptance among union men. No evidence of more than one letter has been found, and the May 5 letter does not suffice to explain the judge's earlier adverse rulings. Nonetheless, Preston's error as to the cause does not alter the validity of his perceptions on the result. He had sat before Judge Langan each day during the trial, attuned to the subtle signals of the judge's voice and face and manner—signals that are not preserved in the written transcript. His sense of the judge's attitude toward him was fully corroborated by the record, all the way to the closing instructions weighted against the defense. The importance of these judicial instructions is nowhere better illustrated than at the Haywood trial, where Debs, among others, believed that what tipped the scales in Big Bill's favor was not the celebrated eloquence of Darrow but the scrupulously correct set of instructions given by Judge Wood.[34]

In a sense, Judge Langan was the Socialist nightmare made flesh, one in a long house-that-Jack-built succession of public officials, any of whom could have reversed the injustice at any number of stages, from the first grand jury to the last pardon hearing—and all of whom failed to act. Labor cases such as Preston's repeatedly brought together a dangerous complex of factors, popular prejudice fanned by an irresponsible press and unscrupulous collusion between legal and political authorities at the behest of private corporations, and yet a single official's resistance to the centripetal forces whirling toward conviction could alter the outcome. Competent counsel and Judge Wood's neutrality led to acquittal in the Haywood case; St. John's Colorado indictment for conspiracy to commit murder died aborning under the skeptical gaze of Judge Stevens.

In the final section of his pamphlet, Preston examined with clarity and fury how public officials had allowed the mine owners to use the state as their instrument. He went on to advise the victims of conspiracy charges. He saw no end to the cycle of injustice until "the Workers change the legal code and give it some semblance of reason and logic, or find some means of abolishing injustice altogether." From his own bitter experience, he tried to distill the common legal remedies that would aid the union man ensnared in a "kangaroo court" and found one of them in Darrow's conduct of the Haywood trial.[35]

Comparison with the Haywood affair is instructive, not only as a lesson in law but also in the very origins of the case, where common themes appear that may also apply to other labor trials of the period. In both cases, the victim was an exceedingly unlikely figure not engaged in a major current dispute with the union. While Steunenberg was not fondly remembered by union miners imprisoned in the bull pens during the Coeur d'Alene troubles of 1899, he had been out of power for several years and no longer retained any importance to the union. In both cases, the press immediately labeled the killing a *union* crime, even when the circumstances did not appear to indicate conspiracy, raising the possibility that the press played an instigating role by fastening the murder on the union in the public mind and creating the opportunity subsequently capitalized upon by the mine owners when they supplied evidence to fit the image. In both cases, the conspiracy hinged on a single witness linked to the mine owners: Harry Orchard, coached by a Mine Owners' Association detective in the one; and in the other William Claiborne,

probably hired by GMOBA, the organization that the press acknowledged was responsible for the conspiracy evidence. In both cases, the
actual crime was secondary to the conspiracy, a factor reaching the
pinnacle of development in the St. John case in Colorado, where the
identity of the killer was not even known. Collectively, these common
themes flowed naturally and logically from a single source: attempts by
the mine owners' associations, repeated as opportunity arose in different
times and places, to use fortuitous acts of violence to discredit the
miners' union.

During 1917 and 1918, Preston's peregrinations in the East continued, as did his recurrent struggles with debt. At one point he sounded
almost entrepreneurial when he wrote to his parole officer of " 'making
good' on my parole" and "doing 'my bit' in the Great Game."[36] In
August 1918, in the midst of World War I, the possibility briefly arose
that Preston might receive his pardon after all if he enlisted in the army.
Preston had written several times to Miller that he was eager to volunteer
"so that I might go to the front if possible," but both believed he was
legally barred from military service because he was still on parole.
Feeling compelled to justify this deviation from pacificism to his Socialist attorney, Preston wrote Miller on August 24:

> While the clap-trap catch-phrases of the militants of our country arouse in
> me only a sort of disgust yet I see clearly the necessity [of] a defensive
> military program and am willing to take part in defeating the militant
> monarchies of Europe. Say what you please I consider commercialism at
> heart pacifistic so far as the sword is concerned and it is only the inherently
> militaristic in America who have tried so insistently to force upon America
> the monarchical militant system.
>   I make this confession without apology and without fear of justifiable
> criticism. I do wish you to know for whom and what you may be working if
> you take the case for me next Spring.[37]

In fact, Preston's position would evoke hearty concurrence from Miller,
who had bolted the Socialists because he favored American participation
in the war. Hoping this proof of patriotism would tip the balance where
all else had failed, the attorney sent a copy of Preston's letter to
Governor Boyle and requested approval for another pardon application.
"He is a rugged young fellow and would make a good soldier," wrote
Miller, "and under the circumstances it seems to me that it would be just
as well to give him a chance."[38]

Governor Boyle responded that Preston's legal status was no bar to enlistment. If he entered the army, his pardon would be forthcoming as quickly as possible. Preston waived the exemption from service to which he was entitled through his work in a munitions factory and registered for service shortly before his thirty-sixth birthday moved him beyond the age limit. Unfortunately the army thought Preston a less rugged young fellow than Miller did, owing to the perforated eardrum suffered in the Nevada state prison. Eight days before the armistice, he reported to his parole officer that he had been listed as deficient and placed in the last class.[39] The prospect of pardon once more eluded him.

In early 1919 Preston was laid off at the munitions factory after government orders were canceled. Apparently he returned to pamphleteering. His July 1919 letter from Pittsburgh reported "traveling by short jumps allmost [sic] constantly."[40] In the spring of 1920, after years of rootless wanderings, far from his adopted mother, far from Western mining camps resembling Goldfield, and far from the desperate struggles of the miners' union, Preston turned west at last to make another pardon application at the spring session and to rejoin the ailing Lillian in Los Angeles. Lillian's failing health may not have been all that drew him home after so long. Zora had apparently returned to California to care for her mother, after her clamorous fights with Liebel culminated in a final parting, and a broken ankle ended her career as a chorus girl, just when she was about to embark on an eagerly anticipated tour of South America.[41] Knowing little more than the bare outlines of Preston's life from his parole reports, we can only hope that these years from 1915 to 1920 were not so unrelievedly grim as they sound, and that along with the constant moves and debts and illnesses and disappointed love, there were also good times of a kind that a man does not report to his parole officer.

As he wended his way westward to Minneapolis, Preston posted his petition for pardon, the first that he had composed by himself. Not only the Minnesota postmark but also the cloudy and amateurish attempts at legal reasoning, the haphazard spelling, and the labored sarcasm, all suggest that it was entirely his own, written without the benefit of an attorney's advice. The Board of Pardons he faced contained none of the original members of 1909 and only two—Governor Boyle and Justice Coleman—from the Board that had heard his last application in 1915.[42] Nothing of what happened at the 1920 hearing is known, except that Governor Boyle at one point asked Preston why he had not taken up a consistent study along some professional line. It was an ironic moment. There sat the governor, his hair straight and black, his glance keen from

behind rimless spectacles. Irish in descent as Preston himself, the son
of a prominent mining man on the Comstock, Boyle had graduated
from college at nineteen and attained swift success as a mining engineer before he turned twenty-one. Just three years older than Preston, he was everything the studious young Morrie, who had avidly attended lectures at the Academy of Sciences, might have become if
he had not lost his father in infancy, been compelled to work since
boyhood to support his mother, spent seven years in jail, and gone
forth branded a murderer. Why had he failed to achieve professional
success? Preston merely replied offhandedly that he feared he was
"too lazy."

After the hearing Preston's usual circumspect attitude to authority
quickly returned, and he wrote to the Board explaining that he simply
did not believe in making excuses for himself:

> My reason for that reply was based on a study of a large number of failures,
> brilliant failures, I may say.
>
> During my travels I have come in contact with a number of men and
> women of power and ability, men of brilliant ideas but who were almost
> utter failures in practical life. Having a sort of faculty for bringing out the
> stories of personal troubles I have listened to the many tales of woe of these
> parties and the several excuses they give for their failure. Prominent among
> those excuses is the holding that society or some powerfull [sic] group in
> society is aligned against them. . . .
>
> I found, in fact, though, that those failures all lacked the tenacity of
> purpose to adhere to a steady course, either in study or work, in every case I
> found that the individual was loath to do the detail work, the "hack" work,
> necessary as a foundation to success — or in sum they were mentally lazy.
> Mostly too I found that they were especially subject to prejudices and
> particularly in favor of some certain personal pet ideas against which they
> would brook no opposition.
>
> Now, having in general discarded the several excuses of failures and
> generalized the cause of their failure in the word laziness I could hardly
> permit myself the luxury of excuse for my failure.[43]

Although Preston may have succeeded in dispelling the "impression
of frivolity" his response had evoked, his request for pardon was again
turned down. The Board's reasoning is not known, but it is clear enough
that the long-sought pardon was beyond his grasp. In 1913, with the
legislative resolutions, the legions of Nevada labor, and four members
of the Board behind him, he had brushed it with his fingertips. Now the
psychological moment had passed, never to return.

The summer found him at home again with his family, after an absence of almost fourteen years, and "quite busy repairing and gardening around my grandmother's place" at Clearwater near Los Angeles. That autumn he cared for Lillian, working only at irregular intervals. Her health was worsening, and for most of 1921 he was compelled to leave work and devote himself to nursing her.[44] His summer was spent at her bedside and in the vegetable garden. "The garden is producing most of the foodstuffs we conserve and we have done nicely," he reported, with the satisfaction of a proletarian Candide.

This is a period of silence where Zora is concerned. The next we know of her it is 1923 and she is living with Louis, whom she has brought west with his young wife and infant son. Zora is working as a dresser for one of the stars during the filming of *The Hunchback of Notre Dame*. She is still beautiful, with a single dramatic strand of white in her upswept black hair. Before her death, probably in 1955, she would add another career to her variegated assortment—farmer's wife, masseuse, seeress of numerology, dancer, actress, dresser, and finally cook in an internment camp for the Japanese during World War II. Yet the period of silence between 1920 and 1922 concerns us, for it is possible that within it lies the end of her connection with Morrie Preston.

However warm Zora's affection for her mother, the woman known to her family as a "nighter" may have had difficulties accommodating to Grandmother Nunnaley's household. The routine of life there was scarcely suited to a former chorus girl used to dancing nights and sleeping late, often found lounging in bed during the afternoon hours smoking and reading and wearing one of the exquisite kimonos she made for herself, and always averse to cooking and housekeeping.[45] In a photograph taken in this period of Lillian seated in a wheelchair, the broad face still much resembles the stern disciplinarian of Zora's youth. Playing the dutiful daughter to her was one of the conventional roles this mercurial Bohemian had always rejected, and the attempt may have been doomed to early failure.

In a sense, Zora's bedroom, strewn with clothes and cosmetics, mirrored her temperament. An ordinary room could no more accommodate the litter of her possessions than an ordinary human relationship could contain her excesses of anger and passion. It is probable that she quarreled with Preston, as she seems to have quarreled with everyone who ever loved her. The point when Preston wrote to his parole officer "the whole care of mother has fallen to me," unless it refers to one of Zora's mysterious truancies, may signify her permanent departure from his life.

The autumn of 1921 found Preston employed as a telephone lineman again—the kind of work he had done before his ill-starred journey to Goldfield fifteen years earlier. Another accident befell him that October when a car ran him down, but he was not long incapacitated. On May 13, 1922, at sixty-one, Lillian died, and Morrie lost the one person whose devotion to him had been steadfast and unwavering. More than a year later he was still working to repay the debt of her medical expenses.[46] His assumption of this obligation indirectly acknowledged that Lillian was closer to her adopted son than to her natural son in San Francisco or any of her other blood relatives.

In the fall of 1923, with dogged persistence, Preston wrote requesting another pardon hearing. But the Board would never listen to this eighth petition for the "tardy and partial reparation" that Preston continued to believe was his by right. On October 9, 1924, shortly after his forty-second birthday, came the last of the unlucky accidents that had plagued him throughout his life. While he was working at the top of a telephone pole on Wilcox Avenue near Sunset Boulevard in Hollywood, the pole began to wobble, and the crosspiece on which Preston was seated broke. He fell thirty-five feet to the ground, crushing his skull, and died a few hours later at the hospital without regaining consciousness. In keeping with his Socialist beliefs, Preston had expressed himself caustically on industrial accidents:

> Men not possessed of wealth or affluence "are of inferior quality mentally and morally, are ignorant and uncultured," "they are such a beastly lot of beggahs, doncha know." And then the unguarded gear in the mills finds it less repulsive to crush the bones and squeeze out the life blood and the rock and earth of the untimbered mine roof have less scruples against tumbling down in death-dealing avalanche.[47]

Once more, as in his Bloody Sunday speech, his angry words had prophesied. The verdict of the coroner's inquest declared that Preston's death had resulted from the carelessness of his employer, the Los Angeles Bureau of Power and Light, because the pole on which he was working had rotted underground at the base.

Unaware that Preston's parole had expired in August and fearful that after he failed to report Nevada authorities might "make public" the fact that he was an ex-convict on parole, Lillian's eighty-four-year-old mother, Mary Nunnaley, wrote the Board of his death. Her shame over his condition, despite his innocence and the passage of many years, bore testament that the stigma of which he used to speak was real indeed.

Besides the shame, grief lay between the neat and clearly penned lines of
Mary Nunnaley's letter, and also pride. "He has been a model man and
beloved by all."[48]

The woman who had named her firstborn child Rockwood, who had
almost certainly been Preston's first and only love, who had done more
than anyone else to win his freedom, apparently did not attend his
funeral. It is possible that Zora had continued to love Morrie in her own
inconstant way and her own occasional time, and he, having long since
despaired of possessing her exclusively, had accepted whatever she was
willing to give. Yet the failure of the Nunnaleys to notify her of
Preston's death may have signified an awareness that her relationship
with him had been severed. There is no sign of contact between them
while Zora was having an affair with a banker a good deal younger than
she during the year preceding Preston's fatal plunge to earth,[49] and the
silence and the absence hint at estrangement and the death of love.

The organization Preston had so swiftly forsworn lasted no longer
than the man. The city had died already. After the Nixon-Wingfield
partnership was dissolved in 1908, essentially turning Nixon's interest
in Goldfield Con over to Wingfield in return for Wingfield's banking
interests, Wingfield had become both formally and financially what he
had long been in fact, the undisputed boss of Goldfield Con. He soon
came to regard the city as a species of company town and its public
officials as his chattels. Once St. John had boasted that union regulations
were "the LAW"; now the law was George Wingfield. "The Western
Federation of Miners and the I.W.W. are now eliminated from the camp
of Goldfield," he wrote in 1911 in response to a query from White, "and
always will be as long as I am identified with it."[50] The great boom was
already slackening as he wrote. Dance halls closed, crime decreased, the
windows of vacant cabins, stripped of their glass panes, seemed to stare
with blind eyes across the empty ground where squatters had fought for
tent space only four years before. The young men who had sung and
marched four abreast under the red banner and dreamed of the Revolution in Our Time moved on to other camps and other battlegrounds, and
Goldfield became a quieter and duller place. All was so calm, so well
under control, that Wingfield found it entirely safe to leave Goldfield
Con in the hands of underlings and move to Reno and his future public
career as a banker and entrepreneur. In his private career as behind-the-
scenes politician, he would rule Nevada's bipartisan political machine
during the twenties, securing a useful place in the U.S. Senate for his
protege, Tasker Oddie, and would finally die on Christmas Day in 1959
in honored old age.

By then the city that had transformed him from a small-time gambler to a millionaire had been a virtual ghost town for years. Large-scale mining had ceased when the mill closed in 1919. After the twenties, when a flash flood roared down from the Malapai and a fire believed to have started in a moonshiner's still raged through the streets, only a small vestige survived of what had once been a city of thousands.

With the downfall of the WFM and the IWW in Goldfield, Nevada's radical unions suffered a mortal blow. WFM organizer Charles Tanner was compelled to report in 1910 that Wingfield's plans to drive the union out of the state were well along the road to success: "In all of the small camps where this man has interests, the locals seem to be practically lifeless."[51] A major strike in the White Pine copper district in 1912, promptly smashed by Governor Oddie, was primarily an echo of events in Bingham Canyon, Utah. Aside from brief flurries of activity in Tonopah in 1914 and 1919 and an abortive attempt at resurgence during the construction of Hoover Dam, the IWW was finished in Nevada. Henceforth these unions' major battles were to be fought in other states. Nevada was not to serve as organizational center and source of sustenance to the radical unions, nor was a strong amalgamated WFM-IWW in Goldfield to act as a unifying force to help cement the breach between the two warring unions at the national level.

In the same way, the great expectations that the Socialists had once attached to Nevada evaporated. Although Goldfield and Tonopah continued to contribute a substantial portion of the Socialist vote, the center of Nevada Socialism shifted away from Goldfield, where Nevada's first state Socialist convention had been held in 1906, to the Reno-Sparks area, stronghold of the railroad brotherhoods, craft unions, and trades alliances. At the same time, following the destruction of the Goldfield unions, the leadership of the Nevada Socialist party passed from flaming revolutionaries such as 1906 congressional candidate Harry Jardine to more conservative, middle-class figures such as Grant Miller, a change that entirely altered the character of the state party. Under Miller's leadership, Nevada Socialism crested at nearly 30 percent of the senatorial vote in 1916, before sinking to a minuscule proportion after the war years, when American Socialism as a whole was experiencing a similar decline. One can only speculate whether a different outcome in Goldfield would have brought Socialists to high office in Nevada, as once seemed within the realm of possibility, and transformed a state the Silver party and massive population growth had already severed from its old political moorings into a Socialist bastion. But the important role the railroad unions played in Nevada Socialism, coupled with the revolutionary Socialists' success in sharply increasing the Socialist vote in such localities as the West Virginia mining regions, suggests that the continued presence and political activity of the Goldfield unions might well have engendered the relatively small increment needed to raise an already sizable Socialist vote to winning levels.[52] In politics, no less than in union affairs, George Wingfield cast a long shadow.

On the national level, the WFM and the IWW went their separate ways, following the Goldfield rout. The WFM, according to the IWW's official historian, "rapidly grew tame" and feared to confront employers after the split with the IWW; it reentered the AFL in 1911, later changing its name to the International Mine, Mill and Smelter Workers, and turned steadily "more innocuous" until the labor revival that attended the Great Depression.[53] No one could accuse the IWW of tameness, but after the sectarian fashion of zealotry, it became ever more fractionated. At the 1908 convention the organization fissured once more as the syndicalists won control, led by St. John and Haywood. Debs stood aside from the quarrel, and DeLeon and his followers abandoned the One Big Union with some parting shots at their opponents as a "bummery" and "slum proletarians." Still more leaders were to be expelled in future years during recurrent fits of schism and apostasy. Historian Sidney Lens believes the IWW organized at least a million workers in its prime and won its demands in a sizable majority of strikes, including the resounding victories at McKees Rocks in 1909 and the Lawrence textile strike in 1912. Yet the union failed to translate these moments of glory into a strong, permanent organization holding signed agreements with employers.[54]

The swollen patriotism of World War I and the accompanying panic over disloyalty lent new impetus to the antagonism many Americans had long felt toward the union's revolutionary doctrine. Many feared that the IWW intended to hinder the war effort, and the organization became the primary target for antiradicalism. On September 5, 1917, agents from the Department of Justice raided IWW units throughout America. Haywood counseled nonresistance; he estimated that two thousand Wobblies were in jail by February. He himself was imprisoned and charged with conspiring to resist the draft and to cause military insubordination, among a long list of subversive acts. In 1918 all the Chicago IWW defendants, including Haywood, were convicted in 101 separate cases. Patrick Renshaw finds the trials a "monumental disaster" for the IWW, which lost its entire leadership in a single stroke.[55]

They were to lose far more when Haywood jumped bail and fled to the Soviet Union in March 1921, after he had given up all hope that the outcome of his attorney's appeal to the U.S. Supreme Court would result in overturning the lower court decision. His flight came as a terrible shock to the union rank and file, but some of the faithful would have found justification in his illness, in the long sentence before him, and in the refusal of eight of the other union leaders to return to Leavenworth. It was a time darkened by the recent lynchings of two more IWW martyrs, Frank Little and Wesley Everett, and darkened, too, by the earlier defection of St. John from union organizing to a new career (or an old temptation) prospecting for gold in New Mexico. And now Haywood. He had changed over the years, from the handsome, imposing young figure who stood tall above the crowd at the birth of the union in 1905 and pounded the convention to order with a board in place of a gavel, to a heavy-faced and embittered old man with a suspicious frown. But he was their leader still, from the very beginning. Did every living hero prove false and only the dead stay true?

Yet another schism, this time between Communist and anti-Communist factions at the 1924 convention, nearly destroyed the IWW, although a small and aging group of diehards remained dedicated to it for years.[56] In time their enemies ceased to find them worth assailing. No longer was the dream contagious, no young "John Brown" wrote angry poems anymore, and the voices that sang the old songs turned tremulous and cracked.

It is said that for years before the burning of the city, the gashes from the miners' hobnailed boots could be seen in Goldfield's saloons on the bars where they had danced on the August night in 1907 when Big Bill Haywood was set free. It was a time when hope raced through the streets with the crazed gallop of a wild horse. They could feel the current of working-class power in the air that night, coursing in like a fresh wind from the north, could believe they saw the dawn of the new age cracking the dark skies. They had fought a long, hard way, but most of it still lay ahead of them then—the jailings, the lynchings, the bloody persecutions, the victories that evaporated, the defeats that inexorably diminished them, the schisms, the betrayals, the inescapable knowledge that the Revolution in Our Time was only a mirage. The year that Morrie Preston died—1924—was the year that the IWW shattered to bits in a final burst of explosive fission. We know now that the men who stamped and whirled on top of the bars in jubilation that night had danced too soon.

NOTES

CHAPTER II: THE GOLDEN AGE

1. Morrie Rockwood Preston, December 1908 pardon application, Nevada Department of Prisons Records, Inmate file 1124 (hereafter cited as Inmate file 1124), in the Nevada State Division of Archives and Records in Carson City (hereafter Nevada Archives), certificate of birth filed Oct. 2, 1882, Shelby County Health Department Vital Records Division, Tennessee.

2. Helen Gomes, telephone interviews, Feb. 25, Apr. 16, 1984.

3. Louis R. Lebel, interview, Apr. 30, 1984.

4. Louis Lebel interview; Esther Lebel, telephone interviews, Feb. 24, Mar. 27, 1982. Lillian Burton is listed in the U.S. census for California, 1900, and in various Los Angeles city directories.

5. See the letters of George C. Pitzer, Dec. 8, 1908: O. B. Zahn and Annie Zahn, Dec. 8, 1908; William B. Harrison, Dec. 2, 1908; M. D. Hall and Lora Hall, Dec. 9, 1908, in Preston's 1908 pardon application, Inmate file 1124. Further information on the Preston family appears in Little Rock city directories, in turn-of-the-century Los Angeles city directories, in the records of Shelby County, Tennessee, and in the 1900 U.S. decennial census for Arkansas. Extensive research over a long period leaves certain facets of Preston's family background still unresolved. For example, we have not yet been able to determine when and where Kate Preston died.

6. Esther and Louis Lebel interviews.

7. On early Goldfield, see Carl B. Glasscock, *Gold in Them Hills* (New York: Grossett & Dunlap, 1932).

8. Wallace Stegner, *Joe Hill* (New York: Doubleday & Company, 1969), 11, 13. Also see Paul F. Brissenden, *The I.W.W.: A Study of American Syndicalism*, Columbia University Studies in History, Economics and Public Law, no. 83 (New York: Columbia University Press, 1919), 41–42, 191, and Melvyn Dubofsky, *We Shall Be All: A History of the Industrial Workers of the World* (Chicago: Quadrangle Books, 1969), ch. 7.

9. Dubofsky, *We Shall Be All*, ch. 5; Sidney Lens, *The Labor Wars: From the Molly Maguires to the Sitdowns* (New York: Doubleday & Company, 1973), 135; and Mark Wyman, *Hard-Rock Epic: Western Miners and the Industrial Revolution, 1860–1910* (Berkeley: University of California Press, 1979), 231.

10. Guy L. Rocha, "Radical Labor Struggles in the Tonopah-Goldfield Mining District, 1901–1922," *Nevada Historical Society Quarterly* 20 (Spring 1977): 6–7. The founding date of the Goldfield WFM is on the seal of Local No. 220. Also see *The Industrial Worker*, Aug. 27, 1910. Brissenden, *The I.W.W.*, 83–110; *Industrial Union Bulletin* (hereafter abbreviated *IUB*), Apr. 6 and Sept. 14, 1907; Philip S. Foner, *History of the Labor Movement in the United States*

(New York: International Publishers, 1947–65), 4:94–95; and Russell R. Elliott, "Labor Troubles in the Mining Camp at Goldfield, Nevada, 1906–1908," *Pacific Historical Review* 19 (1950): 369–84.

11. *Engineering and Mining Journal* 83 (May 25, 1907): 1012, and 84 (Dec. 14, 1907): 1128; *Miners' Magazine* 7 (May 24, 1906): 3; Rocha, "Radical Labor Struggles," 6–8; Joseph R. Conlin, "Goldfield High-Grade," *American West* 20 (May-June 1983), 38–44; and Sally S. Zanjani, "The Mike Smith Case: A Note on High Grading in Goldfield, Nevada, 1910," *Labor History* 24 (Fall 1983): 580–87.

12. Rocha, "Radical Labor Struggles," 6–8.

13. Ibid., 8–9; also see *IUB*, Apr. 6, 1907, and the Tonopah IWW Local No. 325 Records at Special Collections, University of Nevada Library, Reno.

14. Rocha, "Radical Labor Struggles," 8–9; on Branson, see Wells Drury, "Journalism," in *The History of Nevada*, ed. Sam P. Davis (Los Angeles: Elms Publishing Co., 1913), 1:494–95.

15. Nevada Department of Prisons Records, Inmate file 1131—Joseph William Smith, Nevada Archives (hereafter cited as Inmate file 1131); Official Records of Goldfield Precinct No. 1, Oct. 11, 1906, also in the Archives; *Goldfield Sun*, Sept. 6 and 8, 1906; and *Tonopah Sun*, May 10, 1907.

16. Rocha, "Radical Labor Struggles," 3. Also see Laura A. White, "History of the Labor Struggles in Goldfield, Nevada" (master's thesis, University of Nebraska, 1912), 28–29, 30–33; Glasscock, *Gold in Them Hills*, 241–45; *IUB*, Apr. 6, 1907; *Miners' Magazine* 7 (Mar. 8, 1906): 6–7, and 8 (Feb. 14, 1907): 5; Charles McKinnon affidavit, The Goldfield Consolidated Mines Company v. Goldfield Miners' Union No. 220 et al., United States Circuit Court, Nevada (1908), 6.

17. Sally S. Zanjani and Guy L. Rocha, "A Heart for Any Fate: Vincent St. John in Goldfield," *Nevada Historical Society Quarterly* 27 (Summer 1984): 77.

18. *Miners' Magazine* 7 (Apr. 19, 1906): 3; also see the Mar. 29 issue, 9 and 13.

19. *Miners' Magazine* 7 (Sept. 27, 1906): 6–7, and (Sept. 6, 1906): 3; on Stevens, also see John Koontz, *Political History of Nevada*, 5th ed. (Carson City: State Printing Office, 1965), 126.

20. *Miners' Magazine* 7 (Nov. 8, 1906): 8; on the schism, also see Fred W. Thompson and Patrick Murfin, *The I.W.W.: Its First Seventy Years, 1905–1975* (Chicago: Industrial Workers of the World, 1976), 27, and Patrick Renshaw, *The Wobblies* (New York: Doubleday & Company, 1967), 88–95.

21. Vincent St. John, "Shall the Working Class Be Crushed?" *Miners' Magazine* 7 (May 17, 1906): 8; also see White, "Labor Struggles in Goldfield," 41.

22. *Miners' Magazine* 8 (Mar. 21, 1907): 1.

23. Rocha, "Radical Labor Struggles," 4, 9–10.

24. Lens, for example, finds the IWW effort in Goldfield brilliant; see Lens, *The Labor Wars*, 155–56. On the leasing phase, see *Mining and Scientific Press* 94 (May 4, 1907): 548. Also see the *Goldfield Review*, Mar. 9, 1907.

25. On Wingfield's background, see Sally S. Zanjani, *The Unspiked Rail: Memoir of a Nevada Rebel* (Reno: University of Nevada Press, 1981), 101–3, and Barbara C. Thornton, "George Wingfield in Nevada from 1896 to 1932" (master's thesis, University of Nevada, Reno, 1967), 1–16.

26. *Goldfield Chronicle*, Dec. 3, 1907, White, "Labor Struggles in Goldfield," 43, and C. O. Lovell to Sparks, Nov. 28, 1907, John Sparks Executive Records, Nevada Archives.

27. White, "Labor Struggles in Goldfield," 46 n. 5. On Wingfield and on the gunmen, also see Zanjani, *The Unspiked Rail*, chs. 7–8, and the *Carson City Daily Appeal*, May 28, 1920.

28. On the politics of the period, see Russell R. Elliott, *History of Nevada* (Lincoln: University of Nebraska Press, 1973); Mary E. Glass, *Silver and Politics in Nevada* (Reno: University of Nevada Press, 1969); and Sally S. Zanjani, "A Theory of Critical Realignment: The Nevada Example, 1892–1908," *Pacific Historical Review* 48 (1979): 259–80.

29. Zanjani, "A Theory of Critical Realignment," and Zanjani, *The Unspiked Rail*, 187. On the speculations of union leaders, note the story of their arrest (ch. 3), Tregonning's alternate career

(ch. 6), St. John's capitalist phase, and the recurring allegations concerning speculative activities by which union men invariably attempted to discredit their union opponents.

30. Eugene V. Debs, *Debs: His Life, Writings and Speeches* (Chicago: Charles H. Kerr & Company Co-operative, 1908), 372; on Nevada elections, see Koontz, *Political History of Nevada*, 187.

31. Wilbur S. Shepperson, *Retreat to Nevada: A Socialist Colony of World War I* (Reno: University of Nevada Press, 1966), 51–57; Koontz, *Political History of Nevada*, 188; James Weinstein, *Ambiguous Legacy: The Left in American Politics* (New York: New Viewpoints, 1975), 7.

32. Debs, *Debs*, 225.

33. *Goldfield Daily Tribune* (hereafter abbreviated *GDT*), Jan. 21, 1907.

34. Ibid.

CHAPTER III: THE TRIAL BEGINS

1. Vincent St. John, "Review of the Facts in the Situation at Goldfield," *IUB*, Apr. 26, 1907. All newspaper references are for the year 1907 unless otherwise noted. Also see the *Tonopah Sun* (hereafter abbreviated *TS*), Mar. 12 and 13. Although Branson, Preston, and Peter Somers (later Goldfield district judge), with their varying attitudes to Davis, all believed that Davis led the lynch party, one informant told Laura White that he had in fact halted the lynching. See White, "Labor Struggles in Goldfield," 57 n. 3, and Morrie R. Preston, "The Smith-Preston Case," pamphlet (Reno: Journal Press, 1915), 22.

2. Vernon H. Jensen, *Heritage of Conflict* (Ithaca: Cornell University Press, 1950), 78–87.

3. *TS*, Mar. 29, Apr. 8, and Apr. 10, and *GDT*, Apr. 1 and 22.

4. Preston, "The Smith-Preston Case" (1915), 10–11.

5. Ibid.; *TS*, May 10. On the Haywood trial, see Joseph R. Conlin, *Big Bill Haywood and the Radical Union Movement* (Syracuse: Syracuse University Press, 1969), 57, and Irving Stone, *Clarence Darrow for the Defense* (New York: Doubleday & Company, 1941), 102–4, 245–46.

6. *GDT*, Apr. 22.

7. White, "Labor Struggles in Goldfield," 89; also see *GDT*, Apr. 22.

8. *TS*, Mar. 30; also see the *Carson City Daily Appeal*, Mar. 14, and *GDT*, Apr. 22.

9. White, "Labor Struggles in Goldfield," 67, 69, 89. Also see *Mining and Scientific Press* 94 (1907): 358, and the *Carson City Daily Appeal*, Mar. 14.

10. *TS*, Mar. 18–19. Also see the *Reno Evening Gazette*, Mar. 13.

11. *TS*, Mar. 20.

12. *TS*, Mar. 25 and 26; also see the Mar. 20 issue. On attitudes to anarchism, see Richard H. Frost, *The Mooney Case* (Stanford: Stanford University Press, 1968), 263–64; on the "trial by press" similar to Preston's which Mooney underwent, see Curt Gentry, *Frame-up: The Incredible Case of Tom Mooney and Warren Billings* (New York: W. W. Norton & Company, Inc., 1967), 163.

13. *TS*, Apr. 3; also see the Mar. 28 issue and Rocha, "Radical Labor Struggles," 3–15; on St. John, also see Conlin, "Goldfield High-Grade," 65.

14. *GDT*, Apr. 2–3.

15. *TS*, Mar. 30.

16. *GDT*, Apr. 9 and 11; *TS*, Apr. 9; Rocha, "Radical Labor Struggles," 14; White, "Labor Struggles in Goldfield," 80.

17. *Carson City Daily Appeal*, Apr. 10.

18. *TS*, Apr. 12, 17–18, and 22; *GDT*, Apr. 18–19 and 22; *Mining and Scientific Press* 94 (1907): 548, 610; Rocha, "Radical Labor Struggles," 14–15; White, "Labor Struggles in Goldfield," 41–42, 79.

19. Booth M. Malone, "Pen Picture of Hawthorne, Poor Thing," *GDT*, May 5; on Hawthorne, also see Stanley W. Paher, *Nevada Ghost Towns and Mining Camps* (Berkeley: Howell-North Books, 1970), 432–35.

20. *TS*, Apr. 29, and *GDT*, Apr. 19.

21. On Nevada's partisan alignments in this period, see Zanjani, "A Theory of Critical Realignment"; on use of corporation counsel in union cases, see Frost, *The Mooney Case*, 24–25; on Malone and the WFM, see *Miners' Magazine* 7 (Aug. 9, 1906): 4; on use of special counsel in a Goldfield tax assessment case, see the *Goldfield Chronicle*, Sept. 21.

22. White, "Labor Struggles in Goldfield," 86; *GDT*, Apr. 19; Emma F. Langdon, *The Cripple Creek Strike: A History of Industrial Wars in Colorado* (New York: Arno Press & The New York Times, 1969), 101, 178–81; James D. Horan and Howard Swiggett, *The Pinkerton Story* (New York: G. P. Putnam's Sons, 1951), 304–5; George G. Suggs, Jr., *Colorado's War on Militant Unionism* (Detroit: Wayne State University Press, 1972), 101, 116, 189; *Denver Times*, Bench and Bar edition, following the Feb. 18, 1899 issue, 8.

23. *Tonopah Daily Bonanza*, Apr. 15, 1916; *Goldfield Chronicle*, Nov. 14.

24. Boyd Moore, *Persons in the Foreground* (n.p., 1915), unpaged; on Langan's district and elections, see Koontz, *Political History of Nevada*, 125, 188; on Langan and the WFM, see *Miners' Magazine* 7 (Oct. 18, 1906): 4.

25. *GDT*, Apr. 20; *TS*, Apr. 27.

26. Morrie R. Preston, "The Smith-Preston Case" (International Union of Mine, Mill & Smelter Workers, n.d.), 8–9. This second pamphlet, preserved in Inmate file 1124, is different from the 1915 pamphlet and may be tentatively dated around 1917 because it bears the imprint of the International Union of Mine, Mill & Smelter Workers, the new name assumed by the WFM in July 1916, at their twenty-second convention; this pamphlet will henceforth be cited with the 1917 date to distinguish it from the earlier pamphlet of the same title. Also see Jensen, *Heritage of Conflict*, 377.

27. *GDT*, Apr. 21–22, 24, and 26.

28. *TS*, Apr. 24; also see the Apr. 6 issue and *GDT*, Apr. 24. According to the report in the *Sun*, Sexton was arrested in a beer hall.

29. *GDT*, Apr. 24 and 26; *TS*, Apr. 24.

30. William D. Haywood, *Bill Haywood's Book* (New York: International Publishers, 1969), 209; also see Hangs's statement to White, in White, "Labor Struggles in Goldfield," 86, and *GDT*, Apr. 22.

31. *GDT*, Apr. 24.

32. U.S. decennial census for Nevada, 1880; *Reno Evening Gazette*, July 22, 1905; Zanjani, *The Unspiked Rail*, 132–38.

33. *GDT*, Apr. 24.

CHAPTER IV: WITNESSES FOR THE PROSECUTION

1. Preston and Smith v. State, O. N. Hilton brief, Nevada Supreme Court, 1907, 34–35. Also see State v. Preston and Smith, Transcript of witnesses' testimony (hereafter cited as Transcript), First Judicial District of Nevada, 1907, 2–27. Both are in the Nevada Archives.

2. Transcript, 2–27.

3. Ibid., 28–36.

4. Ibid., 37–43.

5. Ibid., 44–52.

6. *GDT*, Apr. 24; *TS*, Apr. 25.

7. Ibid.

8. *Miners' Magazine* 7 (Apr. 13, 1911): 9; Transcript, 53–98.

9. *GDT,* Apr. 26; Transcript, 53–98.
10. Transcript, 99–115.
11. Ibid., 116–32. On Davis's background, see Zanjani, *The Unspiked Rail,* 100–103, 149, and David H. Grover, *Diamondfield Jack: A Study in Frontier Justice* (Reno: University of Nevada Press, 1968). A curious twist on the interlocking destinies of the principal figures in the labor trials of 1907 was the circumstance that Idaho's governor at the time of Davis's conviction was Steunenberg, for whose assassination Haywood was about to stand trial. According to Irving Stone, Steunenberg was offered a $20,000 bribe and a seat in the U.S. Senate to pardon Davis; Steunenberg, incensed by this proposal, smashed his fist down so hard on the table in front of him that he cracked its marble top. The Davis pardon would be issued by a subsequent governor. See Stone, *Clarence Darrow for the Defense,* 194.
12. Transcript, 133–48.
13. Ibid., 149–94.
14. Ibid., 195–212.
15. Ibid., 213–18.

CHAPTER V: WHOSE CONSPIRACY?

1. *TS,* Apr. 27.
2. *GDT,* Apr. 24; *TS,* Apr. 1.
3. Transcript, 219–23.
4. Ibid., 223–46.
5. Ibid., 247–66.
6. Stone, *Clarence Darrow for the Defense,* 217.
7. Transcript, 267–76, 423–36.
8. Ibid., 277–90, 352–62.
9. Ibid., 291–303.
10. Public letter dated Jan. 27, 1907, *Miners' Magazine* 8 (Feb. 14, 1907): 12–13.
11. Sexton had also served on the union committee that negotiated the April labor settlement; Transcript, 271–76.
12. Transcript, 312–19.
13. Ibid., 320–29.
14. Ibid., 330–40.
15. *GDT,* Apr. 22.
16. *GDT,* Apr. 22–24.
17. Transcript, 341–52.
18. Ibid., 363–68; *GDT,* Apr. 28; *TS,* Apr. 30.
19. Transcript, 368–79.
20. Ibid., 379–418, 419–23.
21. Stone, *Clarence Darrow for the Defense,* 232.

CHAPTER VI: PRESTON TAKES THE STAND

1. Transcript, 437–67; *GDT,* Apr. 28; *TS,* Apr. 30; Hilton appeal brief, 69–70; Preston's 1913 pardon application, in Inmate file 1124; and Preston, "The Smith-Preston Case" (1917?), 7, 10. Preston later wrote that he had moved toward Silva in order to get inside the railing at the edge of the sidewalk and reach the corner where he could step off, the sidewalk being considerably above street level at that point; but none of this emerged in his testimony, and the possibility that he may have unintentionally alarmed Silva by his forward movement with gun in hand was never explored in court. On courtroom histrionics in another Goldfield murder trial, see Zanjani, *The Unspiked Rail,* 146–47.

2. Allen Jarvis deposition, May 24, 1907, Preston and Smith v. State, Nevada Supreme Court, 1908, Nevada Archives; on Skinner's indisposition, see Transcript, 468–72.

3. *GDT*, May 2.

4. Ibid., May 7; *TS*, May 6–7; *Carson City News*, May 9.

5. *TS*, May 6.

6. *GDT*, May 7.

7. Stone, *Clarence Darrow for the Defense*, 206.

8. *GDT*, May 7.

9. *Miners' Magazine* 8 (June 6, 1907): 14.

10. Transcript, 472–78; *TS*, May 7; Preston, "The Smith-Preston Case" (1915), 22.

11. Louis Nizer, *My Life in Court* (New York: Pyramid Books, 1963), 273; Transcript, 478–81.

12. Transcript, 481–83.

13. Ibid., 495–509.

14. *TS*, Apr. 15.

15. Ibid., Apr. 18; also see the Apr. 15 issue and *GDT* of the same date.

16. *GDT*, Apr. 18.

17. Transcript, 510–16.

18. Ibid., 516–21, 526–31.

19. Ibid., 521–25.

20. Ibid., 532–40.

CHAPTER VII: THE VERDICT

1. Transcript, 541–42. *TS*, Apr. 30.

2. Transcript, 550–53.

3. Ibid., 554–58.

4. Ibid., 559–77. Preston, "The Smith-Preston Case" (1917?), 5.

5. *TS*, May 9.

6. Ibid.; Preston, "The Smith-Preston Case" (1917?), 7.

7. Hilton appeal brief, 63.

8. The appeal brief recounts that instructions were not "allowed or settled" until after Bowler's address, though some portions may have been read at earlier points; a press report indicates that Bowler made his objections to the prosecution's requested instructions in advance of his address. *TS*, May 9; Appeal brief, 77; Hilton appeal brief, 63; Preston, "The Smith-Preston Case" (1915), 28–29.

9. Conlin, *Big Bill Haywood*, 57; on Bowler's summation, see *TS*, May 9.

10. *TS*, May 9.

11. Ibid.

12. Ibid.; also see Preston, "The Smith-Preston Case" (1915), 27.

13. *TS*, May 9.

14. Preston, "The Smith-Preston Case" (1915), 29. On the decline in stocks, see the *Carson City Daily Appeal*, May 23.

15. Preston, "The Smith-Preston Case" (1915), 27, 29; *TS*, May 9; Appeal brief, 76.

16. Instructions, State v. Preston and Smith, Nevada Archives, 48–49; Appeal brief, 32, 49–50. It will be noted that these instructions diverged from the abstract and formal mode that researchers have observed in California. See Lawrence M. Friedman and Robert V. Percival, *The Roots of Justice: Crime and Punishment in Alameda County, California 1870–1910* (Chapel Hill: University of North Carolina Press, 1981), 186–88; for contrast, see the remarks of Judge Webster Thayer in the Sacco-Vanzetti case, in Francis Russell, *Tragedy in Dedham* (New York: McGraw-Hill Book Company, 1971), 205–11. On the role of instructions, see Appeal brief, 32.

17. Instructions, 55, 57; Appeal brief, 34–35, 57.

18. Instructions, 58, 62–65; Hilton appeal brief, 40–41.

19. Instructions, 72; Appeal brief, 55–58.

20. Appeal brief, 59–60.

21. Ibid., 64–65; also see 60.

22. Instructions, 86–106; Appeal brief, 67–72; Hilton appeal brief, 49–52, 56–58.

23. *TS*, May 10; also see the San Francisco *Call*, May 4 and 10.

24. Ibid.; on the relation between the instructions and Smith's conviction for manslaughter, see Hilton appeal brief, 26; on Goldfield's proclivity for the hung jury, see Zanjani, *The Unspiked Rail*, 131; on Bettles, see the Jarvis deposition. Jarvis's confusion was by no means unusual; a recent study has suggested that the average juror understands only half of the judge's instructions, *New York Times*, June 7, 1981.

25. *TS*, May 10.

26. On frontier homicide convictions, see Roger D. McGrath, *Gunfighters, Highwaymen, and Vigilantes: Violence on the Frontier* (Berkeley: University of California Press, 1984), esp. 256–57; Goldfield homicide convictions were traced through the reports of the state prison warden in the Appendixes to the journals of the Nevada senate and assembly; the occasion when the district attorney failed to appear in court is reported in the *Goldfield Review*, Aug. 3, 1905.

27. *IUB*, June 8.

28. Stegner, *Joe Hill*, 314–15; also see George F. Lewis and D. F. Stacklebeck, eds., *Bench and Bar of Colorado* (Denver: Bench and Bar Publishing Company, 1977), 125.

29. *TS*, May 25; Zanjani and Rocha, "A Heart for Any Fate," 87.

30. *GDT*, May 25.

31. Ibid., May 26. The St. John deposition, apparently a garbled account of a social gathering on May 14, argued that a fair trial before Judge Langan was impossible because he had been present at a meeting shortly after Silva's death at which the threatening letter was discussed and the mine owners conspired to indict the union leaders. On Muller's commission, see *GDT*, June 23.

32. *GDT*, May 28. Also see *TS*, May 27, and Preston, "The Smith-Preston Case" (1917?), 18. For a typical sermon from the bench, see Judge Langan's remarks to convicted murderer J. C. Schwick, reported in the *Goldfield Chronicle*, Nov. 1.

CHAPTER VIII: BURNT OFFERINGS

1. St. John to Smith, June 9, 1907, Inmate file 1131. On the admission of the union leaders to bail, see *Miners' Magazine* 8 (June 6, 1907): 3, and *GDT*, May 29.

2. Smith to St. John, June 12, 1907, Inmate file 1131. Since these letters are typed copies of the originals, some errors in grammar, spelling, and punctuation may be those of the copyist.

3. *Miners' Magazine* 8 (June 20, 1907): 5.

4. *Miners' Magazine* 8 (May 30, 1907): 4; (June 6, 1907): 14; (June 20, 1907): 15; (Sept. 5, 1907): 3; 9 (Feb. 20, 1908): 9; *IUB*, Aug. 31, 1907; *Goldfield Review*, Feb. 15, 1908.

5. Rocha, "Radical Labor Struggles," 15; *GDT*, Sept. 8; McKinnon affidavit, 15–16.

6. *IUB*, Sept. 14.

7. *Miners' Magazine* 8 (Nov. 28, 1907): 14.

8. *Miners' Magazine* 8 (Dec. 26, 1907): 7; also see *IUB*, Nov. 16.

9. Preston, "The Smith-Preston Case" (1915), 5.

10. Haywood, *Bill Haywood's Book*, 25–26.

11. *Goldfield Chronicle*, Nov. 6; also see the Nov. 5 issue and *GDT*, Nov. 6 and 7.

12. *GDT*, Nov. 6 and 7, and May 23, 1908; *IUB*, Nov. 16; Zanjani and Rocha, "A Heart for Any Fate," 88–89. Mullaney later returned to Nevada, where he died in Reno on November 15, 1931, *REG*, Nov. 16, 1931.

13. *GDT*, Nov. 27; McKinnon affidavit, 17–24; for a typical miner's view of scrip, see Les Cupp to Governor Denver Dickerson, Dec. 21, 1908, Dickerson Executive Records, Nevada Archives.

14. *Goldfield Review*, July 13 and Dec. 7; Vice apparently remained in Goldfield.

15. *Goldfield Chronicle*, Dec. 3; *Miners' Magazine* 8 (Dec. 12, 1907): 7. The mine owners' rationale may have been gleaned from a state detective's report submitted to Governor Sparks; it falsely stated that the miners had been denied a referendum vote and that at least 90 percent of them wanted to continue working. See C. O. Lovell to Sparks, Nov. 28, 1907, Sparks Executive Records.

16. *Goldfield Chronicle*, Dec. 10; on Sparks's 1906 campaign, see Zanjani, *The Unspiked Rail*, 94.

17. *Goldfield Chronicle*, Dec. 9.

18. Report of the Roosevelt Commission, 60th Cong., 1st sess., House Exec. Doc. 607, 4–5, 21–22; Russell R. Elliott, *Radical Labor in the Nevada Mining Booms 1900–1920* (Reno: University of Nevada Press, 1963), 131; *GDT*, Dec. 10; *IUB*, Dec. 28; "The Goldfield Situation," *The Outlook*, Dec. 21, 838–39.

19. House Exec. Doc. 607, 8–9, also 5 and 16. Also see "The Situation at Goldfield," *Engineering and Mining Journal* 84 (Dec. 28, 1907): 1177; Jensen, *Heritage of Conflict*, 232; and *Goldfield Chronicle*, Dec. 16.

20. "Troops to Leave Goldfield," *Engineering and Mining Journal* 84 (Dec. 28, 1907): 1227, and "The Nevada State Police," in the Feb. 18, 1908, issue of the same journal, 376; House Exec. Doc. 607, 8–9; Nevada Legislature, *Statutes* (special session, 1908), 21; *IUB*, Feb. 15, 1908; *GDT*, Mar. 7, 1908.

21. *GDT*, Dec. 27–28, and Mar. 7, 1908; *TS*, Mar. 7 and 11, 1908; *Goldfield Chronicle*, Dec. 27.

22. Also see the *IUB* account of the shooting, May 4.

23. *Miners' Magazine* 8 (Dec. 12, 1907): 5; for the analyses of several historians, see White, "Labor Struggles in Goldfield," 187, Jensen, *Heritage of Conflict*, 235, and Wyman, *Hard-Rock Epic*, 239.

24. In October the union did pass a resolution urging support by the national WFM for the St. John faction of the national IWW, but the enactment of a parallel resolution by the WFM in Tonopah, where labor disputes did not occur in this period, indicates that the resolution was not an important factor in the deterioration of labor relations, Thompson and Murfin, *The I.W.W.*, 33. Both White and the press gave much weight to a statement at the June WFM convention by St. John, who said that union members were ignoring the settlement. However, St. John may merely have been putting the best possible face on a humiliating defeat. Evidence is lacking that the union had ignored the sympathetic boycott provision, the two-thirds strike provision, or any other save the one provision favorable to them—jurisdiction. Here they had verbally agreed to forgo jurisdiction over some jobs in order to accommodate the mine owners but later backtracked somewhat from this position. See White, "Labor Struggles in Goldfield," 92–93, and the *Carson City Daily Appeal*, June 22. On the views of management in the 1906 strike, see unsigned letter from Goldfield to George Nixon, Dec. 24, 1906, photocopy in possession of Guy Rocha.

25. "Message of Governor Sparks to the 1907 Legislature," 12–13; *Journal of the Senate, 1907*, 199, 205–6, 209–10; *Journal of the Assembly, 1907*, 206. The bill provided that in the event the governor should remove a sheriff or police official, the state warden would take charge of the office; see the *Carson City News*, Mar. 15.

26. Election data 1902–12 is from Koontz, *Political History of Nevada*, 187–90; referendum turnout was calculated as a percentage of the presidential vote except in nonpresidential elections, when the gubernatorial vote was utilized.

27. Fred G. Clough to Dickerson, Dec. 24, 1909, Inmate file 1124. On the social polarization process in general, see Melvyn Dubofsky, "The Origins of Western Working Class Radicalism,

1890–1905," *Labor History* 7 (Spring 1966): 131–54. On newspaper editorials, see for example the *Goldfield Chronicle,* Dec. 16.

28. Appeal brief and Hilton appeal brief.

29. Zanjani, *The Unspiked Rail,* 144–45.

30. Preston, "The Smith-Preston Case" (1915), 9.

31. On Sweeney's role in the Democratic senatorial primary, see Koontz, *Political History of Nevada,* 207, and on his gubernatorial ambitions, see the *Nevada State Journal,* Aug. 31, 1906; on the backgrounds of the justices, see Davis, *The History of Nevada,* 2:1188–90, 1069–70, 1210–11.

32. White, "Labor Struggles in Goldfield," 85, 120. Socialists might have considered this court a capitalist one in a literal sense: Judge Sweeney had extensive business interests in Goldfield and other mining camps, and Judge Talbot had invested in mining claims in Pioche; see the *Carson City Daily Appeal,* May 10 and 29.

33. State v. M. R. Preston and Joseph Smith, *Nevada Reports* 30 (1909): 301–10.

34. Preston, "The Smith-Preston Case" (1917?), 19.

CHAPTER IX: NOTHING DOING

1. Branson, v. I.W.W., *Nevada Reports* 30 (1909): 270–300.

2. Preston, "The Smith-Preston Case" (1917?), 30.

3. Phillip I. Earl and Guy L. Rocha, "Nevada Convict Was a Presidential Candidate," *Nevada Appeal,* Nov. 9, 1980; Sally Zanjani and Guy L. Rocha, "Nevada's Convict Candidate," *The Nevadan* 23 (Sept. 30, 1984): 6L–7L; *San Francisco Call,* July 7, 1908, July 8, 1908, and July 9, 1908; and *Miners' Magazine* 9 (July 30, 1908): 7. Preston's candidacy apparently evoked scant enthusiasm from his fellow convicts; on Nov. 7, 1908, the *Reno Evening Gazette* reported that a straw poll at the state prison recorded 39 votes for William J. Bryan, 20 for William H. Taft, 19 for Eugene V. Debs, and only 3 for Preston.

4. Supreme court opinion on Preston and Smith petition for rehearing, Sept. 30, 1908, Nevada Archives.

5. Jensen, *Heritage of Conflict,* 84–87; Clough to Dickerson, Dec. 24, 1909, Inmate file 1124, and the petitions in the same file.

6. *Reno Evening Gazette,* Dec. 8, 1908. On Moyer's visit, see the *Tonopah Daily Bonanza,* Dec. 16, 1908.

7. Hilton to Swallow, Dec. 23, 1908, Inmate file 1124; also see Dickerson to Hilton, Dec. 14, 1908.

8. Nevada State Prison, *Reports of the Warden,* 1891–1892 to 1955–1956, see report for 1909–1910, 1; *Carson City News,* Feb. 20 and Sept. 19, 1913. Some prisoners also worked at the prison farm after its acquisition in 1910, and some briefly served on road construction crews between 1911 and 1913.

9. Huffaker to Board of Pardons, Jan. 2, 1908 (probably 1909), Inmate file 1124. Since Huffaker would have had no reason to write to the Board in 1908 when the appeal was still pending, he must have absentmindedly misdated the letter, as people often do just after the New Year.

10. M. O. Hall and Lora Hall letter, Dec. 9, 1908; Dr. George C. Pitzer letter, Dec. 8, 1908; James Punice? (illeg.) letter, Dec. 5, 1908; William Harrison letter, Dec. 2, 1908; Joseph E. Muller letter, Nov. 20, 1908, all in Inmate file 1124.

11. Preston, "The Smith-Preston Case" (1917?), 19.

12. Louis Lebel interview.

13. Steineck to Fischer, Sept. 24, 1908, in Inmate file 1124. On Steineck's background, see the *Tonopah Miner,* Dec. 24, 1904.

14. Steineck to Fischer, Sept. 24, 1908. Also see his letters of Oct. 3, Oct. 16, Dec. 4, and Dec. 29, all in Inmate file 1124.

15. Allen Jarvis statement, Jan. 2, 1909, Inmate file 1124. Jarvis also made a separate deposition dated May 24, 1907, which is included with the appeal briefs and trial transcript in the Nevada Archives.

16. *Miners' Magazine* 10 (Jan. 4, 1909): 6–11.

17. Hilton and Caesar A. Roberts to Board, May 4, 1909; Hilton to Board, May 20, 1909, Inmate file 1124.

18. Preston, "The Smith-Preston Case" (1917?), 17. Data on Bliss has been drawn from extensive materials in the collection of Richard Johnston (Carson City, Nevada).

19. *Daily Forum*, Jan. 6 and 8, 1910.

20. *Reno Evening Gazette*, Jan. 5, 1910. Also see *Western Nevada Miner*, July 30, 1910, and the *Carson City News*, Apr. 15 and July 12, 1910.

21. *Daily Forum*, Jan. 20, 1910.

22. Ibid., Feb. 12, 1910; also see White, "Labor Struggles in Goldfield," 88–89.

23. Clough to Dickerson, Dec. 24, 1909, Inmate file 1124.

24. John O'Malley and Pauline O'Malley deposition, May 28, 1910; R. E. Crosky deposition, June 8, 1910; Hilton deposition, June 8, 1910; Board to Hilton, June 18, 1910, Inmate file 1131.

25. Hilton deposition.

26. *Western Nevada Miner*, June 30, 1910; *Carson City News*, July 12, 1910. On the senatorial preference vote, see Elliott, *History of Nevada*, 244–45.

27. *Carson City News*, July 20, 1910.

28. On Baker and Oddie, see Zanjani, *The Unspiked Rail*, chs. 9–17. Before his diminished fortunes drove him to seek office, Oddie had been a partner of Nixon and Wingfield in the development of the Silverbow townsite. See the *Goldfield Review*, June 29, 1905. On Oddie's career in general, see Loren B. Chan, *Sagebrush Statesman: Tasker L. Oddie of Nevada* (Reno: University of Nevada Press, 1973).

29. Thomas Campbell to Oddie, June 20, 1911; William F. Ayers? (illeg.) to Oddie, June 27, 1911; Joseph Hutchinson to Oddie, July 7, 1911; R. H. Dalzell to Oddie, July 10, 1911; petition letter from W. A. Morgan to Oddie, July 2, 1911, all in Inmate file 1124. Also see the *Sparks Tribune*, July 14, 1911.

30. Tanner to Oddie, July 1, 1911; Somers to Board, June 10, 1911, Inmate file 1124. Note Belford's role in the annual Jackson Day dinner, as reported in the *Reno Evening Gazette*, Jan. 8, 1910. On Belford's background, see Boyd Moore, *Nevadans and Nevada* (H. S. Crocker Company, Inc., 1950), 144-A.

31. *Sparks Tribune*, July 12, 1911; Nevada Legislature, *Journal of the Senate, 1911*, 226. Also see the *Reno Evening Gazette*, Jan. 5, 1910, and the *Carson City News*, July 9 and 14, 1910.

32. Preston to Burton, July 5, 1911; Hilton to Preston, June 12, 1911, Inmate file 1124.

33. Davis to Oddie, Aug. 10, 1911, Tasker L. Oddie Papers, Huntington Library, San Marino, California. Note that there are two collections of Oddie's personal papers, one at the Nevada Historical Society and the other at the Huntington Library. His executive records as governor of Nevada are housed at the Nevada Archives.

34. Wingfield to Oddie, July 2, 1911, Oddie Papers, Huntington Library.

35. Siebert to Oddie, Nov. 22, 1911, Oddie Papers, Huntington Library. On Wingfield's indirect methods, see Zanjani, *The Unspiked Rail*, 320–23; on the Oddie-Siebert relationship, see Mrs. Hugh Brown, *Lady in Boomtown* (Palo Alto: American West Publishing Co., 1968), 51.

36. Belford to Norcross, Oct. 17, 1911, Inmate file 1124.

37. Undated application for pardon, Inmate file 1131.

38. Siebert to Oddie, Nov. 22, 1911, Oddie Papers, Huntington Library.

39. *Nevada State Journal*, Nov. 15, 1911.

40. *Miners' Magazine* 12 (Dec. 28, 1911): 10, and 14 (Jan. 23, 1913): 10.

CHAPTER X: A MORAL VICTORY

1. Preston pardon application, 1913, Inmate file 1124.

2. Wingfield to Oddie, Mar. 13, 1912, Oddie Papers, Huntington Library; *Nevada State Journal*, Aug. 17, 1914; and Zanjani, *The Unspiked Rail*, 148–52, 236–37. On other parolees, see Nevada Executive Office of the Governor, *Messages 1864–1921:* "Message of Governor John Sparks, 1908," 45; "Inaugural Message of Governor Tasker Oddie, 1911," 38, 41; "Message of Governor Tasker Oddie, 1913," 29–40. On eligibility for parole, see *Revised Laws of Nevada, 1912*, 2:2110. The Schwick case was reported in the *Goldfield Chronicle*, Oct. 21, 25, and 28, and Nov. 1; it was another defeat for Hilton, whose large reputation does not seem to have been diminished by repeated failure.

3. On Baker and Thatcher, see Zanjani, *The Unspiked Rail*, 212–14; on McCarran, see Jerome E. Edwards, *Pat McCarran: Political Boss of Nevada* (Reno: University of Nevada Press, 1982).

4. "Assembly Resolution and Memorial, Relative to the Imprisonment of M. R. Preston" (1913), Nevada Archives; on the reaction of the *Carson City News*, see the Feb. 8, 1913 issue; on Miller see the Mar. 23 issue.

5. Preston pardon application, 1913, Inmate file 1124; also see the *Carson City News*, Feb. 8, 1913.

6. Preston, "The Smith-Preston Case" (1917?), 21; *Carson Daily Appeal*, Dec. 29, 1913; on Calumet, see Jensen, *Heritage of Conflict*, 285–86.

7. Davis to Oddie, Oct. 26, 1913, George A. Bartlett Papers, Special Collections, University of Nevada Library (Reno). In Salt Lake City, Davis was visiting Orlando W. Powers, an attorney who had prosecuted him in Idaho and is mentioned in Grover, *Diamondfield Jack*, 156–57; on Davis's financial condition, see the *Carson City Daily Appeal*, Apr. 4, 1913.

8. Preston, "The Smith-Preston Case" (1917?), 21.

9. Ibid.

10. Ibid., 4; on Miller's background, see Davis, *The History of Nevada*, 2:1259, and Koontz, *Political History of Nevada*, 191–92.

11. Esther and Louis Lebel interviews; on Lillian Burton's effort, see Preston "The Smith-Preston Case" (1917?), 21.

12. Douglas to Norcross, Feb. 18, 1914, reprinted in Preston, "The Smith-Preston Case" (1917?), 22.

13. Douglas to Board, Apr. 4, 1914, reprinted in Preston, "The Smith-Preston Case" (1917?), 22–23.

14. Preston, "The Smith-Preston Case" (1917?), 23.

15. When the possible perjury of a prosecution witness in the Tom Mooney case became known two months after Mooney's conviction, Judge Griffin unsuccessfully urged this course on the prosecutors. See Frost, *The Mooney Case*, 316–17.

16. Preston, "The Smith-Preston Case" (1915), 22–24. The published accounts of Goldfield meetings to which Somers alluded probably appeared in March, when a large gap in the preserved copies of Goldfield newspapers occurs.

17. Ibid., 11.

18. Stegner, *Joe Hill*, 287.

19. Preston, "The Smith-Preston Case" (1917?), 25–26.

20. Ibid., 24; also see 9.

21. Thatcher to Board, Apr. 25, 1914, Inmate file 1124; on other parolees, see Nevada Executive Office of the Governor, *Messages 1864–1921*, "Message of Governor Emmet Boyle, 1915," 33–34. On the Oddie-Wingfield relationship during the 1920s, when Oddie was a U.S. senator and Wingfield the undisputed boss of the Nevada bipartisan political machine, see Zanjani, *The Unspiked Rail*, chs. 14–17.

22. Preston, "The Smith-Preston Case" (1917?), 19.

23. On Ludlow, see the *Carson City Daily Appeal*, Apr. 28 and 29, 1914, and Milton Meltzer, *Bread and Roses* (New York: Alfred A. Knopf, 1967), 192–211.

CHAPTER XI: DISCOVERIES OF TIME

1. Preston, "The Smith-Preston Case" (1917?), 26.

2. Preston parole reports, May 18, June 1, June 30, and Aug. 1, 1914, Inmate file 1124. Also see Operative 18, Thiel Detective Agency, Tonopah, Mar. 13, 1915, photocopy of report in the possession of Guy Louis Rocha, Reno.

3. Preston, "The Smith-Preston Case" (1915), esp. 9, 11, 27. Preston also printed a letter from the dean of Vanderbilt law school indicating that Daniel William was the only Claiborne registered in 1903. Also see *Miners' Magazine* 12 (Apr. 13, 1911): 9, 11–12. On Mooney, see Gentry, *Frame-up*, 322–23.

4. Army and railroad pension claims, letters from officials at Vanderbilt, West Point, the Denver Public Library, and the Virginia Archives, and a clipping from the *Los Angeles Times* dated Nov. 7, 1909, all in the Johnston Collection.

5. Rockwell D. Hunt, *California and Californians* (Chicago: Lewis Publishing Company, 1932), 454–55, and other materials relating to Claiborne in the Johnston Collection.

6. Claiborne materials, Johnston Collection. Although Johnston's research has done so much to unmask Claiborne, several mysteries remain, including his birthdate (variously listed as 1880 and 1882), his wives (at least four, possibly five), and his transformation from Daniel to William.

7. Preston, "The Smith-Preston Case" (1915), 27.

8. Ibid., 25–27.

9. Miller to Boyle, Mar. 5, 1915, Inmate file 1124; on the changes in the membership of the Board of Pardons, see Koontz, *Political History of Nevada*, 191, 120.

10. J. D. S. to Miller, Mar. 15, 1915, Inmate file 1124.

11. Langan to Miller, Apr. 22, 1915, Inmate file 1124.

12. Frost, *The Mooney Case*, 204–17, 377–79.

13. *Carson City Daily Appeal*, Apr. 2 and 7, 1913, Feb. 9, 1929; *Carson City News*, Mar. 15, 1921; *Reno Evening Gazette*, Mar. 9, 1921; *GDT*, Jan. 7, 1910; and Koontz, *Political History of Nevada*, 193.

14. Board to Withers, May 25, 1915; Withers to Board, May 31, 1915, Inmate file 1124.

15. *Carson City Daily Appeal*, June 4, 1915.

16. Preston parole reports, June 1 and July 1, 1915, Inmate file 1124.

17. Preston parole report, Oct. 8, 1915; Harry S. Shoneferld to Warden, Oct. 26, 1915. Also see the letters of introduction in Inmate file 1124.

18. Preston parole report, Oct. 1, 1915, Inmate file 1124.

19. Preston parole reports, Nov. 6, 1915, Jan. 1 and Mar. 1, 1916, Inmate file 1124.

20. Preston parole reports, Mar. 1, Apr. 1, June 1, and Sept. 1, 1916. Inmate file 1124.

21. Preston parole report, Aug. 1, 1916, Inmate file 1124.

22. *GDT*, Apr. 15, 1916; also see the *Tonopah Daily Bonanza* of the same date.

23. James W. Byrkit, "Lindley C. Branson and the Jerome *Sun*," *Journal of the West* 19 (Apr., 1980): 51–63; Drury, "Journalism," 494–95.

24. Preston parole reports, Sept. 1, 1916.

25. Louis Lebel interview.

26. Preston, "The Smith-Preston Case" (1917?), 28. The Wisconsin State Historical Society Library has nearly identical versions of this pamphlet printed in New York, possibly in 1916.

27. Ibid., 30.

28. Ibid., 31.

29. Stone, *Clarence Darrow for the Defense*, 206–7.

30. On the Rena Mooney trial, see Frost, *The Mooney Case*, 233.

31. Ibid., 237.

32. A. Grant Miller, "Introduction," April 1915, in Preston, "The Smith-Preston Case" (both versions).

33. *Eastern Utah Advocate*, May 8, July 25, and Sept. 5, 1907, interviews, and other materials in the Johnston Collection.

34. *Miners' Magazine* 8 (Aug. 15, 1907): 4.

35. Preston, "The Smith-Preston Case" (1917?), 31.

36. Preston parole reports, Feb. 28, 1917, and Aug. 1, 1918, Inmate file 1124.

37. Preston to Miller, Aug. 24, 1918, Inmate file 1124.

38. Miller to Boyle, Aug. 27, 1918, Inmate file 1124. Also note Miller's position on the Nevada State Council of Defense, Nevada State Council of Defense Records, Nevada Archives.

39. Preston parole report, Nov. 3, 1918; also see Boyle to Miller, Aug. 29, 1918, both in Inmate file 1124.

40. Preston parole report, July 9, 1919, Inmate file 1124.

41. Esther Lebel interviews.

42. Preston pardon application, Mar. 23, 1920, Inmate file 1124. On the composition of the Board in 1920, see Koontz, *Political History of Nevada,* 111, 114, 120.

43. Preston to Board, May 8, 1920, Inmate file 1124. On Boyle's background, see Myrtle T. Myles, *Nevada's Governors: From Territorial Days to the Present—1861–1971* (Sparks, Nevada: Western Printing and Publishing Co., 1972), 83–85.

44. Preston parole reports, Aug. 8 and Oct. 1, 1920, and Jan. 2 and June 6, 1921, Inmate file 1124.

45. Esther and Louis Lebel interviews. In the 1924 San Fernando Valley Directory, the surname of Zora's son, Louis Rockwood Fischer, is listed as Lebel, a variant of his stepfather's name.

46. Preston parole reports, Oct. 4 and Nov. 4, 1921, and May 23, 1922, Inmate file 1124.

47. Preston, "The Smith-Preston Case" (1917?), 18. Mary Frost Nunnaley to Board, with enclosed newspaper clipping, Oct. 11, 1924, Inmate file 1124.

48. Nunnaley to Board, Oct. 11, 1924, Inmate file 1124.

49. Esther and Louis Lebel interviews.

50. Elliott, "Labor Troubles in the Mining Camp at Goldfield, Nevada, 1906–1908," 384. On Wingfield, also see Zanjani, *The Unspiked Rail,* 140–41. While Wingfield was not successful in permanently eliminating the IWW from Goldfield—the Wobblies organized Metal Mine Workers' Union No. 353 on Aug. 26, 1914—the local did little, if anything, to improve labor conditions during the two and one-half years the union functioned. The organizing activities of IWW Metal Mine Workers Industrial Union No. 800, a regional local based in Phoenix, beginning in 1917 proved equally fruitless. See Rocha, "Radical Labor Struggles," 25–26.

51. *Miners' Magazine* 11 (Dec. 15, 1910): 9.

52. On West Virginia, see Ira Kipnis, *The American Socialist Movement 1897–1912* (New York: Columbia University Press, 1952), 368; on the IWW in Nevada, see Rocha, "Radical Labor Struggles," 3–45, and "The IWW and the Boulder Canyon Project: The Final Death Throes of American Syndicalism," *Nevada Historical Society Quarterly* 21 (Spring 1978): 3–24.

53. Thompson and Murfin, *The I.W.W.,* 30.

54. Lens, *The Labor Wars,* 155, 159–68.

55. Renshaw, *The Wobblies,* 237; also see 241.

56. Ibid., 262–64. Dubofsky, *We Shall Be All,* 142–44.

BIBLIOGRAPHY

Articles and Pamphlets

Byrkit, James W. "Lindley C. Branson and the Jerome *Sun*." *Journal of the West* 19 (April 1980): 51–63.

Conlin, Joseph R. "Goldfield High-Grade." *American West* 20 (May/June 1983): 38–44.

Drury, Wells. "Journalism." In *The History of Nevada*, edited by Sam P. Davis, 1:459–502. Los Angeles: Elms Publishing Company, 1913.

Dubofsky, Melvyn. "The Origins of Working Class Radicalism, 1890–1905." *Labor History* 7 (Spring 1966): 131–54.

Earl, Phillip I., and Guy L. Rocha. "Nevada Convict Was a Presidential Candidate." *Nevada Appeal*, Nov. 9, 1980.

Elliott, Russell R. "Labor Troubles in the Mining Camp at Goldfield, Nevada, 1906–1908." *Pacific Historical Review* 19 (1950): 369–84.

Jardine, Harry. "Letter." *Miners' Magazine* 8 (Feb. 14, 1907): 12–13.

Malone, Booth M. "Pen Picture of Hawthorne, Poor Thing." *Goldfield Daily Tribune*, May 5, 1907.

Miller, A. Grant. "Introduction." In "The Smith-Preston Case," pamphlet by Morrie R. Preston. Page 6 of the 1915 version published in Reno by the Journal Press, and page 4 of the later version published by the International Union of Mine, Mill & Smelter Workers.

Preston, Morrie R. "The Smith-Preston Case." Pamphlet. Reno: Journal Press (1915), 4–30.

———. "The Smith-Preston Case." Pamphlet. International Union of Mine, Mill & Smelter Workers, (n.d., probably 1917), 2–31. Another edition was printed in New York City, possibly in 1916, by Mahonny & Scheid Printing Co., and consisting of 36 pages.

Rocha, Guy L. "Radical Labor Struggles in the Tonopah-Goldfield Mining District, 1901–1922." *Nevada Historical Society Quarterly* 20 (Spring 1977): 3–45.

———. "The IWW and the Boulder Canyon Project: The Final Death Throes of American Syndicalism." *Nevada Historical Society Quarterly* 21 (Spring 1978): 3–24.

St. John, Vincent. "Review of the Facts in the Situation at Goldfield." *Industrial Union Bulletin*, Apr. 26, 1907.

———. "Shall the Working Class Be Crushed?" *Miners' Magazine* 7 (May 17, 1906): 8.

Zanjani, Sally S. "A Theory of Critical Realignment: The Nevada Example, 1892–1908." *Pacific Historical Review* 48 (1979): 259–80.

————. "The Mike Smith Case: A Note on High Grading in Goldfield, Nevada, 1910." *Labor History* 24 (Fall 1983): 580–87.

Zanjani, Sally S., and Guy L. Rocha. "A Heart for Any Fate: Vincent St. John in Goldfield." *Nevada Historical Society Quarterly* 27 (Summer 1984): 75–91.

————. "Nevada's Convict Candidate." *The Nevadan* 23 (Sept. 30, 1984): 6L–7L.

Books

Brissenden, Paul F. *The I.W.W.: A Study of American Syndicalism.* Vol. 83 of Columbia University Studies in History, Economics and Public Law. New York: Columbia University Press, 1919.

Brown, Mrs. Hugh. *Lady in Boomtown: Miners and Manners on the Nevada Frontier.* Palo Alto: American West Publishing Co., 1968.

Brown, Ronald C. *Hard-Rock Miners—The Intermountain West, 1860–1920.* College Station: Texas A & M University Press, 1979.

Chan, Loren B. *Sagebrush Statesman: Tasker L. Oddie of Nevada.* Reno: University of Nevada Press, 1973.

Conlin, Joseph R. *Big Bill Haywood and the Radical Union Movement.* Syracuse: Syracuse University Press, 1969.

Davis, Sam P., ed. *The History of Nevada.* 2 vols. Los Angeles: Elms Publishing Co., 1913.

Debs, Eugene V. *Debs: His Life, Writings and Speeches.* Chicago: Charles H. Kerr & Company Co-operative, 1908.

Dubofsky, Melvyn. *We Shall Be All: A History of the IWW.* Chicago: Quadrangle Books, 1969.

Edwards, Jerome E. *Pat McCarran: Political Boss of Nevada.* Reno: University of Nevada Press, 1982.

Elliott, Russell R. *History of Nevada.* Lincoln: University of Nebraska Press, 1973.

————. *Radical Labor in the Nevada Mining Booms 1900–1920.* Reno: University of Nevada Press, 1963.

Foner, Philip S. *History of the Labor Movement in the United States.* 5 vols. New York: International Publishers, 1947–65.

Friedman, Lawrence M., and Robert V. Percival. *The Roots of Justice: Crime and Punishment in Alameda County California 1870–1910.* Chapel Hill: University of North Carolina Press, 1981.

Frost, Richard H. *The Mooney Case.* Stanford: Stanford University Press, 1968.

Gentry, Curt. *Frame-up: The Incredible Case of Tom Mooney and Warren Billings.* New York: W. W. Norton & Co., Inc., 1967.

Glass, Mary E. *Silver and Politics in Nevada.* Reno: University of Nevada Press, 1969.

Glasscock, Carl B. *Gold in Them Hills: The Story of the West's Last Wild Mining Days.* New York: Grossett & Dunlap, 1932.

Grover, David H. *Diamondfield Jack: A Study in Frontier Justice.* Reno: University of Nevada Press, 1968.

Haywood, William D. *Bill Haywood's Book.* New York: International Publishers, 1969.

Horan, James D., and Howard Swiggett. *The Pinkerton Story.* New York: G. P. Putnam's Sons, 1951.

Hunt, Rockwell D. *California and Californians.* 4 vols. Chicago: The Lewis Publishing Company, 1932.

Jensen, Vernon H. *Heritage of Conflict: Labor Relations in the Non-Ferrous Metals Industry up to 1930.* Ithaca: Cornell University Press, 1950.

Kipnis, Ira. *The American Socialist Movement 1897–1912.* New York: Columbia University Press, 1952.

Koontz, John. *Political History of Nevada.* 5th ed. Carson City: State Printing Office, 1965.

Langdon, Emma F. *The Cripple Creek Strike: A History of Industrial Wars in Colorado.* New York: Arno Press & The New York Times, 1969.

Lens, Sidney. *The Labor Wars: From the Molly Maguires to the Sitdowns.* New York: Doubleday & Company, 1973.

Lewis, George F., and D. F. Stacklebeck, eds. *Bench and Bar of Colorado*. Denver: Bench and Bar Publishing Company, 1977.
Lillard, Richard G. *Desert Challenge: An Interpretation of Nevada*. New York: Alfred A. Knopf, 1942.
McGrath, Roger D. *Gunfighters, Highwaymen, and Vigilantes: Violence on the Frontier*. Berkeley: University of California Press, 1984.
Meltzer, Milton. *Bread and Roses*. New York: Alfred A. Knopf, 1967.
Moore, Boyd. *Persons in the Foreground*. n.p., 1915.
Myles, Myrtle T. *Nevada's Governors: From Territorial Days to the Present—1861–1971*. Sparks, Nevada: Western Printing and Publishing Co., 1972.
Nizer, Louis. *My Life in Court*. New York: Pyramid Books, 1963.
Paher, Stanley W. *Nevada Ghost Towns and Mining Camps*. Berkeley: Howell-North, 1970.
Renshaw, Patrick. *The Wobblies: The Story of Syndicalism in the United States*. New York: Doubleday & Company, 1967.
Russell, Francis. *Tragedy in Dedham*. New York: McGraw-Hill Book Company, 1971.
Shepperson, Wilbur S. *Retreat to Nevada: A Socialist Colony of World War I*. Reno: University of Nevada Press, 1966.
Stegner, Wallace. *Joe Hill*. New York: Doubleday & Company, 1969.
Stone, Irving. *Clarence Darrow for the Defense*. New York: Doubleday & Company, 1941.
Suggs, George G., Jr. *Colorado's War on Militant Unionism*. Detroit: Wayne State University Press, 1972.
Thompson, Fred W., and Patrick Murfin. *The I.W.W.: Its First Seventy Years, 1905–1975*. Chicago: Industrial Workers of the World, 1976.
Weinstein, James. *Ambiguous Legacy: The Left in American Politics*. New York: New Viewpoints, 1975.
Wyman, Mark. *Hard-Rock Epic: Western Miners and the Industrial Revolution, 1860–1910*. Berkeley: University of California Press, 1979.
Zanjani, Sally S. *The Unspiked Rail: Memoir of a Nevada Rebel*. Reno: University of Nevada Press, 1981.

Newspapers and Periodicals

Call (San Francisco)
Carson City Daily Appeal
Carson City News
Daily Forum (Sparks)
Denver Times
Eastern Utah Advocate
The Engineering and Mining Journal
Goldfield Chronicle
Goldfield Daily Tribune
Goldfield Review
Industrial Union Bulletin
The Industrial Worker
Miners' Magazine
Mining and Scientific Press
Nevada Appeal
Nevada State Journal
Nevada Workman
The New York Times
The Outlook
Reno Evening Gazette
Sparks Tribune
Times (Los Angeles)

Tonopah Daily Bonanza
The Tonopah Miner
Tonopah Sun
Western Nevada Miner

Manuscript Collections and Unpublished Materials

Bartlett, George A. Papers. Special Collections, University of Nevada Library, Reno.

Branson, L. C. v. the Industrial Workers of the World. Nevada Supreme Court, 1908. Nevada State Division of Archives and Records, Carson City.

Brinley, Jr., John E. "The Western Federation of Miners." Ph.D. dissertation, University of Utah, 1972.

Dickerson, Denver S. Executive Records. Nevada State Division of Archives and Records, Carson City.

The Goldfield Consolidated Mines Company v. Goldfield Miners' Union No. 220 et. al. United States Circuit Court, Nevada, 1908.

Johnston, Richard. Collection of materials relating to Thomas O. Bliss and William L. Claiborne (private), Carson City.

Nevada State Council of Defense. Records. Nevada State Division of Archives and Records, Carson City.

Oddie, Tasker L. Papers and Executive Records. Huntington Library, San Marino, California, Nevada Historical Society, Reno, and Nevada State Division of Archives and Records, Carson City.

Sparks, John. Executive Records. Nevada State Division of Archives and Records, Carson City.

State v. Morrie R. Preston and Joseph W. Smith. First Judicial District of Nevada, 1907. The transcript of testimony, appeal briefs, records of Preston (Inmate file 1124) and Smith (Inmate file 1131), and other materials relating to the case are preserved at the Nevada State Division of Archives and Records, Carson City.

Thornton, Barbara C. "George Wingfield in Nevada from 1896 to 1932." Master's thesis, University of Nevada, Reno, 1967.

Tonopah Industrial Workers of the World Local 325. Records. Special Collections, University of Nevada Library, Reno.

White, Laura A. "History of the Labor Struggles in Goldfield, Nevada." Master's thesis, University of Nebraska, 1912.

Government Documents

Congress. House. 60th Cong., 1st sess., House Exec. Doc. 607 [Report of the Roosevelt Commission].

Nevada Executive Office of the Governor. *Messages 1864–1921.*

Nevada Legislature. "Assembly Resolution and Memorial, Relative to the Imprisonment of M. R. Preston." 1913. Nevada State Division of Archives and Records, Carson City.

————. *Journal of the Senate.* 1907, 1908, 1911.

————. *Journal of the Assembly.* 1907, 1908.

————. *Statutes.* Special session, 1908.

————. *Revised Laws of Nevada, 1912.*

Nevada Reports. 1909.

Nevada State Prison. *Reports of the Warden,* 1891–1892 to 1955–1956.

Interviews

Gomes, Helen (telephone), Feb. 25 and Apr. 16, 1982.

Lebel, Esther (telephone), Feb. 24 and Mar. 27, 1982.

Lebel, Louis R., Apr. 30, 1982.

INDEX